CRYSTAL
BASICS

POCKET ENCYCLOPEDIA

The Energetic, Healing, and Spiritual Power of
450 GEMSTONES

NICHOLAS PEARSON

DESTINY
BOOKS

Destiny Bo[...]
Rochester, Vermont

T0054687

Destiny Books
One Park Street
Rochester, Vermont 05767
www.DestinyBooks.com

Destiny Books is a division of Inner Traditions International

Note to the reader: *This book is intended as an informational guide. The remedies,*
approaches, and techniques described herein are meant to supplement, and not to be a
substitute for, professional medical care or treatment. They should not be used to treat a
serious ailment without prior consultation with a qualified health care professional.

Cataloging-in-Publication Data for this title is available from the Library of Congress

ISBN 978-1-64411-503-9 (print)
ISBN 978-1-64411-504-6 (ebook)

Printed and bound in China by Reliance Printing Co., Ltd.

10 9 8 7 6 5 4 3 2 1

Text design and layout by Virginia Scott Bowman
This book was typeset in Myriad Pro and Garamond Premier Pro with Minion Pro and
Gill Sans used as display typefaces
Photographs and illustrations by Steven Thomas Pearson-Walsh

To send correspondence to the author of this book, mail a first-class letter to the author c/o
Inner Traditions • Bear & Company, One Park Street, Rochester, VT 05767, and we will forward
the communication, or contact the author directly at **www.theluminouspearl.com**.

CONTENTS

ACKNOWLEDGMENTS

As this book approaches its publication date, I'm reflecting on the many ways that my community has supported this and many other projects. Thank you to everyone who has helped shape this book.

Special thanks go to my husband, Steven, for the photos and diagrams—and for being my biggest supporter over the years.

Thank you to Sharron Britton of High Springs Emporium for letting us visit to take photos of your incredible selection of rocks and minerals. Many thanks to Miranda and the team at Avalon for allowing me to borrow crystals for photos as well. Thanks are owed to Lisa of the Lemurian Rose for introducing me (and the rest of the world) to fascia jasper and for sending me the perfect piece for a photo. Thank you also to Ashley Leavy for support, encouragement, and so much more.

Finally, a huge wave of gratitude and appreciation to Jamaica and the team at Inner Traditions for helping me bring another book to life.

INTRODUCTION

THE BEAUTY AND POWER OF CRYSTALS

That the mineral kingdom has inspired humankind since the beginning of time will surprise no one who has spent time marveling over any crystal. Mother Nature's rocks and gems elicit awe, stimulate the imagination, and please the eye of anyone who takes notice of them. Stones were among the first tools, adornments, pigments, and ritual objects used by humans, and they have been woven into the fabric of human society ever since. In present times crystals and gemstones are celebrated for more than just their beauty and mystery; they have been accessed by countless people around the globe for their healing gifts and spiritual blessings.

WHAT ARE CRYSTALS?

To better understand how crystals work, we must first understand what crystals are. A crystal is defined as a (usually) solid substance with a homogeneous composition and a repeating symmetrical structure. In other words, crystals have a predictable and regular list of constituents, and those components are arranged in repeating geometric patterns. Crystals can be found in everything, from every rock and mineral of the Earth's crust to the human body. There are crystals in our food, our walls, our electronics, and almost everywhere else we look.

When crystals are naturally occurring and inorganic in origin, we call

■ A mineral, such as quartz, is a naturally occurring inorganic crystal. A rock, such as granite, is formed from a mixture of different minerals.

them *minerals*. The vast majority of the tools we colloquially refer to as crystals and healing stones are minerals. Some may be polished, tumbled, or otherwise shaped in ways that obscure their original crystal form, or their constituent crystals may be so tiny as to be invisible to the naked eye. Common examples of minerals include quartz, calcite, hematite, gypsum, and topaz. The same mineral may take many forms, each with its own name. A prime example of this is quartz, which under varying conditions may be called amethyst, citrine, smoky quartz, agate, chalcedony, or jasper.

When minerals aggregate we call the resulting formation a *rock*. Rocks have variable textures, structures, and compositions. Although they are usually formed from minerals, which are crystalline, we cannot always see the component crystals with the naked eye. A rock may be composed primarily of a single mineral, such as limestone (mostly calcite) or quartzite (mostly quartz), or it may consist of many different minerals. Common rocks include granite, marble, gneiss, slate, and schist. Some popular healing stones, such as lapis lazuli and dalmatian stone, are actually rocks rather than single minerals.

There are times when geologic forces come together to form something that doesn't quite meet the definition of rock or mineral. Sometimes it lacks the necessary crystalline structure, or it might be the result of organic processes. In these instances the material is called a *mineraloid,* meaning "mineral-like." Obsidian, opal, moldavite, amber, and the calcium carbonate in shells and pearls are common examples of mineraloids.

The word *stone* is more nebulous in definition. It usually connotes any hard substance of geologic origin, particularly if it has been shaped or changed in any way by human hands. Similarly, any of the above terms—crystal, mineral, rock, and mineraloid—can be transformed into *gemstones* when used for ornamental purposes. Gems can be drilled into beads, faceted like precious stones, or otherwise prepared to be worn or displayed.

What ties all these meanings together is their relationship to the concept of crystallinity and their geologic origins. Crystals are the outer form of a mineral's inner order, so to be crystalline is to have a perfect or near-perfect inner order. This regular, repeating, rhythmic structure is called a *crystal lattice,* and this lattice is largely responsible for the way in which crystals heal. There is a relationship between crystal energy and the structure and formation of crystals, and that energy can improve our lives.

1
CRYSTALS AND ENERGY

Many crystal healers, psychics, and other sensitive people discuss the energy of crystals as if it were a discrete, tangible, and universal experience. While I personally believe the science behind crystals and energy supports this idea, much of what we experience in the realm of crystal healing results from subtle energy, which is to say that it is some sort of energy or phenomenon that science has no means of measuring—at least not yet. To better understand subtle energy I find it helpful to explore through the lens of physics, as it provides a thorough platform for comprehending how and why crystal energy works. Throughout this book, if you encounter expressions like *subtle energy* that you aren't familiar with, please refer to the glossary of metaphysical terms on page 275.

UNDERSTANDING ENERGY

The word *energy* is bounced around in a lot of different contexts. We talk about subtle energy, crystal energy, personal energy, as well as the energy of planets, elements, and other people. But what exactly is energy?

To a scientist, energy is defined as the capacity to animate or to perform work. The nature of this work is relative; it might include moving, heating, or changing a substance or a system.

Energy can be converted from one form to another, but it can never disappear altogether. Energy is often visualized or expressed as waves—as opposed to matter, which is described as particles. However, the separation between wave and particle, energy and matter, is not exactly black and white.

Everything in the cosmos is made of tiny bits of matter, which are made of still tinier particles. Each and every one of these particles is part of a cosmic dance, in a constant state of motion. Further, between particles there is a lot of empty space that can be repeatedly divided until something very curious happens: these units start to behave as both particles and waves. Whether we observe particles (specific masses) or waves (disturbance in the mass) largely depends on the observer. Ultimately the subtle realm of energy and concrete world of matter are inextricably linked.

Vibrating systems are known to generate energy fields, like those found on the electromagnetic spectrum. Matter of all varieties produces these fields, which expand from their point of origin and move outward at the speed of light toward infinity. The closer you are to the source of such an energy field, the easier it is to detect; its strength diminishes with distance. Everything produces such a field: crystals, carpets, cows, and every tissue in your body. The nature of these electromagnetic fields (and their counterparts in the realm of subtle energy) is influenced by how organized a particular source is.

Crystals, therefore, are more than just solid, inert matter. The precision inherent in their composition and structure results in an energy field that is similarly perfect. Orderly, coherent fields have a tendency to influence the fields around them to become more orderly, too. Thus crystals, with their innate perfection, help us achieve this state of coherence. Let's look at the mechanisms responsible for how crystals do this.

ESSENTIAL CRYSTAL FUNCTIONS

The precise and orderly makeup of crystals (and therefore of rocks and minerals) enables them to perform a broad range of actions. Not only can they encourage other energy fields to become more harmonious as mentioned above, but crystals can also amplify, transmit, and store energy as a result of the crystal lattice. The essential functions of all crystals can be expressed in the following list:

▸ Crystals *harmonize* energy fields to make them more coherent.
▸ Crystals *amplify* our energy and intentions, since coherent fields can be detected farther away from their source.
▸ Crystals *reflect* and *refract* by enhancing and redirecting the focus of our energy and psyche, just as prisms and lenses do.
▸ Crystals act as antennae to *transmit* and *receive* energy and information, due to their precise oscillations.
▸ Crystals *record* energy because of tiny imperfections and variations in their lattices.
▸ Crystals *translate* energy from one state to another, thus converting our intentions or ideas into vibrations that can have a greater impact on our lives and the world around us.

Taken as a whole, these essential crystal functions illustrate the mechanisms we harness when we co-create with crystals for healing, personal growth, and transformation. Other, more subtle and symbolic functions of crystals will be described in chapter 2.

CRYSTALS AND THE HUMAN BODY

Crystal healing relies on the principles outlined above to create change in our lives. There are several models that demonstrate how crystals help us achieve these changes, and we will explore a couple of them below.

First and foremost, let's look at what happens when two electromagnetic fields interact. Two resonant oscillating fields will typically undergo some sort of harmonization or synchronization, a process referred to as *entrainment*. It is important to note that the energy field with the higher amplitude (like a louder volume) will always entrain the field of lower amplitude. Due to their highly ordered, coherent structures, crystals have high-amplitude energy fields. This gives them the ability to harmonize our unique individual energy fields, which are in a state of constant flux. As the human energy field becomes more ordered and crystalline there are subtle shifts in mood and perception, which in turn trigger a cascade of chemical and electrical signals that move through the body. Science has shown that increasing coherence of the human energy field, particularly the fields generated by the heart and brain, improves overall health and well-being. Thus we can conclude that energy transcends pathology through this mechanism.

The human body is also composed of many crystalline and semi-crystalline substances. Collagen, hemoglobin, DNA, and many other substances in the human body exhibit high degrees of order and symmetry, thus resembling and behaving like crystals in many ways. Our teeth and bones contain minerals that provide their structure, and the liquids within and around every cell are organized into liquid crystal states. We are literally made of crystals, from head to toe. Every part of us works the way crystals do, exhibiting the same essential functions as other crystals. When we introduce our favorite healing stones to the energy field, our bodies, made of living crystals, interact with the energies of the mineral kingdom to effect palpable change.

In short, crystals are powerful tools that transform and organize the energies around them. Working with crystals invites greater healing and balance on all levels—body, mind, and spirit.

2

CRYSTAL CORRESPONDENCES

In addition to examining the energy of crystals through the lens of science, there are many ways of categorizing the subtle energies and spiritual properties of crystals (and other substances). These other levels of understanding can be called *correspondences* because they are said to correspond, or vibrate in harmony with, other principles, symbols, and forces in the universe. This concept is based on the occult principle of correspondence, often summarized in the expression "As above, so below." Throughout this chapter we will take a look at some of the major correspondences used in crystal healing today, including color, chakra, elemental, planetary, and zodiacal correspondences. But we begin with a brief geology lesson, so we can explore how the science of crystals corresponds with their energy.

GEOLOGICAL CORRESPONDENCES

When I first began my crystal journey I relied on the clues provided by color, shape, and traditional correspondences to discover the healing power of rocks and minerals. However, as I learned more about the structure, makeup, and formation processes of my favorite stones I saw correlations between these geological features and the energies I read about and experienced firsthand. I saw that metamorphic rocks provided assistance during periods of change, and minerals rich in iron were grounding, as were those that belonged to the cubic crystal system. Over the years I've found that the geologic clues encoded in crystals are the most reliable indicators of a crystal's energy. In the following paragraphs we'll explore the fundamental correspondences and energies of a crystal's formation process and crystal system. Although a full discussion of the composition, structure, and formation process is beyond the scope of this book, you can find a more complete exploration of this topic in chapter 2 of my book *Crystal Basics: The Energetic, Healing & Spiritual Power of 200 Gemstones*.

Formation Process

All of the rocks and minerals of Earth are formed through a sequence of events known as the rock cycle. Their origins are generally classified as igneous, sedimentary, or metamorphic. Igneous rocks and their constituent minerals form when molten rock cools; they are also referred to as primary minerals because they are the start of the rock cycle. Sedimentary rocks and minerals are made from other rocks and minerals that are broken down from some kind of weathering or erosion in their environments. The resulting particles are put back together to create new formations. Metamorphic rocks are the result of either igneous or sedimentary rocks that are transformed by exposure to heat and/or pressure, which causes their components to reorganize themselves.

A crystal's formation process usually indicates the level of its action. Learning about the formation process of your healing tools provides insight into where and how they direct their healing energy. Refer to the list below for some key words describing the effects of the different formation processes.

▸ **Igneous:** symbolizes new beginnings, sparks inspiration and creativity, inspires freedom, burns away stuck and stagnant energies, provides stability, helps recognize and manifest your potential, reaches into the source of an issue

- ▸ **Sedimentary:** reveals how the environment affects you, enhances memory and recall, reveals subconscious mind, dissolves longstanding issues, highlights how karma shapes your life, facilitates past-life recall
- ▸ **Metamorphic:** assists all processes of transition and change, alleviates sense of overwhelm, promotes strength and courage, increases stamina, protects during vulnerable periods of change, stimulates self-reflection

Crystal System

The seven crystal systems (cubic, tetragonal, orthorhombic, monoclinic, triclinic, trigonal, and hexagonal) are groups of crystals defined by their shared geometry. Each crystal system has unique relationships of their internal axes based on the shapes of their crystal lattices. Minerals that belong to the same crystal system generally exhibit similarly shaped crystals. In addition to the seven known crystal systems, there is also a group of materials that have no discernible crystal structure; they are referred to as *amorphous,* meaning "without form."

While the formation process indicates the level to which a crystal directs its energy, the crystal system (or lack thereof in the case of amorphous stones) represents the direction and focus of a crystal's energy. In a way the crystal systems are rather like different personality types of the mineral realm. The list below provides some key phrases to describe the energy of the various crystal systems.

- ▸ **Cubic:** grounding and stabilizing, brings order out of chaos, enforces healthy boundaries, supports manifestation, promotes focus and motivation
- ▸ **Tetragonal:** absorbs and transmutes negative energies, inspires creativity, attracts new opportunities, provides balance between giving and receiving, facilitates contact with higher self
- ▸ **Orthorhombic:** invites greater balance, fosters sense of belonging,

improves focus, helps prioritize important tasks, imparts decisiveness, releases old programming

▸ **Monoclinic:** drives forward momentum, protects and purifies energy, helps strive for your dreams, soothes tension, highlights link between emotions and physical health

▸ **Triclinic:** integrates new energies and ideas, helps access higher consciousness, deepens intuition, promotes adaptability, balances polarities, transforms trauma, releases limiting beliefs

▸ **Trigonal:** brings clarity and understanding, boosts personal energy, symbolizes positive change, promotes simplicity and contentment, helps use resources effectively

▸ **Hexagonal:** improves efficiency, communication, and learning; stimulates creativity and curiosity; expands perspective; facilitates meditation and other spiritual growth

▸ **Amorphous:** stimulates creativity, catalyzes profound growth, symbolizes change and flux, reveals subconscious patterns, imparts flexibility, releases deeply held ideas, calms the spirit

THE POWER OF COLOR

Color presents one of the most personal and meaningful sets of correspondences that inform our relationship with crystals. Many crystal healers and collectors begin their understanding of crystals' effects around the perceived meaning of color, especially with regard to the chakras (refer to the next section for a discussion of chakras). While color is often deeply meaningful to practitioners, it represents only a tiny fraction of the measurable energy of crystals—not much more than 7 percent of their total energy. In spite of this, color has an impact on our psychological state, not just the energetic, so it continues to serve as a useful tool for many crystal lovers. Here is an overview of the properties of the most common colors found in the mineral kingdom:

- **Red:** grounding, vitality, strength, determination, courage
- **Orange:** energy, creativity, passion, stamina, optimism
- **Yellow** and **gold:** happiness, charisma, will, letting go, focus, wealth, joy
- **Green:** growth, regeneration, healing, balance, love, abundance
- **Blue:** connection, serenity, communication, clarity, hope, cooling
- **Indigo:** intuition, introspection, calm, memory, structure, rest
- **Violet** and **purple:** transformation, spirituality, psychic development, dispel illusion, meditation
- **Pink:** emotional balance, reassurance, self-esteem, love, romance, inner child
- **White** and **colorless:** purification, protection, clarity, fresh perspective, amplify intentions
- **Black:** grounding, protecting, strengthening, self-reflecting, detoxifying
- **Gray** and **silver:** balancing, dreams, cloaking, impartiality, intuition
- **Brown:** stability, support, grounding, earthy, regeneration, connection to nature

It is important to remember that since color plays only a small part in the energetics of crystals, the above associations can be highly mutable and your personal relationship with a certain color can supersede the textbook definitions. Also bear in mind not to limit a crystal's effects to just the meaning of its color; just like you, each and every stone is a dynamic entity composed of many levels of existence.

CHAKRAS AND CRYSTALS

You may already be familiar with the term *chakra,* derived from the Sanskrit word for wheel.* Today, chakras are viewed as spinning vortices of energy, rather like organs in your energy field. They are responsible for

---

*The word *chakra* is properly pronounced with the hard *ch,* as in *change.*

integrating, processing, transforming, and releasing life-force energy in different ways. The most widely used chakra systems are those with seven energy centers, though sources both ancient and modern vary in the number of chakras they depict.

The Western chakra system familiar to most readers is the result of approximately two hundred years of adaptation. Although it bears little resemblance to the original chakras of ancient literature, this system is a useful therapeutic map for the energies, emotions, and themes of a human being. Each center reflects different physical, psychological, and spiritual themes that are accessible by working with that chakra. In the late 1970s it became popular to depict these seven energy centers with the colors of the rainbow, as seen in the image on the following page.

Crystal healers and other practitioners of complementary, integrative, and energy modalities often rely on the chakras as a means of understanding the out-of-balance patterns that lead to disease. The chakras serve as energetic doorways to the subconscious and the energy field as a whole, thus making them powerful focal points for the laying-on of stones during crystal healing. Each chakra is typically said to resonate with particular colors. Let's take a look at the basic meanings of the chakras so you can better apply their corresponding crystals to your everyday life:

- ▸ **Root:** survival, strength, grounding, motivation, sexuality, metabolism, circulatory system, reproductive system
- ▸ **Sacral:** sexuality, creativity, passion, fertility, identity, connection, reproductive system, kidney, bladder
- ▸ **Solar plexus:** personal power, will, self-esteem, intellect, manifestation, digestive and elimination systems, adrenal glands
- ▸ **Heart:** emotions, relationships, balance, compassion, heart and circulatory system, immune and respiratory systems

Soul Star

Causal

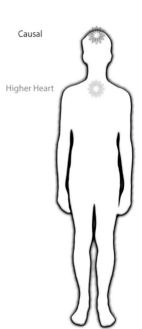

Higher Heart

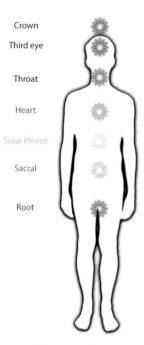

Crown

Third eye

Throat

Heart

Solar Plexus

Sacral

Root

■ The seven main energy centers
of the Western chakra system

Earth Star

■ Four minor chakras

14

- **Throat:** expression, communication, truth, mind, mouth and throat, vocal cords, nervous system, sensory organs
- **Third eye:** intuition, higher mind, dreaming, insight, understanding, sense of purpose, brain, pineal gland, sensory organs (especially eyes)
- **Crown:** divine connection, spiritual journey, self-realization, enlightenment, brain, nervous system

To work with the chakras you can choose a corresponding stone to wear, carry, or use in meditation. Many practitioners place crystals directly on (or near) the chakras to bring balance and healing to the specific energy centers. In addition to the seven main chakras outlined above, there are also minor chakras found throughout the body and energy field. Four important ones I use in my practice are earth star, higher heart, causal, and soul star chakras.

- **Earth star** (located below the feet): profound grounding, nourishes entire being, connects to past lives and karmic patterns, contains information regarding soul's origin and purpose
- **Higher heart** (positioned between heart and throat chakras): acts as a window into the overall health of energy field, unconditional love and compassion, unifies inner masculine and feminine energies, immune and lymphatic systems
- **Causal** (located at the back of the head): aligns and integrates higher energies, connects to higher mind, perception of cause and effect (or karma), helps connect to destiny
- **Soul star** (located above the head): heightens relationship to the universe, integrates cosmic energies, transcends ego, spiritual expansion

ELEMENTAL ENERGY

The elements of the wise are another avenue for understanding the energy of crystals and other tools for healing and ritual. The elemental correspondence or signature describes the relationship between the crystal and the alchemical elements of earth, air, fire, water, and spirit. Each element conveys an energy of its own, which can be directed through crystals for healing, magic, and manifestation.

- **Earth** (▽ with line): stabilizing, grounding, abundance, growth, fertility, protection, healing, manifestation, physical body, home
- **Water** (▽): emotions, cleansing, ancestry, subconscious, empathy, love
- **Fire** (△): willpower, passion, sexuality, transformation, illumination, purification, intuition, movement
- **Air** (△ with line): thought, logic, communication, language, expression, clarity, truth, flux
- **Spirit** (☆): deep transformation and healing; exists at the intersection of the other four elements, creation, divinity, harmony, sanctity

ASTROLOGICAL CORRESPONDENCES

Once again we refer to the axiom "As above, so below," which is clearly evident in the astrological correspondences assigned to crystals and gemstones. Gemstones have been thought to vibrate in harmony with the stars, planets, and constellations since early antiquity—a tradition that continues today under the guise of birthstones.

You can tap into the power of a celestial body or sign of the zodiac by working with a corresponding crystal or wearing it on your person. The various planets and luminaries, like the Sun and Moon, focus their energy through the mineral kingdom quite tangibly. Here is a brief overview of the energies associated with planetary correspondences:

- **Sun** (☉): success, sovereignty, identity, health, manifestation
- **Moon** (☽): intuition, calming, emotions, magic, divination

- **Mercury** (☿): mind, movement, communication, travel, guidance
- **Venus** (♀): love, beauty, inspiration, fertility, attraction
- **Mars** (♂): action, decisiveness, conflict, ambition, drive, protection
- **Jupiter** (♃): expansion, joy, luck, prosperity, purpose, goals
- **Saturn** (♄): discipline, karma, banishment, protection, restriction, time
- **Uranus** (♅): imagination, innovation, new ideas, rebellion, freedom
- **Neptune** (♆): mysticism, transcendence, unconditional love, creativity, dreams
- **Pluto** (♇): death and resurrection, subconscious, hidden patterns, deep transformation

Similarly, each crystal can be interpreted through the lens of the twelve signs of the zodiac, much in the way the modern jewelry industry correlates different birthstones to the months of the year and various signs of the zodiac. You might choose a crystal to enhance a quality you possess already (whether or not it's associated with your sign) or to integrate a new skill or lesson. Here is a short overview of the meaning of zodiacal correspondences:

- **Aries** (♈): courage, ambition, drive, leadership, boldness
- **Taurus** (♉): comfort, luxury, stability, sensuality, wealth
- **Gemini** (♊): mental power, communication, movement, learning, multitasking
- **Cancer** (♋): tenderness, family, boundaries, healing, empathy
- **Leo** (♌): confidence, creativity, performance, leadership, courage, justice
- **Virgo** (♍): organization, analysis, service, pragmatism, precision
- **Libra** (♎): balance, harmony, love, romance, cooperation, charm
- **Scorpio** (♏): transformation, power, psychic ability, revelation, mystery
- **Sagittarius** (♐): philosophy, freedom-loving, learning, goal-planning, exploration

- **Capricorn** (♑): practical, stability, career, achievement, tradition, responsibility
- **Aquarius** (♒): unconventional, idealistic, rebellious, egalitarian, innovative
- **Pisces** (♓): adaptable, fluid, empathic, psychic, mystical

Speaking more broadly, a crystal's correspondences reflect the energies offered by any rock, mineral, crystal, or gemstone. The information provided throughout this chapter is but a starting point intended to help launch your exploration of the inner workings of each crystal, and going above and beyond the key words that summarize their physical, psychological, and spiritual effects, which we will explore in chapter 5. Deeper explorations of the color, chakra, elemental, and astrological correspondences can provide deep insight into the energy of any crystal, and I encourage you to spend time getting to know each stone's relationship to these corresponding forces.

3

GETTING STARTED

The world of crystal and gemstone healing can feel overwhelming when you are just starting out. I've put together this chapter to guide you through the basic steps of selecting, storing, cleansing, and programming (or charging) crystals to help you dive into a rewarding relationship with your crystal allies.

CHOOSING CRYSTALS

These days most people won't have any trouble finding crystals. Not only are they available at your local metaphysical, occult, and nature shops, they have crept their way into many mainstream retail stores. You can also buy crystals online and at rock and gem shows, jewelry shows, and metaphysical expos. When faced with so many opportunities, the real challenge is in choosing the right stones.

I think it's a great idea to start with the crystals that grab your attention. Perhaps the rich, violet hues of amethyst or the sparkling, cerulean druse of celestite draws you in. It might be the tactile feel of a polished jasper in your hands or the comforting heft of rhodonite that signals you've found the right stone. Sometimes it's just an inner knowing. However you find yourself attracted to a crystal, begin with ones that call to you. Trust your instincts; there's a good chance that when you look up the properties of these crystals they'll be a perfect reflection of your current scenario.

You might also choose to use a reference book (such as this one) to look up a crystal whose properties correspond to challenges you're facing in life. Just be sure to remember that crystals are multifaceted—just as you are—and their entire stories cannot be told in a few key words and phrases.

It might seem rather surprising, but crystals you feel a strong aversion to can also be important for your personal growth. Often crystals that feel uncomfortable hold the potential for profound healing. They feel uneasy because they vibrate to or represent an energy, lesson, or pattern you've not yet mastered. Working with them a little at a time in a safe space offers an opportunity to close the gap between where you are and where your destiny lies, so be sure not to ignore stones that seem to be repelling you.

When sourcing your crystals remember that size, quality, color, and provenance all affect the value and energy of any given stone. While there is no need to drive yourself to bankruptcy to get the biggest and finest specimens, it is important to remember that all these factors affect the work you will do. Large stones produce larger, louder energy fields, but they aren't useful for carrying with you or laying on the body. When shopping for crystals be mindful of the purpose or goal you have for working with them.

Also bear in mind that many stones are heat-treated, irradiated, dyed, stabilized, or outright simulated/synthesized. Most of these processes render the resulting stones unfit for healing. Heat treatment is the gentlest and most acceptable of these treatments, but irradiated, dyed, and coated stones may be energetically damaged beyond repair. My best advice is generally to stick to natural, untreated stones, either raw or polished. For a full discussion of sourcing crystals, including information about the many kinds of treated, simulated, and synthetic stones available, check out chapter 4 of my book *Crystal Basics: The Energetic, Healing & Spiritual Power of 200 Gemstones.*

Are Your Crystals Ethical?

One of the hottest topics in the world of crystal healing is the concept of ethically sourced crystals. As the world awakens to the harsh reality of mining processes and their connection to colonialism, many crystal healers are seeking alternative, conscious sources for their crystals. The persistent injustice, both to our fellow humans and the planet itself, is exacerbated by crystals' steep growth in popularity. There is no definitive set of criteria for what constitutes an ethically sourced crystal; in fact, many retailers have begun to advertise that their stones come from ethical sources even when their actual provenance is, at best, unknown. While there is no easy solution to the question of ethics in mining and the crystal industry at large, here are some helpful tips for finding ethically sourced stones:

- Buy directly from the source wherever possible. Many rockhounds dig their own stones and offer them for sale online and at rock and mineral shows.
- Purchase vintage and historic rocks and minerals from old collections. These are often available online and at rock and mineral shows, often at very affordable prices.
- Dig your own! Visiting mines and digging sites can be a fun vacation. Don't underestimate the power of common rocks, too; you'll find the healing qualities of many common rocks described in chapter 5.
- Always ask for provenance. The reality is that most stones' exact stories aren't known, but requesting information about where a stone came from and how it got to you

can provide clues as to whether it was sourced responsibly. It also reminds purveyors that it's important to their customers.

- Beware trademarked names and other nomenclature that sounds like a metaphysical term with the suffix *-ite* added to the end, as these are often sold with massively inflated prices and hidden provenance.
- Learn about how crystals, gemstones, and industrially important minerals are mined in different countries. If you find places that frequently engage in human rights violations, consider a personal ban on crystals from such locations.

STORING CRYSTALS

Once you've started a collection of crystals and gemstones, you'll need a method to store them safely. Large or beautiful specimens lend themselves well to display, as do small stones grouped in decorative dishes or other containers, but eventually you may have too many crystals to keep on display at all times.

You may want to sort your crystals by size, type, or color in order to better locate them. I like to keep my smaller rough and tumbled stones organized in plastic containers with small compartments, which are easy to find at your local craft store. I also have some larger wooden and plastic boxes I use for crystals that need more space. If you'll be placing multiple stones into the same box, it is helpful to wrap stones in cloth, undyed tissue paper, or something similar to protect them. I recommend checking the Mohs scale of hardness of the various stones you plan to store together (this is listed for each entry in chapter 5), as softer stones can be damaged by harder ones. The Mohs scale rates stones from 1 to 10, with 10 being the hardest, based on the stone's relative resistance to scratching. For example, you would not want a beautiful, clear piece of amber (2–2.5) to be scratched by an equally gorgeous amethyst (7).

Bear in mind that some crystals can be damaged by humidity or direct sun exposure, so you may need to store certain specimens out of sight to protect them between uses.

CLEANSING CRYSTALS

As discussed in chapter 1, crystals are natural recorders of the energies they meet. This means that crystals need to be cleansed in order to work optimally. If they become fully saturated with the energies around you, they will reflect those energies. Imagine a crystal you wear on a stressful day; it will absorb some of that stress, thereby alleviating you of it, but once saturated it will release that stressful energy back to you. It's also difficult to know what kind of energy a crystal has encountered on its long journey from mine to store, so cleansing is an important first step in getting to know your new crystal allies.

Certain crystals are better suited to particular cleansing methods over others, as salt, water, and sunshine can damage some of your beloved stones, particularly the softer ones. Here is a short list of popular cleansing methods:

- ► Sunlight and moonlight
- ► Salt
- ► Water
- ► Smoke from cleansing herbs, such as sage, cedar, or frankincense
- ► Sound

■ There are many ways to cleanse crystals, including sound, salt, smoke, and using other crystals.

▸ Breath
▸ Burying in earth
▸ Rain, snow, or wind
▸ Immersing in flower petals, cleansing herbs, or brown rice
▸ Placing atop other crystals, such as selenite or an amethyst cluster
▸ Flower and gem essences

It is important to stress that salt, sunlight, and water are especially challenging to work with if you are unfamiliar with the chemical composition and physical properties of your crystals. Avoid using salt or water for minerals softer than 5 on the Mohs scale, and be mindful that some rocks and minerals are soluble, friable, or can otherwise be damaged by salt or water. Sunlight causes many transparent colored gems to fade, including amethyst, kunzite, aquamarine, rose quartz, fluorite, and many others.

My three favorite methods for cleansing are sound, smoke, and breath, as they are safe for all your crystals. To cleanse your crystals with sound you can use singing bowls, chimes, bells, or anything else that makes noise—so long as it is intentional. I've also cleansed with my voice, a French horn, and clapping my hands. Set an intention and visualize the sound waves moving through the crystal(s), shaking loose any energies that no longer serve. Similarly, smoke is a very simple method and you can use a variety of herbs including sage, cedar, palo santo, hyssop, rose, cedar, juniper, rue, lemongrass, copal, and frankincense. Say a prayer or set the intention to cleanse your crystals, then light your herbs or incense. Waft the smoke over your stones, or gently pass them through the smoke. Couple this action with a visualization of the smoke's energy moving through the crystals and wiping them clean.

Breath is my go-to cleansing method because it's always handy and requires no props or tools. The breath can be harnessed, alongside intention and visualization, to enact what is perhaps the most powerful cleansing method available. Releasing the breath in a short, sharp pulse through the nose generates a tiny ionic charge that interacts with your crystal to leave it cleansed and clear.

✧ Cleansing with Breath

Select the stone that you'd like to cleanse, and spend a moment or two setting your intention to purify it. As your mind focuses on this, grasp your stone between the thumb and index finger of your dominant hand, or if it is large or heavy, hold it in the palm of one or both hands. Breathe deeply and rhythmically while making a conscious connection to the stone. Visualize white light or any other symbol of purification flowing into your body with the breath as you inhale, then exhale any stagnant or disharmonious energy. When you feel totally saturated with this cleansing force, you are ready to cleanse your stone. Take a deep breath, filling your whole being with this energy; raise the stone before you and exhale with a powerful pulse of air through the nose. Imagine this pulse of air carrying white light into your chosen stone and sweeping away any old or unneeded energy, leaving behind a clean slate.

No matter how you choose to cleanse your stones, be sure to repeat it often. A good rule of thumb is to cleanse them after every use. It's a bit like washing your hands or your clothes; better to be too clean than not clean enough. There are also persistent myths that some stones—namely selenite, hematite, kyanite, and citrine—do not need to be cleansed. This is inaccurate. All crystals have memory, so all crystals retain information that may not match your intention. Therefore, all crystals must be cleansed.

CHARGING AND PROGRAMMING CRYSTALS

There is a popular notion that crystals need to be charged like batteries. Many people place their crystals under the full moon or atop a slab of selenite hoping to charge them, not realizing that these methods are actually cleansing, not charging their stones. So what exactly does it mean to charge a crystal?

When I began my crystal journey there was virtually no talk of charging; rather, most authors and practitioners talked about *programming* crystals. Essentially these are two terms that describe the same practice. The idea behind this is that crystals work best with direction. Programming is an essential step wherein we can imbue crystals with our intentions, in the same way an app or computer software gives direction to our devices.

Originally the word "charge" was used in this context to convey the meaning of "entrust with a task or responsibility." Over the past decade or two the connotation of the word has changed with our technology. Since we so frequently charge the batteries of our phones and other devices, crystal lovers perceive it to mean something similar when it comes to crystals. However, unlike the energy in batteries, the energy in crystals can't be depleted. They can, however, soak up a lot of energies that make them less effective, and this is why frequent cleansing is imperative. You can also charge or program a crystal with your intention, which is another step that enhances your crystal work. Not only does it set the stage for the crystal to have a specific task to focus on, but it also programs your mind! My favorite programming technique uses the breath and is similar to the cleansing method described above.

✧ Programming Crystals

Start with a cleansed crystal and select the intention you'd like to use to program or charge your crystal for this session. I recommend distilling your intention to a single word or a short phrase. Relax and breathe deeply and rhythmically, focusing on your desired intention. As you breathe, imagine that you are inhaling not only air but the energy of your goal; visualize breathing in any colors or symbols you associate with your goal and allowing them to fill your body and aura. Once you are saturated with this intention, hold your crystal between the thumb and forefinger of your dominant hand, or in one or both palms if this is not comfortable or possible. Breathe in deeply, and consciously connect to your crystal. Release the breath in a short, sharp pulse through the nose, while picturing the breath carrying your intention into the crystal. Once finished, spend a moment in gratitude to the crystal before returning to your normal awareness.

4

WORKING WITH CRYSTALS

Once you've gotten familiar with the foundational practices of select-ing, cleansing, and programming crystals, it's time to get down to the real work of healing and personal development. Throughout this chap-ter you'll find information about different applications for crystal energy, from exploring the shape of crystals to partnering with crystals for healing, divination, and everyday wear.

CRYSTAL SHAPES

Crystals and gemstones are available in a wide array of natural and polished shapes, each of which offers fresh possibilities for working with crystals in different ways. I'm often asked how the energy of a crystal is affected by its shape. In fact, not much. If the predominant determinants of a crystal's energy are its formation process, chemical composition, and the internal arrangement of its atoms, ions, and molecules, then the outer form has very little to do with its energy.

Two crystals that are otherwise equal except for their shape will have the same fundamental energy. However, the shape of a stone affects the *distribu-tion* of the energy. It's a bit like listening to the same song on two different kinds of speakers; chances are the sound through your phone's speakers is different from what you hear on your car speakers. Ideally, when choosing a crystal you can keep in mind that different crystal shapes may not change

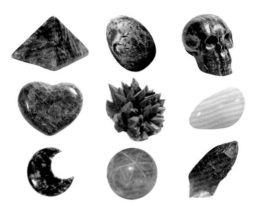

■ An assortment of crystal shapes

the energy itself, but they influence the way we use that energy. The popular axiom says that form follows function, and it's true of crystals, too. For example, it's difficult to lay a sphere on the body for a healing layout, and a large cluster makes a terrible choice for a pocket rock, so our practice is adapted to the shape of our stones. Here's a brief overview of some of the key themes and applications for various shapes that crystals can take:

▶ **Point:** The classic crystal shape with a single termination, or point, directs energy through its tip. It may be natural or polished into this shape.

▶ **Double terminated:** Double terminated crystals have points at each end. They send and receive energy simultaneously, while also symbolizing connection. Naturally double-terminated crystals are more effective than those polished into this shape.

- **Cluster:** Many minerals form as groups of crystals attached to a common matrix or base. Clusters disperse energy in many directions, making them helpful for uplifting the vibes in a room. Crystal clusters also symbolize group harmony.

- **Rough:** Rough stones are unpolished and uncut. They tend to have a less refined energy than polished ones and may be more grounding than some polished shapes.

- **Tumbled:** Tumbled stones are irregular, rounded shapes produced by a machine called a rock tumbler. These are among the most readily available shapes, and they are perfect for carrying in your pocket or adding to a crystal grid or layout.

- **Palm stone:** Palm stones, also called *gallets,* are rather like tumbles in that they are smooth and rounded, but they are large enough to fill the palm of your hand. They are excellent for using around the home or for an extra-large dose of crystal energy on the go.

- **Sphere:** Spherical stones emit a gentle, pervasive energy that flows evenly in all directions at once. Spheres are balancing, nourishing, and unifying.

- **Egg:** Eggs represent fertility, creativity, and growth. They are also gently anchoring and serve as excellent massage tools.

- **Pyramid:** Pyramids offer a simultaneously anchoring and uplifting influence. Pyramid-shaped stones support manifestation, confer protection, and align the entire energy field.

- **Obelisk and generator:** Obelisks are usually polished pillars with square bases and pyramidal terminations. Generators are polished crystal points with flat bases that stand upright. Also called towers, these shapes exhibit the same directional flow of energy as crystal points.

- **Cabochon:** A cabochon is a gemstone cut with a dome-shaped top and a flat underside. Usually intended for jewelry-making, a cabochon also makes an excellent healing tool because it lays flat on the body.

- ▶ **Wand:** Crystal wands, both natural and polished, are made from many different materials. Wands can activate crystal grids, direct energy in a healing session, and serve as focal points in meditation and ritual.
- ▶ **Heart:** Gemstone hearts are tokens of love, affection, and emotional balance.
- ▶ **Worry stone:** Oval-shaped with an indentation for the thumb, worry stones are wonderful allies for your pocket. They are tactile tools that can be rubbed to bring comfort and ease stress.
- ▶ **Skull:** Crystal skulls are powerful tools for expanding consciousness, deepening spiritual practice, and communing with guides, ancestors, devas, and other spiritual beings. They are dimensional doorways and bring healing to the soul.

EVERYDAY CRYSTALS

There are countless ways to incorporate crystal energy into your life. You can carry or wear crystals, place them around the home or office, and even bring them to bed. Crystals can support your garden, protect your car, and offer healing energy virtually anywhere you place them.

Carrying and Wearing Crystals

Perhaps the simplest way to benefit from crystal energy is to wear crystals as jewelry or carry them in your pocket or purse. Jewelry makes for the easiest way to benefit from the influence of crystals all day long. Gem and crystal jewelry is ubiquitous, from inexpensive bracelets and pendants to fine gemstones available in a range of styles. Wearing crystals as pendants, bracelets, rings, and other jewelry is most effective when they are cleansed regularly and charged with your intention before leaving the house.

A small, smooth, tumbled stone, such as a polished heart or palm stone, is ideal to take on the go. Small stones can be tucked directly into a pocket or purse, or one or more stones can be placed into a pouch for safekeeping

■ Wearing gemstone jewelry is a wonderful way to benefit from crystal energy.

while you're out and about. Less is usually more in this instance, as combining too many crystals in an attempt to manifest too many things usually produces muddled results. Don't forget to cleanse and program your stones regularly for best results.

Crystals in the Home and Office

One of the very first books I ever read on crystals illustrated the various ways that stones could be placed around the home, garden, and office to bring health and harmony to every space. Ever since, I've kept crystals in each room (and on virtually every horizontal surface available) to enhance my daily life.

You can choose relaxing, restorative crystals for the bedroom; cleansing and energizing crystals for the bathroom; and nourishing, joyful ones for the kitchen. Romantic and empowering crystals can be a good choice anywhere in your personal living space. Large stones may be best suited to project their energy throughout the space available; clusters and geodes are particularly helpful for this. Bookends, sculptures, and other decorative pieces are excellent additions to the home. Try stones like fluorite, carnelian, or pyrite in your office or workspace to boost productivity. Gardening with crystals is also rewarding; add moss agate, quartz, or shungite (or any other stone that feels appropriate) to containers or beds to encourage healthy plant growth.

Crystal Dreaming

Many people enjoy adding a crystal to the nightstand or tucking a gem under the pillow to support better and more restful sleep. Your bed can even be gridded (see page 35 for a discussion of grids) to encourage better rest and healing. Often crystal lovers will bring a new stone to bed to get to know it better, and in hopes that their dreams may reveal something about the nature of the stone. This can be a rewarding practice but bear in mind that it isn't a substitute for meditation or otherwise consciously working with a crystal. Remember that crystals are reflectors of the subconscious, so much of what is revealed in your dreams may not be a representation of the crystal's energy but of your own.

When it comes to sleeping with crystals, be mindful about which ones and how many you have nearby. "Less is more" is a good guideline, as too many energies can negatively impact your sleep cycle. I try to limit the number of stones on my nightstand and I avoid taking stimulating, energizing, or overly intense crystals to bed without being prepared for the possibility that I may not sleep well. Like all other applications of crystal energy, the stones in, around, or near your bed benefit from frequent cleansing.

CRYSTAL HEALING

Many people are drawn to crystals for hands-on healing and related applications. Crystals can be placed directly on and around the body for healing layouts, and they catalyze profound healing and personal development when used in meditation. Even those stones placed around the home or worn as jewelry gently support well-being on every level.

Meditating with Crystals

The very first step in using crystals for healing is cultivating a meditation practice with your stones. Crystal meditation doesn't require formal training, but it does require practice, patience, and persistence. The goal of meditation is not a state of no thoughts; rather it is an opportunity for quiet reflection. When coupled with crystals, meditation fosters a deeper relationship with your healing stones and offers deep insight into the ways they can benefit your spirit, mind, and body.

For best results when meditating, seat yourself with good posture in a comfortable place, free from distractions. The breath is an important gateway to entering meditative states, so I often encourage students and clients to focus on their breathing without forcing it; observe the breath coming and going. After you get some practice with the basics of meditation, you can add crystals to the mix. Holding or visualizing a crystal during meditation is a way to observe how its energy influences you. It gives you the opportunity to explore crystal energy in an intimate, personal way. Below you'll find a grounding and centering exercise to get you started.

✧ *Grounding and Centering*

Some of the most universally appreciated techniques are grounding and centering. Grounding creates a conscious link between your energy field and the Earth's. This results in a complete circuit of energy to discharge and release the energies that do not serve us, and receive healing and nourishing energy from the planet. Centering helps gather our awareness and instill a sense of focus. Grounding and centering work best when used in sequence, and they are a solid way to start any form of meditation.

Once you have gotten settled into your comfortable place, begin to breathe rhythmically and comfortably, merely observing the breath. Set your intention to ground and center. As you breathe, imagine that luminous roots are growing from the soles of your feet and/or the base of your spine. They dig deep into the planet, connecting you to the heart of Mother Earth. Exhale any worry, tension, stress, or other disharmony through those luminous roots into the molten core of the Earth, where they are transmuted into positive energy. Reverse that flow of energy on the in-breath, drawing healing, nourishing energy into the core of your being.

Once you feel grounded and supported, take mental note of your spiritual center. In what ways, if any, do you feel out of balance? Perhaps you'll get an impression of your aura or chakras being out of alignment, or get an image of your mind feeling scattered and thin. As you draw forth healing energy from the planet beneath you, imagine that it realigns and balances you in every way, helping you feel more centered. When you feel completely grounded and centered, thank Mother Earth and draw your awareness back to the room around you. Open your eyes and spend a moment breathing normally before returning to normal activities.

Grids and Layouts

Making crystal grids and practicing laying-on-of-stones are two of my favorite applications for crystal energy. Both rely on intentional arrangements of crystals and gemstones to effect change and invite greater balance and wholeness into your life. Crystal grids can be made on virtually any flat surface that won't be disturbed, while layouts are created on and around the body during a healing session.

Crystal grids can be used to confer protection, enhance the manifestation of any goal, or beam healing to someone remotely. Grids can be small enough to fit on a shelf or end table, or large enough to fill an entire room. It's easy to find books devoted to grid-making, so we'll start with the basics.

You can place a rough or tumbled stone within a ring or other defined shape of quartz crystals to broadcast that stone's energy into your space. If the quartz crystals are directed inward, consider that they are attracting an intention toward you, whereas outward-turned points might be sending energy away or broadcasting it to another location. More elaborate grids, such as the one pictured below, might incorporate many stones to support your goals.

Crystal layouts are rather like large grids meant to bring change directly to the human body and aura. They can be as simple as a handful of strategically placed clear quartz points or tumbled stones, or they can be elaborate arrays of stones consisting of dozens and dozens of stones. Three of my favorite all-purpose layouts are pictured on page 37. The first requires

■ This is an example of a grid for manifesting prosperity. It consists of a central citrine surrounded by rings of aventurine, tiger's eye, and clear quartz.

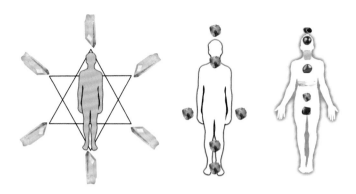

■ Three easy-to-use crystal layouts: Solomon's seal,
the carnelian net, and a chakra-balancing layout

only six points of clear quartz; direct the points outward to expel unwanted energies, or inward to recharge and rebalance. The second layout, called the *carnelian net,* makes use of six tumbled or rough carnelian to release trauma, bring harmony, and revitalize your entire being. The third and final layout can be made from any seven stones that feel appropriate for balancing the seven major chakras. I like to add clear quartz points to the hands to enhance the flow of energy through the entire energy field. Use your intuition and creativity to create your own crystal grids and healing layouts.

Crystal Elixirs

Crystal energy can be transferred to your drinking water to bring healing to body, mind, and spirit. Crystal- and gem-infused waters have been in use for centuries, if not millennia, and offer new ways of catalyzing the healing process. Care should always be taken when making elixirs or essences from crystals, as many rocks and minerals are toxic and pose considerable threat if ingested in even small amounts.* In light of this, consider using only indirect methods for imprinting your drinking water with crystal energy until you can effectively identify those that are safe for other uses.

Allow your water to infuse for several hours in sunlight if it's safe for the crystal; otherwise consider moonlight or ambient lighting. Then remove the stones and either bottle the water as an elixir or drink it as a gem water.

Crystal elixirs and gem waters have a multitude of uses. Gem waters are made to be used immediately, as they are not preserved. Elixirs (also called essences) require preservation with vegetable glycerin, apple cider vinegar, or an alcohol such as brandy or vodka; they are used only a few drops at a time. You can add them to food and beverages, apply them to the skin, spray them around the aura, or infuse them into a bath. You can read more about making essences in my earlier books: *Crystal Basics* (pages 128–40) and *Flower Essences from the Witch's Garden*.

Other Applications

The only limits to working with crystals are the stones available to you and your imagination. You can hold them for meditation, use them as focal points for astral journeys, and incorporate them into rituals. Use crystal wands and similar shapes to cut karmic cords or remove harmful energies from your aura.

---

*There is a persistent myth that crystals whose names end in -*ite* are not water-safe. This is completely untrue; the suffix only denotes that a substance is a rock or mineral and conveys no information about solubility or safety. Many minerals with names ending in -*ite* are water-safe (andradite, mookaite, indicolite, etc.) while others without this suffix (galena, orpiment, realgar) can be deadly when placed in your drinking water. Please refer to the safety guidelines in chapter 7 of *Crystal Basics* for detailed information about precautions when making elixirs.

■ The safest way to make elixirs is via the indirect method (pictured at right). Place your crystals in a smaller vessel that can be placed inside a container filled with water. Since the stones do not make contact with the water, they can safely energize your water without fear of contamination.

Try using crystal clusters to brush or sweep the aura clean. Below you'll find an example of another crystal healing ritual: aura cleansing with selenite.

✧ Aura Clearing with Selenite

Begin by cleansing your favorite piece of selenite. I like to use a longer wand- or blade-shaped crystal, but any handheld piece will do. Set your intention to cleanse your aura and consider programming the selenite with this goal in mind. Next, hold the stone over the crown of your head and gently sweep it downward along the midline of your body toward the feet. Use gentle, continuous movements—although shorter, more vigorous motions can break up particularly stagnant energies. Give the crystal a quick and gentle flick or shake after reaching the feet, and visualize it releasing any disharmonious energies and transmuting them into white light. Repeat along each side of the body. Finish by gently sweeping upward from the feet to the crown, envisioning that the selenite is restoring balance and harmony to your entire energy field.

5
ENCYCLOPEDIA OF CRYSTALS

The sheer diversity of the mineral kingdom inspired me to put together this compendium of healing crystals. This directory includes 450 rocks, minerals, fossils, and gemstones, from the most common and humble of ordinary rocks to truly precious and rare gems. I've aspired to include a mix of both common and rare stones, including several that have yet to be included in other books. Each entry includes some important geological information related to the formula, hardness, crystal system, and formation process, all of which provide important clues about a crystal's energy. You may also, if you like, cross-reference this information with chapter 2 of *Crystal Basics* to uncover the deeper meaning and primary influences for every stone. Some entries may indicate that the composition includes other minerals, as in the case of fire agate, which is composed of quartz and limonite; consulting the specific entry for limonite can expand your understanding of the energy of fire agate. Every crystal entry also includes associated chakras and the elemental, planetary, and zodiacal correspondences for each stone.

While it is an impossible task to catalog every mineral species and variety of rock (there are tens of thousands when we consider the myriad ways they combine), this guide is meant to be a useful starting point for your practice. Whether you use this encyclopedia for quick reference to get to know a new stone or take it along to help you navigate the variety of crystals in your favorite store, may this book inspire and support your crystal journey.

Actinolite

Formula: $Ca_2(Mg,Fe)_5Si_8O_{22}(OH)_2$ Hardness: 5–6
Crystal system: monoclinic   Formation process: metamorphic
Chakra: root, solar plexus, heart   Correspondences: earth,
Mars, Aries, Scorpio

Physical healing: supports processes of growth, regeneration in the body; improves health of kidneys and liver; hastens healing of open wounds

Psychological healing: fosters motivation, determination, and follow-through; helps with maintaining a clear head during stressful periods; imparts honesty, integrity, and willingness to serve; assuages loneliness and inspires friendly, openhearted attitude

Spiritual healing: shines a light in times of darkness and despair; protects and nourishes; clears blockages and stagnant energies from the aura and chakras; invites a sense of belonging, brotherhood, and connection

Note: Fibrous, asbestiform actinolite should be handled with care so that no airborne particles are inhaled or ingested.

Adamite

Formula: Zn_2AsO_4OH Hardness: 3.5   Crystal system: orthorhombic
Formation process: sedimentary   Chakra: sacral, solar plexus,
heart   Correspondences: fire, air, Jupiter, Sagittarius

Physical healing: balances endocrine system and hormones, alleviates conditions of the lungs, enhances metabolism, boosts energy, dispels lethargy and fatigue

Psychological healing: instills mental clarity; cuts through confusion and depression, replacing them with joy, wonder, and love; nourishes the inner child; links emotions to will, helping you attain your heart's desire; ignites both creativity and motivation

Spiritual healing: helps radiate love, positivity, and light; enhances contact with spirits, guides, angels, and other beings while repelling harmful or dangerous entities; deepens your connection to and trust in the Divine

Note: Adamite may be toxic if mishandled.

Aegirine

Formula: $NaFeSi_2O_6$ Hardness: 6   Crystal system: monoclinic
Formation process: igneous or metamorphic
Chakra: earth star, root   Correspondences: earth, fire,
Jupiter, Sagittarius

Physical healing: stabilizes the physical body and stimulates repair of physical tissue, boosts immune system, enhances absorption of minerals and nutrients

Psychological healing: invites positivity; grants courage, confidence, and conviction; helps stand up to peer pressure; encourages attainment of wisdom; offers strength to reflect your true self in the world

Spiritual healing: strongly protective and deeply grounding, extracts foreign and harmful energies from the body and aura, helps integrate life lessons before moving on, facilitates astral travel, offers sense of belonging and cohesion among groups, boosts and harmonizes the effects of other crystals

Agate

Formula: SiO_2 with impurities   Hardness: 6.5–7
Crystal system: trigonal   Formation process: igneous or
sedimentary   Chakra: various   Correspondences: earth,
Mercury, Gemini

Physical healing: promotes overall health and well-being; nourishes and protects body; stabilizes metabolism; regenerates tissue; stimulates digestion and elimination; especially supportive of skin, lymphatic system, and eyes; promotes sleep

Psychological healing: considered lucky and protective; invites pragmatism, self-awareness, and analysis; promotes peace, grace, harmony, and personal development

Spiritual healing: protects and nourishes aura, reveals root causes, gently grounds, sustains in times of transition

Agate, Blue Lace

Formula: SiO$_2$ with impurities   Hardness: 6.5–7   Crystal system: trigonal   Formation process: igneous   Chakra: solar plexus, heart, throat   Correspondences: water, Neptune, Pisces

Physical healing: supports health of respiratory system, relieves congestion, soothes lungs; promotes healthy skin, alleviates rashes and other disorders of skin; supports healthy eyes and vision; strengthens bones and nails; prevents dizziness

Psychological healing: stone of harmony that invites peace and happiness into the home; promotes peace, lightheartedness, and happiness; soothes and calms; invites self-forgiveness; supports self-confidence, resiliency, and self-esteem

Spiritual healing: allows you to be more truly yourself; helps accept life lessons with ease and grace; aids in releasing unwanted fears, energies, and attachments; instills inner and outer strength

Agate, Botswana

Formula: SiO$_2$ with impurities   Hardness: 6.5–7   Crystal system: trigonal   Formation process: igneous   Chakra: sacral   Correspondences: earth, Mercury, Gemini, Scorpio

Physical healing: supports health of brain and nervous system; may be used to break bad habits and addictions, particularly smoking

Psychological healing: eliminates repressed guilt; supports healthy sexual expression; improves self-image; eliminates programming from family; encourages harmony; assists communication and creative self-expression, making it a good stone for artists, writers, dancers, and other creatives

Spiritual healing: protects and cleanses the aura, facilitates astral travel

Agate, Crazy Lace

Formula: SiO_2 with impurities   Hardness: 6.5–7   Crystal system: trigonal   Formation process: igneous   Chakra: solar plexus, crown   Correspondences: air, Mercury, Gemini, Leo

Physical healing: supports healthy metabolism; boosts body's ability to fight off infections; alleviates conditions affecting blood vessels and nerves, including sciatica

Psychological healing: encourages mental flexibility, problem-solving skills, and creativity; encourages you to put plans into motion by taking decisive action

Spiritual healing: increases personal magnetism; inspires elegance and grace; helpful during periods of rapid change, especially by reinforcing a positive outlook during challenging times

Agate, Dulcote

Formula: SiO_2 with calcite ($CaCO_3$), goethite [$Fe^{3+}O(OH)$], and iron (Fe)   Hardness: 6.5   Crystal system: trigonal   Formation process: sedimentary   Chakra: sacral, heart   Correspondences: water, Moon, Cancer

Physical healing: promotes overall healing and stimulates cellular repair, ensures healthy pregnancy and safe birth, helpful for releasing addiction

Psychological healing: fosters hope and optimism; offers renewal of mind and body; releases trauma, painful memories, and unhealthy feelings rooted in the past; promotes mother-child bonding; eases childhood trauma

Spiritual healing: protective stone, traditionally carried for safe travel; facilitates connection to nature spirits; encourages perception and celebration of beauty in all forms; invokes wisdom of nature to inspire magic and spiritual practice

Agate, Fire

Formula: SiO_2 with limonite $[FeO(OH) \cdot nH_2O]$
Hardness: 6.5–7   Crystal system: trigonal
Formation process: igneous   Chakra: sacral, solar plexus
Correspondences: fire, water, Sun, Mars, Aries, Leo

Physical healing: warms, energizes, and promotes overall healing and rejuvenation; boosts metabolism and digestion; alleviates conditions of intestines; supports healthy reproductive system and libido

Psychological healing: enhances inspiration, creativity, problem-solving skills; eliminates fear and doubt while inviting a sense of passion and purpose, thereby enabling you to feel more decisive and content; fosters warm and bright disposition

Spiritual healing: deflects harmful energy and sends it back to its source, purifies aura and strengthens aura's natural defenses, activates kundalini and helps you reach ecstatic states in meditation

Agate, Flower

Formula: SiO_2 with impurities   Hardness: 6.5–7
Crystal system: trigonal
Formation process: igneous   Chakra: sacral, heart
Correspondences: earth, water, Venus, Taurus, Virgo

Physical healing: promotes nutrient absorption and health of digestive system, stimulates healing of urinary and reproductive systems

Psychological healing: stone of sacred sexuality, inspires the pursuit of beauty and stimulates creative impulses, cultivates inner and outer beauty and enhances self-esteem, soothes and releases old emotional patterns

Spiritual healing: boosts manifestation, abundance, and following your bliss; realigns subtle bodies with physical; offers support during phases of transformation and change; facilitates connection to devas

Agate, Gobi Desert

Formula: SiO_2 with iron (Fe) and other impurities
Hardness: 6.5–7   Crystal system: trigonal   Formation process: igneous or sedimentary   Chakra: root, sacral, solar plexus   Correspondences: earth, air, Saturn, Uranus, Aquarius

Physical healing: strengthens bones, dispels parasites and infection, expedites recovery after dehydration

Psychological healing: inspires patience, stillness, and quietude; helps eliminate repetitive thinking and repressed emotions; teaches lessons of acceptance and helps in embracing diversity

Spiritual healing: enhances meditation; helps to attain states of surrender; connects the core of your being with ancient wisdom and earth energies; clears the aura, especially good at removing karmic debris and past-life trauma

Agate, Iris

Formula: SiO_2 Hardness: 6.5–7   Crystal system: trigonal
Formation process: igneous   Chakra: crown, soul star
Correspondences: earth, air, fire, water, spirit, Moon, Neptune, Uranus, Aquarius, Pisces

Physical healing: brings light to physical body for overall healing and repair; promotes healthy skin, hair, and nails; soothes eyes

Psychological healing: stone of optimism, happiness, and hope; helps you see the silver lining; promotes friendship and peace

Spiritual healing: clears unhealthy patterns from the aura, stimulates psychic development and clairvoyance, helps shamanic journeys to higher planes

Agate, Lake Superior

Formula: SiO_2 with hematite (Fe_2O_3)   Hardness: 6.5–7
Crystal system: trigonal   Formation process: igneous
Chakra: root   Correspondences: earth, water, fire, Mars,
Saturn, Aries, Leo, Scorpio

Physical healing: draws out pain and tension, especially in neck and shoulders;
improves sleep; supports health of the brain and nervous system, particularly
the medulla oblongata

Psychological healing: boosts confidence; enhances logic and reasoning; helpful
for learning and studying, as it enhances memory and recall; balances work
and play

Spiritual healing: connects to ancient wisdom, facilitates contact with spirit
guides and teachers, links you to ancestral wisdom, helps release karmic
patterns and break harmful ancestral cycles

Agate, Montana Moss

Formula: SiO_2 with manganese (Mn), iron (Fe)
Hardness: 6.5–7   Crystal system: trigonal
Formation process: igneous   Chakra: root, crown
Correspondences: earth, Pluto, Scorpio

Physical healing: helpful for conditions of the skin and circulatory system

Psychological healing: counters sense of aimlessness by helping you find
purpose and direction, sparks curiosity and draws out latent talents

Spiritual healing: deepens meditation and enhances visionary states, promotes
attunement to earth energies, stimulates flow of kundalini energy, draws out
negative energies and clears the aura and chakras

Note: also exhibits the properties of moss agate (p. 48)

Agate, Moss

Formula: SiO_2 with celadonite $[K(Mg,Fe^{2+})Fe^{3+}(Si_4O_{10})(OH)_2]$ or hornblende $[(Ca,Na)_{2-3}(Mg,Fe,Al)_5(Al,Si)_8O_{22}(OH,F)_2]$

Hardness: 6.5–7   Crystal system: trigonal

Formation process: igneous   Chakra: root, heart

Correspondences: earth, Venus, Mercury, Jupiter, Virgo

Physical healing: soothes pain and reduces inflammation, alleviates excess mucus, detoxifies, supports immune system, helps body regulate blood sugar

Psychological healing: nourishes and balances mind and emotions, stabilizes mood, decreases excessive worry

Spiritual healing: fosters connection to the natural world; facilitates contact with nature spirits and devas; great for gardens, supports healthy plant growth; boosts manifestation skills

Agate, Pink

Formula: SiO_2 with manganese (Mn), iron (Fe)

Hardness: 6.5–7   Crystal system: trigonal

Formation process: igneous

Chakra: heart   Correspondences: water, air, Venus, Libra

Physical healing: soothes inflammation; treats eyes, skin, digestive system, pancreas, and reproductive system; stimulates metabolism

Psychological healing: assuages fear, alleviates emotional pain, soothes childhood trauma and painful memories, boosts self-esteem

Spiritual healing: invites unconditional love and compassion; promotes tolerance, acceptance, and kindness for all life

Agate, Polyhedroid

Formula: SiO_2 with impurities   Hardness: 6.5–7
Crystal system: trigonal   Formation process: igneous   Chakra: third eye
Correspondences: air, spirit, Mercury, Uranus, Aquarius

Physical healing: promotes health and healing of visceral organs, promotes healing and recovery after transplant surgeries

Psychological healing: stimulates creative thinking, helpful for relating to and understanding people from other cultures and backgrounds

Spiritual healing: engenders sense of belonging; facilitates spiritual growth, adaptation, and personal development; cultivates sense of wonder and awe

Agate, Snakeskin

Formula: SiO_2 with impurities   Hardness: 6.5–7
Crystal system: trigonal   Formation process: sedimentary   Chakra: root, sacral
Correspondences: earth, air, Mercury, Pluto, Gemini, Scorpio

Physical healing: soothes and rejuvenates skin, relieves congestion and reduces irritation of mucous membranes, calms upset stomach

Psychological healing: boosts mental faculties, problem-solving skills, rational thinking; promotes confidence and self-esteem; stimulates direct, open, and honest communication

Spiritual healing: symbolizes transformation, rebirth, and renewal; facilitates shamanic journey, soul retrieval, and kundalini activation

Agate, Stick

Formula: SiO_2 with pseudomorph inclusions
Hardness: 6.5–7   **Crystal system:** trigonal
Formation process: sedimentary   **Chakra:** sacral, third eye
Correspondences: earth, air, fire, water, spirit, Mercury, Gemini, Virgo

Physical healing: strengthens blood vessels, myelin sheaths on nerves, and connective tissue; expedites processes of digestive system, especially intestines; supports respiratory health

Psychological healing: centers, nourishes, and balances emotions; eases panic, fear, and overwhelm; sweeps away fear of change, loss, and death; promotes learning and adaptation

Spiritual healing: supports all processes of growth, change, and transformation; enhances spirit communication, shamanic journeys, and shapeshifting; removes attached entities and energies; strongly boosts psychic senses; connects to elements and natural world

Agate, Tree

Formula: SiO_2 with celadonite $[K(Mg,Fe^{2+})Fe^{3+}(Si_4O_{10})(OH)_2]$ or hornblende $[(Ca,Na)_{2-3}(Mg,Fe,Al)_5(Al,Si)_8O_{22}(OH,F)_2]$ **Hardness:** 6.5–7
Crystal system: trigonal   **Formation process:** igneous
Chakra: root, heart   **Correspondences:** earth, Venus, Taurus

Physical healing: balances microbiome, thus supporting health of digestive and immune systems; reduces symptoms of seasonal allergies; promotes smooth functioning of skin and liver

Psychological healing: stabilizes heart and mind; alleviates trauma and emotional pain; invites joy and pleasure; balances mood swings; eases anxiety, tension, and worry

Spiritual healing: gently grounds and reconnects to nature; promotes group harmony; facilitates contact with nature spirits, devas, and fairies

Agate, Turritella

Formula: SiO_2 with fossils   Hardness: 6.5–7
Crystal system: trigonal
Formation process: sedimentary   Chakra: earth star, root
Correspondences: earth, water, Mercury, Virgo, Pisces

Physical healing: cleanses and detoxifies body; protects against environmental toxins, pathogens, and allergens; supports healthy digestion, elimination, and nutrient absorption; balances adrenals and alleviates fatigue

Psychological healing: assuages feelings of guilt, homesickness, and loneliness; sparks motivation and helps you to pursue goals

Spiritual healing: protects and grounds, promotes connection to natural world and communication with spirit realms, combats egotism, helps reveal and transform karma, heals polluted or desecrated land

Note: see also fossil (p. 123)

Ajoite

Formula: $(K,Na)Cu_7AlSi_9O_{24}(OH)_6 \cdot 3H_2O$ Hardness: 3.5
Crystal system: triclinic   Formation process: sedimentary
Chakra: heart, throat, crown   Correspondences: water, spirit, Venus, Neptune, Virgo, Aquarius

Physical healing: draws out physical pain, often by revealing its source; improves health of blood and circulatory system; balances hormones; treats conditions of reproductive system

Psychological healing: brings deep peace; alleviates anger, sorrow, spite, grief; cultivates compassionate, loving, and nurturing attitude; promotes emotional honesty; mends relationships

Spiritual healing: expands awareness; connects to the Divine Feminine and to the earth; facilitates communication with angels, nature spirits, and other spiritual beings; removes energetic cords and implants

51

Amazonite

Formula: KAlSi$_3$O$_8$ with lead (Pb)   Hardness: 6–6.5
Crystal system: triclinic   Formation process: igneous
Chakra: heart, throat   Correspondences: water, Saturn,
Uranus, Aquarius

Physical healing: relieves cramps, disorders of liver, and seasonal allergies; promotes healthy skeletal system; supports female reproductive system

Psychological healing: reduces stress and stress-related conditions, encourages communication, resolves conflict, removes mindset of victimhood

Spiritual healing: excellent karmic healer, develops sense of freedom, emboldens you to achieve and live your personal truth, encourages group harmony

Amber

Formula: complex; mostly C, H, O, S and trace organic
compounds   Hardness: 2–2.5   Crystal system: amorphous
Formation process: organic (sedimentary)   Chakra: root,
solar plexus   Correspondences: fire, spirit, Sun, Leo

Physical healing: heals childhood conditions, such as colic and teething pain; relieves pain and inflammation; detoxifies; promotes healthy digestion and elimination; alleviates seasonal affective disorder

Psychological healing: brings comfort, warmth, and hope; dispels timidity and doubt; promotes confidence, creativity, flexibility, and joy; clears emotional baggage and brings mental clarity

Spiritual healing: stone of ancient wisdom; gently protects, particularly psychic and empathic people; prevents psychic attack; grounds and centers energy; brings awareness to karma, especially ancestral karma; facilitates connection to natural world

Amblygonite

Formula: (Li,Na)AlPO$_4$(F,OH)   Hardness: 5.5–6
Crystal system: triclinic   Formation process: igneous
Chakra: solar plexus, crown   Correspondences: fire, Uranus, Taurus

Physical healing: supports health of digestive system, promotes regular elimination, facilitates repair of broken bones, eases disorders of nervous system and sensory organs, helpful for peaceful end-of-life transitions

Psychological healing: soothes, calms, and nourishes mind and emotions; excellent for ameliorating anxiety; improves concentration and focus; dissolves paralyzing fears; overcomes procrastination; boosts creativity

Spiritual healing: clears blockages from solar plexus chakra; strengthens willpower; helpful for struggles involving authority and power, particularly in those fearful of hurting others; plants seeds of inner peace; ushers in a sense of purpose and fulfillment

Amethyst

Formula: quartz (SiO$_2$) with iron (Fe)   Hardness: 7
Crystal system: trigonal   Formation process: igneous
Chakra: third eye, crown   Correspondences: air, spirit, Jupiter, Neptune, Aquarius, Pisces, Sagittarius

Physical healing: supports healthy nervous system, bones, and endocrine system; promotes overall healing; may treat indigestion, tumors, headaches, broken bones, blood sugar imbalances

Psychological healing: assuages worry, fear, anxiety, and stress; supports breaking bad habits and overcoming addiction; promotes equanimity and serenity

Spiritual healing: represents wisdom, alchemy, and magic; enhances meditation, dreaming, psychic development, and other spiritual pursuits; cleanses and transmutes negative energy; promotes connection to higher realms

Amethyst, Brandberg

Formula: quartz (SiO_2) with aluminum (Al), iron (Fe), hematite (Fe_2O_3)   Hardness: 7   Crystal system: trigonal
Formation process: igneous   Chakra: all, especially crown, soul star   Correspondences: air, spirit, Jupiter, Neptune, Aquarius, Pisces, Sagittarius

Physical healing: supports immune function, especially helpful for autoimmune conditions; restores vitality and aids in recovery from fatigue and exhaustion; addresses conditions affecting nervous and digestive systems

Psychological healing: enhances memory, assists introspection and shadow work, helps to heal broken heart, relieves stress

Spiritual healing: powerful karmic healer; clears away stagnant, harmful, and negative energy; removes cords, attachments, entities; facilitates astral travel and psychic development

Amethyst, Chevron

Formula: quartz (SiO_2) with iron (Fe)   Hardness: 7   Crystal system: trigonal   Formation process: igneous   Chakra: all, especially third eye   Correspondences: air, spirit, Jupiter, Neptune, Aquarius, Pisces, Sagittarius

Physical healing: in addition to general properties of amethyst, treats skin, liver, lungs, liver, and pancreas; stimulates thymus gland and immune system; repairs damaged DNA; coordinates body's organs and systems for overall health

Psychological healing: releases deeply held beliefs, behaviors, and feelings; improves sense of self-worth; connects to reserves of inner strength; supports in setting and attaining goals; relieves anxiety

Spiritual healing: useful for meditation, psychic development, and manifestation; shields and strengthens aura and protects against psychic attack; promotes empathy, compassion, and unity

Amethyst, Lavender

Formula: quartz (SiO$_2$) with iron (Fe) **Hardness:** 7 **Crystal system:** trigonal **Formation process:** igneous **Chakra:** all, especially third eye **Correspondences:** air, spirit, Jupiter, Neptune, Uranus, Sagittarius, Aquarius, Pisces

Physical healing: supports health of joints, connective tissue, and cartilage; reduces pain and inflammation; promotes better alignment of spine and other joints; clears confusing or contradictory symptoms; supports general healing

Psychological healing: alleviates grief, loss, and emotional turmoil; improves negotiation skills; brings mental clarity

Spiritual healing: fosters greater alignment with higher self and sense of purpose; promotes wisdom and facilitates psychic development; integrates body, mind, and spirit; invites peace; instills sense of justice

Note: also called cape amethyst, lavender quartz, and lavender

Amethyst, Pink

Formula: quartz (SiO$_2$) with iron (Fe) and hematite (Fe$_2$O$_3$) **Hardness:** 7 **Crystal system:** trigonal **Formation process:** igneous **Chakra:** earth star, heart, higher heart, crown **Correspondences:** water, fire, Venus, Uranus, Libra, Aquarius

Physical healing: treats conditions of heart and circulatory system; supports health of stomach, thymus; relieves pain and cramps of hands and feet

Psychological healing: improves self-esteem and promotes self-love; promotes emotional honesty, especially by facilitating the processing of uncomfortable emotions

Spiritual healing: helps heal inner child, releases trauma from current and past lives, initiates state of unconditional love and compassion, links heart and crown chakras, protects and guides via contact with angels, invokes wisdom from the heart of Mother Earth

Amethyst, Red-Capped

Formula: quartz (SiO_2) with iron (Fe) and hematite (Fe_2O_3)
Hardness: 7   Crystal system: trigonal
Formation process: igneous   Chakra: root, crown
Correspondences: air, earth, Jupiter, Mars, Sagittarius, Aries

Physical healing: supports physical detoxification; may lessen symptoms of withdrawal; helpful for headaches, migraines, and managing pain from chronic conditions

Psychological healing: alleviates anger, fear, tension, and resentment; assists conflict resolution; promotes compassion and empathy

Spiritual healing: strengthens connection between body and soul, stimulates flow of kundalini energy, transmutes harmful energy in environment, helps integrate spiritual practice into everyday life

Note: See also chevron amethyst (p. 54), hematite (p. 138). It is often labeled "auralite" or "super seven" depending on location of origin.

Amethyst, Veracruz

Formula: quartz (SiO_2) with iron (Fe)   Hardness: 7
Crystal system: trigonal   Formation process: igneous
Chakra: higher heart, third eye, crown, soul star
Correspondences: air, spirit, Moon, Jupiter, Uranus, Sagittarius, Aquarius

Physical healing: especially effective for understanding spiritual underpinnings of disease, helpful for conditions of nervous and endocrine systems, gently eases pain

Psychological healing: helps discover and create beauty; dissolves attachment; instills humility, gratitude, and compassion

Spiritual healing: stone of ascension, spiritual development, and dissolution of ego; expands consciousness; enhances meditation, astral travel, and inspiration; links the crown and heart chakras; awakens latent healing abilities; useful in grids for creating sacred space and healing the earth

Amethyst with Goethite

Formula: quartz (SiO_2) with iron (Fe) and inclusions of goethite [α-FeO(OH)]   Hardness: 7   Crystal system: trigonal
Formation process: igneous   Chakra: solar plexus, crown
Correspondences: air, fire, spirit, Mars, Jupiter, Neptune, Aquarius, Pisces, Sagittarius

Physical healing: boosts metabolism, helps regulate adrenal glands, supports healthy digestion, promotes longevity and youthfulness, helps rid the body of parasites and infections

Psychological healing: links intuitive with rational parts of mind; helps better harness the mind for understanding of emotions; strengthens ability to channel willpower and motivation into productive, meaningful tasks

Spiritual healing: supports manifestation, meditation, and personal development; aligns willpower with the divine plan; provides continuous spiritual support during periods of uncertainty and transition

Note: Goethite is usually mislabeled "cacoxenite" in amethyst.

Ametrine

Formula: quartz (SiO_2) with iron (Fe)   Hardness: 7
Crystal system: trigonal   Formation process: igneous
Chakra: solar plexus, third eye, crown   Correspondences: air, fire, spirit, Mercury, Jupiter, Gemini, Sagittarius

Physical healing: balances brain and nervous system, supports healthy digestion and elimination, balances metabolism and supports weight loss, may mitigate symptoms of dementia and stroke

Psychological healing: incites optimism, joy, and encouragement; empowers taking decisive action; dispels indecision and anxiety stemming from introversion; promotes perception and analysis; releases fear

Spiritual healing: stone of guidance and clarity; boosts psychic skills, including clairvoyance and channeling; balances spiritual and worldly pursuits; helps you feel worthy of prosperity

Note: see also amethyst (p. 53) and citrine (p. 101)

57

Ammonite

Formula: variable, often SiO_2, $CaCO_3$, or Fe_2SO_4
Hardness: variable   Crystal system: variable, usually trigonal or cubic   Formation process: sedimentary
Chakra: earth star, root   Correspondences: water, spirit, Neptune, Aquarius, Virgo, Gemini

Physical healing: heals conditions of head, especially eyes and ears; promotes fertility
Psychological healing: regenerative and rejuvenating, helps connect to subconscious mind, inspires hope and renewal
Spiritual healing: symbolizes wisdom, immortality, and regeneration; activates and connects to earth energies; supports past-life regression and karmic healing; assists prophecy, divination, dowsing, and dreamwork; furthers connection to the gods

Anhydrite

Formula: $CaSO_4$ Hardness: 3.5   Crystal system: orthorhombic   Formation process: sedimentary
Chakra: heart, third eye, crown   Correspondences: air, Saturn, Uranus, Aquarius

Physical healing: promotes overall healing and balance; regulates fluids; helpful for swelling, congestion, and water retention; good for bones, skin, joints, liver, nails, and hair
Psychological healing: brings mental peace and clarity; improves sense of self-worth; cools hot emotions of anger, bitterness, hate, and resentment; encourages forgiveness
Spiritual healing: brings stagnant energies back into motion, cleanses aura and chakras, facilitates angelic contact, initiates astral travel and shamanic journeys, improves meditation, encourages feelings of belonging and connection

Anhydrite, Blue (Angelite)

Formula: $CaSO_4$ Hardness: 3.5   Crystal system: orthorhombic   Formation process: sedimentary
Chakra: heart, throat, third eye, crown
Correspondences: air, Saturn, Uranus, Aquarius

Physical healing: regulates body fluids; promotes healthy skeletal system, kidneys, and liver; strengthening for the uterus; helps reduce inflammation and promotes flexibility; alleviates arthritis; promotes blood circulation to extremities

Psychological healing: reduces insecurity and boosts confidence; improves communication; imparts tact and eloquence; mitigates obsession, phobia, and self-harm; heals a broken heart and soothes troubled mind

Spiritual healing: assists angelic communication, gently awakens third-eye chakra and promotes clairvoyance and other psychic skills, imparts a sense of belonging

Anhydrite, Purple

Formula: $CaSO_4$ Hardness: 3.5   Crystal system: orthorhombic
Formation process: sedimentary   Chakra: third eye, crown
Correspondences: air, spirit, Uranus, Aquarius

Physical healing: strongly detoxifies, strengthens organs of elimination and skeletal system, resolves conditions of pineal gland and eyes

Psychological healing: dissolves guilt, shame, trauma, and shock; reduces tendency to hide personal matters or keep others at arm's length; softens rigid beliefs and habits; soothes emotional pain

Spiritual healing: gently grounds, cleanses, and stabilizes aura; improves psychic development, opens contact with spirit guides and communication with ancestors; grounds high-frequency energy into the body and mind

Apatite, Blue

Formula: $Ca_{10}(PO_4)_6(OH,F,Cl)_2$ Hardness: 5   Crystal system: hexagonal   Formation process: igneous, sedimentary, or metamorphic   Chakra: third eye   Correspondences: air, Mercury, Saturn, Gemini, Capricorn, Pisces

Physical healing: among the best stones for the skeletal system; nourishes bone marrow, repairs and strengthens cartilage; alkalizes body; promotes healthy teeth and gums; may be used to treat viral infections; beneficial for people with autism

Psychological healing: brings order and structure to the mind; ameliorates restlessness, aloofness, and irritability; encourages independence; helps overcome eating disorders

Spiritual healing: may increase synchronicities in daily life; boosts psychic skills, deepens meditation, improves telekinesis; imparts generosity and humanitarianism; facilitates kundalini awakening

Apatite, Golden

Formula: $Ca_{10}(PO_4)_6(OH,F,Cl)_2$ Hardness: 5   Crystal system: hexagonal   Formation process: igneous or metamorphic   Chakra: solar plexus   Correspondences: fire, Mercury, Sun, Gemini, Leo

Physical healing: nourishes skeletal system, relieves pain, promotes healthy eating habits, improves metabolism and supports weight loss, realigns posture, combats low energy, promotes sperm production, improves digestion, balances endocrine system

Psychological healing: releases apathy, sorrow, guilt, anger, and mania; inspires motivation and mental clarity, thereby dispelling laziness and inactivity; strengthens willpower; inspires hope

Spiritual healing: clears blocks in solar plexus chakra, helps integrate life lessons, stimulates underactive chakras, improves manifestation skills, generates prosperity and abundance

Apatite, Green

Formula: $Ca_{10}(PO_4)_6(OH,F,Cl)_2$ Hardness: 5
Crystal system: hexagonal Formation process: igneous,
sedimentary, or metamorphic Chakra: heart, third eye
Correspondences: water, earth, Mercury, Saturn, Gemini,
Capricorn

Physical healing: supports healthy skeletal system, especially cartilage and
marrow; combats infection, especially in bone marrow; maintains health
of kidneys and spleen; neutralizes harmful effects of radiation; improves
strength, stamina, and coordination; treats conditions of the heart

Psychological healing: attracts peace and contentment; assists in overcoming
mental and emotional depletion; brings hope, harmony, and emotional
balance; reminds you to value your energy, time, and other resources

Spiritual healing: promotes abundance, prosperity, and financial freedom; helps
to heal your relationship with money; reveals karmic underpinnings of disease

Apatite, Pink

Formula: $Ca_{10}(PO_4)_6(OH,F,Cl)_2$ with manganese (Mn)
Hardness: 5 Crystal system: hexagonal
Formation process: igneous Chakra: heart
Correspondences: water, earth, Venus, Taurus, Libra

Physical healing: supports healthy skeletal system, treats fatigue and exhaustion,
promotes healthy heart and circulatory system, helpful for metabolic
disorders, helps manage sensory processing disorders

Psychological healing: helps you to communicate from the heart with tact and
eloquence, imparts optimism, helpful for oversensitive emotions, calms frayed
nerves, fosters sense of acceptance and tolerance, encourages embracing
diversity, alleviates jealousy and angst

Spiritual healing: cultivates feelings of compassion and loving-kindness for all
beings, unites hearts of all members of a group

Apatite, Red

Formula: $Ca_{10}(PO_4)_6(OH,F,Cl)_2$ with hematite (Fe_2O_3)
Hardness: 5   Crystal system: hexagonal
Formation process: igneous   Chakra: root, third eye
Correspondences: air, fire, Mercury, Mars, Aries

Physical healing: nourishes circulatory system; promotes production of blood cells in marrow; supports healthy eyes, bones, teeth; helps in coping with chronic illness and viral infections; benefits male reproductive system; helps strengthen muscles and cartilage

Psychological healing: quells anger, restlessness, and irritability; alleviates despondency, anxiety, and worry; promotes confidence and belief in yourself; brings motivation and resolution to your healing journey and self-improvement

Spiritual healing: accelerates healing and manifestation on all levels; improves psychic skills, especially by providing psychic sensations in the body; helps you to act upon psychic information

Apophyllite

Formula: $(K,Na)Ca_4Si_8O_{20}(F,OH)\cdot8H_2O$ Hardness: 4.5–5
Crystal system: tetragonal   Formation process: igneous
Chakra: third eye, crown   Correspondences: air, Moon, Uranus, Cancer, Aquarius

Physical healing: soothes eyes, skin, and mucous membranes; alleviates allergies; improves sleep; beneficial for lungs and respiratory system; lowers blood pressure; helpful for addiction, especially tobacco

Psychological healing: brings clarity, insight, and illumination to the mind; releases insecurity, anxiety, and nervousness; teaches restraint and self-control

Spiritual healing: inspires regular spiritual practice; enhances meditation, psychic development, energy healing, and astral travel; facilitates past-life recall and access to Akashic records; improves dream recall and lucid dreaming; illuminates soul's blueprint; releases intense, recurring karmic cycles, especially generational patterns

Apophyllite, Green

Formula: $(K,Na)Ca_4Si_8O_{20}(F,OH) \cdot 8H_2O$ with iron (Fe)
Hardness: 4.5–5   Crystal system: tetragonal
Formation process: igneous   Chakra: heart, third eye, crown
Correspondences: water, earth, Venus, Taurus

Physical healing: detoxifies the body, regenerates damaged or diseased tissues, offers excellent support for respiratory system

Psychological healing: imparts tenderness, hope, and love; nourishes the inner child; encourages exuberant joy and wonder; overcomes fear with gratitude; especially helpful for victims of abuse, trauma, and oppression

Spiritual healing: promotes abundance and breaks negative financial cycles; lovingly connects to nature and the spirits, devas, and other forces in the natural world; promotes the health of plants and gardens; helps you attune to ley lines, vortices, and earth energies

Apophyllite, Red

Formula: $(K,Na)Ca_4Si_8O_{20}(F,OH) \cdot 8H_2O$ with inclusions
Hardness: 4.5–5   Crystal system: tetragonal
Formation process: igneous   Chakra: root, heart
Correspondences: water, fire, Mars, Venus, Aries, Libra

Physical healing: fights infection; mitigates the growth of unhealthy cells; engenders rejuvenating and peaceful sleep; reminds you to practice good self-care

Psychological healing: inspires tender, nurturing love of self and others; can give you the courage to ask for help; assuages feelings of loss, suffering, disappointment, envy, greed, and isolation; clarifies heart and mind and removes internal conflict

Spiritual healing: opens the heart to greater compassion; gently links the heart and root chakras; improves connection to clients in healing practices; deeply nourishes at the soul level; helps with attunement to the natural world, particularly the consciousness of rock, stone, and soil

63

Aquamarine

Formula: $Be_3Al_2(SiO_3)_6$ with iron (Fe)   Hardness: 7.5–8
Crystal system: hexagonal   Formation
process: igneous   Chakra: heart, throat, crown
Correspondences: water, Moon, Neptune, Venus, Pisces, Taurus

Physical healing: versatile stone for overall healing; reduces inflexibility, pain, swelling; treats calcification and water retention; promotes healthy, youthful skin and complexion

Psychological healing: brings clarity, inspiration, and adaptability; invites courage, clear communication, and peace; balances the heart and mind; releases old mental and emotional patterns, especially related to grief and trauma

Spiritual healing: inspires lightheartedness, healthy detachment, and joy; awakens the soul's blueprint for perfect health of body, mind, and spirit; enhances awareness, deepens meditation, and supports spiritual growth; helps you to understand and act upon spiritual guidance and psychic information

Note: see also beryl (p. 76)

Aquaprase

Formula: chalcedony (SiO_2) with chromium (Cr) and
nickel (N)   Hardness: 6.5–7   Crystal system: trigonal
Formation process: igneous   Chakra: higher heart, throat
Correspondences: water, earth, Venus, Neptune, Cancer, Pisces

Physical healing: promotes healthy digestion and elimination, supports female reproductive system, relieves pain and inflammation, initiates detoxification

Psychological healing: imparts tranquility, brings light and movement to stagnant emotional patterns, resolves inner and outer conflict, encourages clear and concise expression of emotions, harmonizes emotions and intellect

Spiritual healing: balances earth and water elements, strengthens yin/receptive energies, enhances meditation, activates higher heart and throat chakras, helps in attainment of inner peace, releases stagnant energies from aura and chakras

Aragonite

Formula: CaCO$_3$ Hardness: 3.5–4   Crystal system: orthorhombic   Formation process: sedimentary
Chakra: heart, throat, third eye
Correspondences: Saturn

Physical healing: stabilizes, centers, and balances the body and its processes; builds and repairs muscle; cools the body; supports digestive, circulatory, and skeletal systems

Psychological healing: combats nervousness, restlessness, and indecision; boosts mental abilities; eliminates bias and promotes fairness and equity; soothes and calms both mind and emotions

Spiritual healing: generally protects, particularly against geopathic stress (earth energies that may cause physical or mental harm to humans), grounds and connects to nature, promotes commitment to your spiritual path

Aragonite, Blue

Formula: CaCO$_3$ with iron (Fe) or copper (Cu)
Hardness: 3.5–4   Crystal system: orthorhombic
Formation process: sedimentary   Chakra: heart, throat, third eye   Correspondences: air, water, Saturn, Venus, Capricorn, Virgo

Physical healing: clears toxins and cools the body, excellent for hastening resolution of fever and the common cold, balances brain and nervous system, supports respiratory health, improves sleep and prevents nightmares

Psychological healing: calms and balances mind and heart; grants greater emotional awareness (both yours and that of others); facilitates sincere, effective communication; soothes anger; helps with navigating life during stressful times

Spiritual healing: gently stimulates intuition, encourages you to use psychic skills for the benefit of others, aids dream interpretation

Aragonite, Brown

Formula: $CaCO_3$ Hardness: 3.5–4   Crystal
system: orthorhombic   Formation process: sedimentary
Chakra: sacral   Correspondences: earth, Saturn, Capricorn

Physical healing: balances digestive system, especially stomach and small
  intestine; strengthens knees, spine, and other joints
Psychological healing: invites patience and resilience; exerts grounding, calming,
  and motivating influence; releases guilt and shame resulting from old
  emotional burdens; brings a level head to times of crisis
Spiritual healing: ally for meditation and mindfulness, helps you be more present
  in the now, promotes stability and patience along a spiritual path

Aragonite, Green

Formula: $CaCO_3$ Hardness: 3.5–4   Crystal
system: orthorhombic   Formation process: sedimentary
Chakra: heart   Correspondences: earth, Venus, Taurus

Physical healing: excellent aid in resolving skin conditions, promotes healthy hair
  and scalp, treats nausea and upset stomach
Psychological healing: enhances discernment and critical thinking skills, brings
  emotional balance, helps you to organize and process emotions, alleviates old
  emotional wounds
Spiritual healing: connects to nature; facilitates communication with devas,
  nature spirits, and other spiritual beings; softens the heart and alleviates
  spiritual burdens; invites a state of surrender; teaches you to go with the flow

Aragonite, Purple

Formula: $CaCO_3$ **Hardness:** 3.5–4   **Crystal system:** orthorhombic   **Formation process:** sedimentary   **Chakra:** third eye, crown, soul star   **Correspondences:** air, fire, Jupiter, Pluto, Scorpio, Sagittarius

Physical healing: strengthens skeletal system, promotes cellular regeneration, mitigates physical conditions resulting from mental or spiritual causes

Psychological healing: draws upon the power of unconditional love to promote healing of emotional pain and trauma, helps you develop empathy and improves your ability to relate to others

Spiritual healing: grounds higher spiritual energies into the body; excellent for manifestation; promotes psychic development, especially clairvoyance, clairsentience, and prophetic dreams; may be useful for animal communication

Aragonite, Sputnik

Formula: $CaCO_3$ **Hardness:** 3.5–4   **Crystal system:** orthorhombic   **Formation process:** sedimentary   **Chakra:** all, especially earth star and solar plexus   **Correspondences:** earth, air, fire, water, spirit, Saturn, Uranus, Cancer, Capricorn

Physical healing: strengthens and supports the skeletal system, hastens healing of wounds and boosts immune function, promotes health of nervous system

Psychological healing: excellent aid to concentration for multitasking, ensuring all tasks are followed through to completion; allows you to let go and surrender, especially when hypercritical of yourself and others; boosts confidence, promotes tact, and protects against criticism of others

Spiritual healing: clears, aligns, and strengthens aura; clears blockages in the chakras; facilitates astral travel, shamanic journeys, dreams, and angelic communication; enhances meditation; restores soul fragments; promotes group harmony and cohesion

Aragonite, White

Formula: CaCO$_3$ Hardness: 3.5–4
Crystal system: orthorhombic
Formation process: sedimentary   Chakra: crown
Correspondences: air, water, Moon, Cancer

Physical healing: promotes healthy digestive and skeletal systems; reduces pain, especially from pinched nerves and misaligned vertebrae

Psychological healing: lessens feelings of self-doubt, inconstancy, and anxiety; helps you find a place where you belong; encourages self-expression; balances emotions

Spiritual healing: promotes regular, pragmatic spiritual practice; enables you to integrate psychic skills and spiritual insights without distracting you from the everyday world

Aragonite, Yellow

Formula: CaCO$_3$ with iron (Fe)   Hardness: 3.5–4   Crystal system: orthorhombic   Formation process: sedimentary   Chakra: sacral, solar plexus   Correspondences: air, Sun, Mercury, Gemini, Leo

Physical healing: supports skeletal, digestive, and lymphatic systems; relieves pain, especially from chronic conditions

Psychological healing: imparts thoughtful, responsible, and diplomatic attitude; gently eases guilt and regret; inspires optimism; helps thoughtful consideration of actions and their consequences; helps to clarify and resolve conflict

Spiritual healing: offers attunement to higher self, helps you feel safe and nurtured by Source, supports prayer and helps in following a spiritual path with diligence

Arfvedsonite

Formula: $[Na][Na_2][Fe^{2+}_4Fe^{3+}]Si_8O_{22}(OH)_2$ Hardness: 5–6
Crystal system: monoclinic   Formation process: igneous
or metamorphic   Chakra: earth star, solar plexus
Correspondences: earth, air, fire, water, spirit, Pluto, Scorpio

Physical healing: excellent for relieving ringing and pressure in the ears, helps
the nervous system to adapt and recharge when overstimulated, supports the
health of the kidneys and all organs of elimination

Psychological healing: wonderful stone for relinquishing feelings of guilt;
conquers fear; stabilizes during periods of intense stress, trauma, and
transition; guides toward reconciliation and forgiveness; promotes creativity,
action, and adaptability

Spiritual healing: very protective and cleansing to the energy field; brings hope
and solace during dark night of the soul; promotes curiosity and wonder, even
during troubled times

Astrophyllite

Formula: $K_2NaFe^{2+}_7Ti_2Si_8O_{26}(OH)_4F$ Hardness: 3   Crystal
system: triclinic   Formation process: igneous   Chakra: all,
especially causal, soul star   Correspondences: earth, air, fire,
water, spirit, Mars, Pluto, Scorpio

Physical healing: treats conditions of large intestine and promotes healthy
elimination, balances hormones, supports the brain and reproductive system,
protects against harmful radiation

Psychological healing: creates balance in life, which is helpful for both
workaholics and procrastinators; facilitates revealing and integrating the
shadow self; promotes understanding and forgiveness of self and others

Spiritual healing: assists the pursuit of truth, justice, and liberation; clears harmful
energy from aura and body; boosts psychic abilities and promotes contact
with ETs and starbeings; facilitates past-life recall; extracts entities from people
and places

Aventurine, Blue

Formula: SiO_2 with dumortierite [$Al_7BO_3(SiO_4)_3O_3$], nitrogen (N), copper silicates (Cu, Si, O), or other minerals
Hardness: 6.5–7   Crystal system: trigonal
Formation process: igneous, sedimentary, or metamorphic
Chakra: throat, third eye   Correspondences: air, water, Mercury, Libra, Sagittarius, Aquarius

Physical healing: reduces fever and inflammation, and otherwise cools the body; maintains balance of endocrine and nervous systems
Psychological healing: imparts patience, stillness, and calmness; heightens awareness and helps in detachment from bias; banishes bad habits and helps create positive ones to replace them
Spiritual healing: inspires deeply-rooted peace, advantageous for cultivation of Buddha-nature, enhances meditation and psychic development

Aventurine, Green

Formula: SiO_2 with fuchsite [$K(Al,Cr)_3Si_3O_{10}(OH)_2$] and other minerals   Hardness: 6.5–7   Crystal system: trigonal
Formation process: igneous, sedimentary, or metamorphic
Chakra: heart   Correspondences: earth, water, air, Venus, Mercury, Libra, Sagittarius, Aquarius

Physical healing: soothes the physical body, alleviates pain, detoxifies the body, fights infection and regulates blood pressure
Psychological healing: calms and soothes the mind, nurtures feelings of self-love, encourages adequate self-care, lessens irritability and aggression, sharpens risk-assessment
Spiritual healing: attracts luck, fortune, and love; represents growth in all areas of life; helps new projects blossom

Aventurine, Peach

Formula: SiO_2 with hematite (Fe_2O_3)   **Hardness:** 6.5–7
Crystal system: trigonal   **Formation process:** igneous,
sedimentary, or metamorphic   **Chakra:** solar plexus, heart
Correspondences: air, earth, Mercury, Gemini, Virgo

Physical healing: supports health of circulatory system, encourages blood cell production in marrow, promotes healthy liver, ameliorates pain and numbness in extremities

Psychological healing: calms heart and mind; quiets inner saboteur and assuages feelings of inadequacy or imposter syndrome; counteracts shyness and anxiety; inspires dignity, patience, and a calming presence

Spiritual healing: encourages hope, helps you aim for and achieve your goals, promotes continuous self-improvement

Aventurine, Red

Formula: SiO_2 with hematite (Fe_2O_3) and/or piemontite
$[Ca_2(Al,Mn^{3+},Fe^{3+})_3(SiO_4)(Si_2O_7)O(OH)]$ **Hardness:** 6.5–7
Crystal system: trigonal   **Formation process:** igneous,
sedimentary, or metamorphic   **Chakra:** root
Correspondences: fire, Mars, Aries

Physical healing: energizes, without being too stimulating; excellent for fortifying the blood and circulatory system; promotes fertility; boosts libido; revitalizes and rejuvenates body; improves sluggish metabolism

Psychological healing: jump-starts motivation; imparts courage, pragmatism, and level-headedness; inspires friendliness, open-mindedness, and a desire to learn and grow; inspires inner strength and confidence

Spiritual healing: promotes sense of generosity and humanitarianism, dynamically grounding and pairs well with higher-consciousness stones to prevent spaciness, enables spiritual growth through humor

Aventurine, Yellow

Formula: SiO_2 with iron (Fe)   Hardness: 6.5–7
Crystal system: trigonal   Formation process: igneous,
sedimentary, or metamorphic   Chakra: solar plexus
Correspondences: fire, earth, Sun, Mars, Aries, Leo

Physical healing: supports mucous membranes, diaphragm, and stomach; supports organs of elimination, including skin, kidneys, and liver; improves digestion and alleviates overly acidic stomach

Psychological healing: imparts cheerful optimism and helps you believe anything is possible; promotes decision-making skills, ends procrastination, and boosts motivation; stokes creative fire within

Spiritual healing: brings peace, hope, and action to spiritual practice; balances yin and yang energies

Note: Some yellow aventurine is sold under the trade name "Himalayan gold azeztulite."

Axinite

Formula: $(Ca,Fe,Mn,Mg)_3Al_2BSi_4O_{15}(OH)$ Hardness: 6–7.5
Crystal system: triclinic   Formation process: igneous or
metamorphic   Chakra: root, third eye   Correspondences: earth,
spirit, Mars, Aries

Physical healing: excellent for joints, bones, ligaments; alleviates conditions affecting sensory organs and sensory processing; general tonic for nervous system; boosts energy

Psychological healing: sharpens the mind, improves memory, and dispels doubt; promotes diplomacy and tact, while also prompting courage and empowerment; helps set and enforce boundaries; may be used to help release relationships that no longer serve you

Spiritual healing: promotes grounding and alignment of body, mind, and spirit; removes unwanted energies, cuts cords, and purifies aura; assists pursuit of truth and justice

Azurite

Formula: $Cu_3(CO_3)_2(OH)_2$ Hardness: 3.5–4   Crystal system: monoclinic   Formation process: sedimentary
Chakra: third eye   Correspondences: air, Venus, Sagittarius

Physical healing: supports healthy liver, thyroid, and nervous system; may alleviate pain

Psychological healing: reveals and releases limiting beliefs and old habits; invites honest and critical self-reflection; reveals emotions to the conscious mind for greater understanding; offers excellent support for learning, as it helps the mind to accept new information

Spiritual healing: initiates deep states of reflection, meditation, and introspection; enhances intuition and psychic development; excellent for use in channeling, mediumship, and similar pursuits; assists past-life recall

Azurite-Malachite

Formula: $Cu_3(CO_3)_2(OH)_2$ and $Cu_2CO_3(OH)_2$ Hardness: 3.5–4
Crystal system: monoclinic   Formation process: sedimentary
Chakra: earth star, solar plexus, heart, third eye
Correspondences: earth, water, Venus, Libra

Physical healing: slows abnormal cellular growth; relieves pain, tension, and cramps; detoxifies the body; nourishes and replenishes vital energy for overall healing

Psychological healing: balances heart and mind; deepens awareness of sources of memories, beliefs, and behaviors so they are easier to release; nourishes emotional body

Spiritual healing: inspires harmony; awakens information stored in earth star chakra; facilitates meditation; dissolves egotism, conceit, arrogance, and vanity; taps into the oneness of all life; accelerates planetary healing

Note: see also azurite (above) and malachite (p. 168)

Barite

Formula: BaSO$_4$ Hardness: 3–3.5 Crystal system: orthorhombic Formation process: igneous, sedimentary, or metamorphic Chakra: earth star, third eye, crown Correspondences: air, spirit, Uranus, Aquarius

Physical healing: among the best stones for the brain; warms and detoxifies; combats parasites and infections, particularly viral and fungal; treats upset stomach, gas, and bloating; helps to alleviate sore throat; soothes irritated skin; improves posture

Psychological healing: boosts the mind, clears confusion, enhances memory, alleviates social anxiety and shyness, helps enforce healthy boundaries, promotes friendship and responsibility

Spiritual healing: facilitates spiritual growth and psychic development; improves dream recall and assists astral travel; protects against harmful energies and precludes attachments and psychic attack; helps you shine your light as a beacon for the world; reveals purpose

Barite, Blue

Formula: BaSO$_4$ Hardness: 3–3.5 Crystal system: orthorhombic Formation process: igneous, sedimentary, or metamorphic Chakra: earth star, throat, third eye, crown Correspondences: air, Uranus, Aquarius

Physical healing: largely effective for the brain and nervous system; detoxifies, soothes, and strengthens the physical body overall; cools fevers and warms cold extremities; balances overactive metabolism

Psychological healing: excellent for sharpening memory, promotes resilience and hope, excellent support for addiction recovery (as an adjunct to other treatments), helps in articulating abstract ideas for all to understand, enhances communication across all media

Spiritual healing: facilitates angelic communication, promotes compassion and loving kindness, excellent for lucid dreaming, brings hope and light

Barite, Gold

Formula: BaSO$_4$ with iron (Fe)   Hardness: 3–3.5
Crystal system: orthorhombic   Formation
process: igneous, sedimentary, or metamorphic
Chakra: earth star, solar plexus, crown
Correspondences: fire, Sun, Leo, Sagittarius

Physical healing: strongly detoxifies and warms, like all barite; especially good
for the stomach and intestines; stabilizes and detoxifies the body for recovery
following chemotherapy and radiation

Psychological healing: increases feelings of contentment and gratitude; helps
overcome unhealthy cravings and bad habits; eliminates guilt; improves
charisma, powers of persuasion, and enthusiasm

Spiritual healing: helps you break out on your own, especially with regard to
spiritual practice; links willpower to higher consciousness; boosts manifestation

Basalt

Formula: variable   Hardness: 6   Crystal system: mostly
monoclinic and triclinic   Formation process: igneous
Chakra: earth star, root, sacral   Correspondences: earth,
fire, Pluto, Scorpio, Capricorn

Physical healing: grounds and tones physical body; encourages stamina, strength,
and vitality; reduces tension, blockages, pain, and constipation; mitigates
headache and migraine; improves digestion and circulation

Psychological healing: helps maintain level head during transitions; ally for when
life feels stuck or stagnant; strengthens problem-solving skills, creativity, and
inspiration; facilitates authentic connection and communication; catalyzes
safe emotional release

Spiritual healing: strongly grounds and protects; offers relief, renewal, and
rebirth; sparks pursuit of inner truth; brings vivid, prophetic dreams

Beryl

Formula: $Be_3Al_2Si_6O_{18}$ **Hardness:** 7.5–8
Crystal system: hexagonal **Formation process:** igneous
Chakra: all, especially heart, throat, crown
Correspondences: water, Moon, Cancer, Leo

Physical healing: alleviates upset stomach, restores balance after illness or injury, palliates conditions of nervous system
Psychological healing: promotes reconciliation, emotional clarity, and tender love; enhances communication and understanding; brings courage
Spiritual healing: good medium for scrying (crystal gazing); traditionally used for protection; connects you to the bigger picture and reveals life's divine blueprint; promotes psychic development, especially clairvoyance; promotes past-life recall, supports karmic healing
Note: See entries for aquamarine, emerald, heliodor, and morganite for more beryls.

Beryl, Red (Bixbite)

Formula: $Be_3Al_2Si_6O_{18}$ with manganese (Mn) and lithium (Li) **Hardness:** 7.5–8 **Crystal system:** hexagonal
Formation process: igneous **Chakra:** root, heart
Correspondences: fire, Venus, Neptune, Libra

Physical healing: boosts physical energy and vitality, counteracts low blood pressure and sluggish metabolism, stimulates reproductive system, fortifies bone marrow, reduces physical effects of stress, strengthens nerves and liver
Psychological healing: promotes deep, loving energy; clarifies emotions and enables you to better communicate them; directs compassion toward yourself and others; raises self-esteem; excellent ally for recovering from abuse
Spiritual healing: grounds the energy of unconditional love into the material world, links heart and root chakras, helps you tackle challenging situations with love and courage

Beryl, White (Goshenite)

Formula: $Be_3Al_2Si_6O_{18}$ Hardness: 7.5–8
Crystal system: hexagonal Formation process: igneous
Chakra: all, especially crown Correspondences: water,
spirit, Moon, Cancer, Aquarius

Physical healing: beneficial for lymphatic system, aids in purification and detoxification, alleviates inflammation, supports immune health, cleanses and rejuvenates at the cellular level, improves eyesight, supports nerve and stomach health

Psychological healing: brings light, clarity, and purpose to the psyche; enhances memory and recall; overcomes feeling scattered mentally or spread too thin from too many tasks; helps maintain sense of control and composure when facing difficult circumstances

Spiritual healing: ushers in brilliant white light for healing and purification of body, mind, and spirit; offers solace during periods of transition and transformation; reveals and releases persistent karmic patterns playing out

Biotite

Formula: $K(Mg,Fe)_3AlSi_3O_{10}(F,OH)_2$ Hardness: 2.5–3
Crystal system: monoclinic Formation process: igneous
or metamorphic Chakra: third eye Correspondences: air,
Mercury, Mars, Gemini, Scorpio

Physical healing: decreases overly acidic states, regulates bile production and secretion, alleviates sciatic pain, helps to purify kidneys, may reduce size of tumors and other growths, promotes healthy elimination

Psychological healing: gently grounds the mind and invites clarity and stillness, engenders flexibility and adaptability, inspires creativity and boosts problem-solving skills, reveals layers of pain built around suppressed trauma

Spiritual healing: enhances psychic development, helps clear obstacles from path, gently protects, promotes self-awareness

Black Onyx
Formula: SiO_2 with carbon (C) and/or iron (Fe)
Hardness: 6.5–7 **Crystal system:** trigonal
Formation process: igneous or sedimentary **Chakra:** root
Correspondences: earth, water, Saturn, Capricorn

Physical healing: treats conditions of teeth, bones, ligaments; helps detoxify for fungal infections, such as candidiasis; helps you to feel more safe and secure in your physical body

Psychological healing: one of the best stones for overcoming bad habits, enables you to face your fears, teaches acceptance and surrender, promotes self-discovery, helps you to create and maintain healthy boundaries

Spiritual healing: grounds, stabilizes, and protects; calms and clarifies when you feel overwhelmed or unfocused; highlights internal conflicts so you can resolve them

Note: Black onyx is a variety of chalcedony or jasper, and their respective properties also apply.

Bloodstone
Formula: quartz (SiO_2) with hematite (Fe_2O_3)
Hardness: 6.5–7 **Crystal system:** trigonal **Formation process:** igneous **Chakra:** root **Correspondences:** earth, fire, Mars, Aries, Scorpio

Physical healing: boosts immune function and bolsters body's defenses; offers support, strength, stability, and vitality to the body; combats colds, allergies, and infections; purifies the body, especially the blood; improves nutrient absorption; stanches bleeding and encourages recovery after injury, illness, and surgery

Psychological healing: imparts courage and fights fear, alleviates anxiety and irritability, keeps you grounded during challenging times, wards off feelings of disappointment and discouragement

Spiritual healing: very protective; helps you to feel more courageous and open-hearted, especially during vulnerable moments; supports new endeavors

Note: a variety of jasper (see p. 148)

Brazilianite

Formula: $NaAl_3(PO4)_2(OH)_4$ Hardness: 5.5
Crystal system: monoclinic Formation process: igneous
Chakra: sacral, solar plexus, heart Correspondences: air, fire,
Saturn, Neptune, Capricorn, Pisces

Physical healing: excellent for pain relief; combats conditions involving heat
and light, including sunstroke, sunburn, fever, and inflammation; supports
endocrine health and hormonal balance; promotes health of reproductive
system; alleviates dry skin

Psychological healing: reduces judgmental tendencies; improves self-worth,
mitigates need to seek approval; releases victimhood; strengthens willpower
and creative impulses; assuages anger and resentment; sparks passion and joy

Spiritual healing: helps the body, mind, and spirit adjust to new and higher energies;
improves flow of energy through aura, chakras, meridians, and *nadis* (channels
for prana, the body's vital energy); encourages pursuing your dreams

Bronzite

Formula: $(Mg,Fe)SiO_3$ Hardness: 5–6 Crystal
system: monoclinic Formation process: igneous or
metamorphic Chakra: root Correspondences: earth, fire,
Sun, Mars, Aries, Leo

Physical healing: relieves pain; combats fatigue, exhaustion, and burnout;
promotes health of nervous system; soothes cramps; good first aid for injuries;
restores vitality

Psychological healing: invokes powers of discernment, resolve, and decisiveness;
imparts courtesy, tact, and compassion; promotes equitable thoughts and deeds;
strengthens resolve; helps in navigating stressful situations; boosts confidence

Spiritual healing: protects and grounds; returns negativity to the sender,
particularly jealous thoughts and harmful magic; inspires spiritual (and social)
activism, and promotes acts of service; promotes harmony among groups;
alleviates compassion fatigue

Brookite

Formula: TiO_2 Hardness: 5.5–6 Crystal system: orthorhombic Formation process: metamorphic Chakra: third eye, crown, soul star Correspondences: spirit, Mars, Pluto, Aries

Physical healing: helps eyes, brain (especially pineal gland), and nerves; promotes better absorption of minerals and nutrients; strengthens liver, kidneys, and heart; stimulates repair of physical and subtle anatomy after surgery

Psychological healing: prompts reflection and better self-awareness, centering when you feel lost or stuck, can help you process emotions with more clarity and detachment, cools hot tempers

Spiritual healing: strongly activates upper chakras; accelerates psychic development, supports astral travel and communication with non-physical beings; inspires broader worldview; enables access to Akashic records

Brucite

Formula: $Mg(OH)_2$ Hardness: 2.5–3 Crystal system: trigonal Formation process: metamorphic Chakra: solar plexus, throat Correspondences: air, fire, Sun, Aries, Leo

Physical healing: promotes wound healing; alleviates pain, reduces physical effects of stress; promotes better sleep; helpful for seasonal allergies

Psychological healing: cools tempers and facilitates conflict resolution, helps you see a situation with a new perspective, improves communication, improves sense of self-worth and eradicates feelings of inferiority, dissolves shyness, encourages outgoing attitude

Spiritual healing: stone of new beginnings, gently protects and helps neutralize harmful energy, purifies the energy of a space, facilitates letting go

Calcite

Formula: $CaCO_3$ Hardness: 3 Crystal system: trigonal
Formation process: igneous, sedimentary,
or metamorphic Chakra: all (varies by type)
Correspondences: water, Mercury, Gemini (varies by type)

Physical healing: promotes health of bones, skin, teeth, and endocrine system; exerts cooling effect on body; combats parasites; has a gentle diuretic effect; promotes overall health and well-being

Psychological healing: generally supports healthy mind and balanced emotions, invites clarity and organization to the emotions, improves memory and sparks creativity, promotes adaptation, helps integrate change in thoughts and emotions

Spiritual healing: supports spiritual growth, links parallel realities, boosts manifestation, clarifies sense of purpose, enhances willpower, encourages spontaneity, can remove blockages in the aura and chakras

Calcite, Aqua

Formula: $CaCO_3$ with iron (Fe) Hardness: 3
Crystal system: trigonal Formation process: sedimentary
Chakra: heart, higher heart, throat, third eye
Correspondences: water, Moon, Neptune, Cancer, Pisces

Physical healing: soothes overtaxed nervous system; supports health of circulatory system; combats conditions affecting throat, larynx, esophagus, and lymph nodes

Psychological healing: nourishes and soothes the emotional body; assuages stress, worry, fear, and anxiety; helps tap into unconscious and repressed emotions; resolves issues from childhood; excellent for students, as it improves memory

Spiritual healing: improves meditation; promotes past-life recall; enhances lucid dreaming, psychic development (especially telepathy), and accessing wisdom from the planet; powerfully connects to Lemuria and the element of water; connects to Atlantis

Calcite, Black

Formula: $CaCO_3$ with carbon (C), manganese (Mn), and/or iron (Fe) Hardness: 3 Crystal system: trigonal
Formation process: igneous, sedimentary, or metamorphic
Chakra: earth star, third eye Correspondences: earth, spirit, Pluto, Scorpio

Physical healing: especially effective for releasing physical illness stemming from past-life and karmic sources, as well as psychosomatic conditions; promotes healthy teeth and bones

Psychological healing: breaks down limiting beliefs and behaviors; transmutes fear; supports grieving process; provides strength and resilience for personal growth; sparks foresight, caution, and careful planning

Spiritual healing: connects to mystery and wonder; improves manifestation skills; facilitates past-life recall and shamanic journeys; facilitates contact with spirit guides; enhances and supports soul retrieval; protects and cleanses, especially for out-of-body travel and during dreams

Calcite, Blue

Formula: $CaCO_3$ with iron (Fe) Hardness: 3
Crystal system: trigonal Formation process: sedimentary
Chakra: throat Correspondences: water, Neptune, Pisces

Physical healing: treats sore throat, tonsillitis, and swollen lymph nodes; alleviates water retention; reduces headaches and ameliorates neurological conditions; promotes liver detox, cleanses lymphatic system; reduces high blood pressure

Psychological healing: very calming, reduces anxiety and tension; boosts confidence; improves communication; helps with overcoming creative blocks; excellent for writers; helps you achieve your ambitions

Spiritual healing: dismantles ingrained judgments while promoting discernment and clarity, improves psychic and intuitive skills

Calcite, Cobaltoan

Formula: $(Ca,Co)CO_3$ Hardness: 3 Crystal system: trigonal
Formation process: sedimentary Chakra: heart, higher heart,
third eye Correspondences: water, fire, Venus, Pluto, Leo,
Libra

Physical healing: promotes smooth function of circulatory system; improves
absorption and assimilation of iron; supports health of thyroid, nervous
system, and reproductive system; promotes aging with grace
Psychological healing: promotes love, kindness, and forgiveness; encourages
emotional honesty and maturity; balances emotions and intellect; transforms
negative thoughts into positive; inspires sensuality and evokes inner beauty
Spiritual healing: stone of initiation; reveals latent talents, including psychic skills;
deeply connects to the Divine Feminine; balances yin and yang energies;
imparts feelings of oneness with Source

Calcite, Gold

Formula: $CaCO_3$ with iron (Fe) Hardness: 3 Crystal
system: trigonal Formation process: igneous or sedimentary
Chakra: solar plexus, crown Correspondences: fire, Sun, Leo,
Sagittarius

Physical healing: maintains and balances endocrine system, helps regulate blood
sugar, helps physical body integrate changes made in aura and chakras
Psychological healing: improves confidence, persistence, and resilience; brings
clarity, insight, and action; stimulates intellectual pursuits and strengthens the
mind
Spiritual healing: represents spiritual evolution and initiation, strengthens
potential for manifestation, aligns willpower with divine will, facilitates access
to higher consciousness, clears the way for connection to higher truth, fosters
abundance and prosperity

Calcite, Green

Formula: $CaCO_3$ with iron (Fe), copper (Cu), or chromium (Cr)
Hardness: 3 Crystal system: trigonal
Formation process: igneous or sedimentary Chakra: heart
Correspondences: water, earth, Venus, Taurus

Physical healing: strongly supportive of skeletal system; eases congestion and soreness in chest; promotes cardiac health; helps ease heartburn, shortness of breath, and high blood pressure; reduces inflammation and stimulates detox; promotes health of reproductive system

Psychological healing: releases bitterness, resentment, and anger; promotes forgiveness; brings mental clarity

Spiritual healing: increases love, passion, and peace; sparks imagination and helps you dream big; initiates balance and renewal

Calcite, Mangano

Formula: $(Ca,Mn)CO_3$ Hardness: 3 Crystal system: trigonal
Formation process: igneous or sedimentary Chakra: solar plexus, heart Correspondences: fire, water, Venus, Libra

Physical healing: promotes healthy digestion and elimination, may be used alongside medical treatments for cancer, supports healthy circulatory system and heart, regulates blood pressure and heart rate, alleviates shortness of breath

Psychological healing: invites relaxation and forgiveness; soothes troubled emotions; helps in overcoming anxiety, worry, bitterness, and fear; promotes an open-minded, friendly attitude

Spiritual healing: brings a sense of freedom, confidence, and inner peace; anchors consciousness in the present moment, releases pain from the past and worries about the future; invites you to view and understand love and all emotions from the soul's perspective

Calcite, Optical

Formula: $CaCO_3$ Hardness: 3 Crystal system: trigonal
Formation process: igneous or sedimentary Chakra: third
eye, crown Correspondences: air, Mercury, Gemini

Physical healing: releases blockages by bringing light into the body; stimulates absorption of water and balance of body's fluids; promotes healthy metabolism; alleviates pain; supports health of bones and teeth, mucous membranes, and connective tissues

Psychological healing: invites insight, mental clarity, and a fresh perspective; improves relationships and brings understanding; quells overactive sex drive

Spiritual healing: activates all the chakras, particularly third eye and crown; infuses body, aura, and chakras with white light and clears blockages; accelerates manifestation; attracts prosperity and abundance; enhances meditation and psychic development; supports spiritual growth

Calcite, Orange

Formula: $CaCO_3$ with hematite (Fe_2O_3) Hardness: 3
Crystal system: trigonal Formation process: sedimentary
or igneous Chakra: sacral Correspondences: fire, Sun, Leo

Physical healing: promotes health of skin, teeth, bones, and digestive system; balances metabolism and may support weight loss; increases energy

Psychological healing: boosts creativity and confidence; instills self-respect, motivation, and enthusiasm; promotes pragmatic approach to achieving goals; lends confidence to overcome shyness and dissolves guilt and shame, especially around sex and intimacy; encourages open and honest communication

Spiritual healing: translates inspiration, willpower, and creativity into action; lends stamina to pursuit of a spiritual path

Calcite, Peach

Formula: $CaCO_3$ with hematite (Fe_2O_3), iron (Fe), and/or manganese (Mn) Hardness: 3 Crystal system: trigonal Formation process: sedimentary or igneous Chakra: sacral, solar plexus Correspondences: fire, water, Venus, Mars, Libra

Physical healing: brings balance to over- or underactive metabolism, supports health of reproductive system, treats conditions affecting sensory organs

Psychological healing: brings clarity to heart and mind; promotes sincerity, intimacy, and love; brings relief during states of inner conflict; synthesizes instincts with intellect; enhances ability to organize to-do lists and take tests; raises self-esteem and encourages love for self and others

Spiritual healing: unites complementary forces, represents marriage of knowledge and wisdom, invites action inspired by higher wisdom, symbolizes union of inner Divine Feminine and Divine Masculine

Calcite, Red

Formula: $CaCO_3$ with hematite (Fe_2O_3) Hardness: 3 Crystal system: trigonal Formation process: igneous or sedimentary Chakra: root, heart Correspondences: earth, fire, Mars, Aries

Physical healing: stimulates immune system, promotes healthy skin and healing of wounds, maintains healthy circulatory system, detoxifies, may curb insomnia, accelerates bone marrow and blood cell production, promotes fertility

Psychological healing: stabilizes, grounds, and increases confidence; boosts efforts to overcome laziness and procrastination; helps to channel mental activity into concrete action; may help with food addiction and conflict resolution

Spiritual healing: offers support for grounding energy field, circulates energy through entire aura and chakra system, boosts capacity for manifestation, helps you feel more at ease in your body

Calcite, Stellar Beam

Formula: CaCO₃ Hardness: 3 Crystal system: trigonal
Formation process: igneous Chakra: solar plexus, crown, soul star Correspondences: fire, spirit, Sun, Uranus, Leo, Aquarius

Physical healing: like all calcite, excellent for bones and teeth; may help with conditions affecting nervous system and sensory organs; supports pineal and pituitary gland functions

Psychological healing: helps reveal and transform negative belief systems; reprograms mind for success, personal growth, and healing; opens psyche to new concepts and is excellent for learning

Spiritual healing: aligns personal will with divine will; activates and aligns chakra system; supports astral travel, lucid dreaming, connection to higher planes, and communication with guides and angels; profoundly enhances spiritual development and manifestation skills

Note: The energy of the corresponding color also applies to stellar beam calcite.

Calcite, Yellow

Formula: CaCO₃ Hardness: 3 Crystal system: trigonal
Formation process: sedimentary Chakra: sacral, solar plexus
Correspondences: fire, Sun, Mercury, Leo

Physical healing: calms upset stomach; improves digestion; regulates endocrine function; excellent for strengthening skin, bones, and teeth

Psychological healing: bolsters self-esteem, improves focus and memory, encourages expression and creativity, dissolves emotional blockages

Spiritual healing: symbolizes the soul's freedom, joy, and happiness; helps you stay present; inspires originality and authenticity in spiritual practice

Cancrinite

Formula: $Na_6Ca_2[(CO_3)_2|Al_6Si_6O_{24}]\cdot2H_2O$ Hardness: 5–6
Crystal system: hexagonal Formation
process: metamorphic Chakra: all, especially sacral, throat
Correspondences: water, Uranus, Aries, Aquarius

Physical healing: eases tension in the neck and shoulders; helpful for congestion, sore throat, laryngitis, and tonsillitis; supports health of connective tissues

Psychological healing: promotes straightforward, clear thinking; strengthens connection, communication, and feeling of support; inspires adaptability, creativity, and innovation; boosts willpower; reduces need for approval from others

Spiritual healing: shields aura; aligns chakras; draws out inner skills and talents, both mundane and mystical; promotes simplicity in spiritual practice; brings hope and warmth to counteract feeling lost or unsupported

Carnelian

Formula: SiO_2 with hematite (Fe_2O_3) Hardness: 6.5–7
Crystal system: trigonal Formation process: igneous or
sedimentary Chakra: sacral Correspondences: fire, Mars, Aries

Physical healing: energizes, nourishes, and strengthens; reduces inflammation; excellent palliative for allergies and colds; supports immune, lymph, and circulatory systems; promotes healthy reproductive system

Psychological healing: promotes enthusiasm, optimism, and a positive outlook; curbs procrastination and sparks decisive action; supports concentration and memory; alleviates deeply held trauma

Spiritual healing: mediates between extremes and dissolves tendencies toward spiritual bypassing (avoiding feelings by hiding behind spiritual practices) and toxic positivity (dismissing negative emotions with false reassurances), imparts sense of resolve and trust in your spiritual practice, helps break free from karmic cycles and ignites kundalini energy

Note: The properties of agate (p. 42) and chalcedony (p. 92) also apply.

Cassiterite

Formula: SnO_2 Hardness: 6–7 Crystal system: tetragonal
Formation process: igneous Chakra: earth star, root, sacral, solar plexus Correspondences: earth, Jupiter, Sagittarius

Physical healing: helpful for liver, endocrine system, and stomach; supports death and dying with dignity and peace; improves metabolism of fats

Psychological healing: combats fear; cultivates organization, strategy, and motivation; imparts joy and optimism; heals inner child; improves work-life balance; dissolves destructive habits

Spiritual healing: strongly protects and grounds; attracts luck and good fortune; boosts manifestation; breaks down spiritual obstacles; increases synchronicity; imparts equity, tolerance, and compassion for all; strengthens feelings of stewardship for, and sacredness of, the earth

Cat's Eye

Formula: quartz (SiO_2) with hornblende $[(Ca,Na)_{2-3}(Mg,Fe,Al)_5 (Al,Si)_8O_{22}(OH,F)_2]$ Hardness: 6.5–7 Crystal system: trigonal, monoclinic Formation process: metamorphic Chakra: third eye Correspondences: air, fire, Sun, Venus, Leo, Pisces

Physical healing: helpful for conditions of the eyes; relieves pain, especially headaches; soothes nerves; balances overactive metabolism; supports liver health

Psychological healing: boosts mental faculties, especially reasoning and problem-solving skills; boosts confidence; assuages jealousy

Spiritual healing: awakens psychic vision; guards against harmful energy; promotes insight, detachment, and deep meditation; often used to attract abundance

Note: Cat's eye gemstones in other minerals will exhibit properties similar to those listed above, as well as those of their parent mineral.

Cavansite

Formula: $Ca(VO)Si_4O10·4(H2O)$ Hardness: 3–4
Crystal system: orthorhombic   Formation process: igneous
Chakra: heart, higher heart, throat   Correspondences: water, Neptune, Pisces

Physical healing: prevents bone loss and tooth decay; treats conditions of the eyes and ears; relieves irritation, inflammation, and redness; helps to regulate conditions of the blood

Psychological healing: deeply healing and supportive to the emotions; invites self-expression and open, honest communication; encourages love and expression of all forms of love; encourages nurturing of self and others; inspires creativity

Spiritual healing: symbolizes pursuit of truth and beauty, prompts states of compassion and empathy, cleanses and aligns entire energy field and chakras, boosts psychic abilities, inspires joy, helps communicate spiritual ideas and messages

Celestite

Formula: $SrSO_4$ Hardness: 3–3.5   Crystal system: orthorhombic   Formation process: sedimentary
Chakra: throat, third eye, crown   Correspondences: water, air, Venus, Neptune, Gemini

Physical healing: encourages healthy bones and teeth, regulates metabolism, helps the body fight infection, detoxifies

Psychological healing: invites peace, hope, and stillness; releases fear; helps overcome psychosomatic conditions; fuels creativity and artistic endeavors; improves communication

Spiritual healing: strongly cleanses aura and chakras of attachments, stagnant energies, and cords; brings grace and angelic support; enhances psychic communication, especially with angels, spirits, and guides; balances and opens the upper chakras; improves dream recall

Celestobarite (Barytocelestine)

Formula: $(Sr,Ba)SO_4$ Hardness: 3–3.5 Crystal system: orthorhombic Formation process: sedimentary Chakra: all, especially earth star, root, third eye, crown Correspondences: air, earth, Mercury, Gemini, Libra, Aquarius

Physical healing: supports health of brain, nervous system, stomach, and skin; reveals karmic spiritual patterns underpinning disease

Psychological healing: encourages reconciliation, diplomacy, and excellent negotiation skills; cuts through doom and gloom; improves decision-making; invites impartiality

Spiritual healing: strongly grounds and protects; inspires transgressive, creative impulses for personal and planetary change; facilitates astral travel, psychic development, and shamanic journeys; accesses and integrates higher consciousness

Note: Celestobarite also exhibits properties similar to barite (p. 74) and celestite (p. 90).

Cerussite

Formula: $PbCO_3$ Hardness: 3–3.5 Crystal system: orthorhombic Formation process: sedimentary Chakra: root, crown, causal Correspondences: earth, spirit, Saturn, Aquarius

Physical healing: relieves restlessness and insomnia, assuages disorders of the brain and nervous system, improves and stabilizes coordination, supports recovery from chronic and/or hereditary conditions

Psychological healing: assuages feelings of homesickness, loneliness, and anguish; relieves anxiety; strengthens relationships; provides stamina and resilience when obstacles loom

Spiritual healing: powerfully grounds, draws light into the physical realm, facilitates past-life recall and identifies karmic relationships, helps in finding the path to enlightenment

Note: Cerussite can be toxic if mishandled.

Chalcedony

Formula: SiO_2 Hardness: 6.5–7 Crystal system: trigonal
Formation process: igneous or sedimentary
Chakra: various Correspondences: water, Moon, Mercury, Cancer

Physical healing: soothes and cleanses the body; treats conditions of female reproductive system; palliates colds, flu, and seasonal allergies; reduces heat and inflammation

Psychological healing: inculcates peace and tranquility; offers comfort during times of stress; relieves nervousness, anxiety, tension, and fear

Spiritual healing: imparts charity and sparks service; connects to the Divine Feminine; balances yin and yang energies; promotes overall healing and positive change, both personal and planetary; instills compassion; gently protects

Chalcedony, Blue

Formula: SiO_2 with impurities Hardness: 6.5–7
Crystal system: trigonal Formation process: igneous or sedimentary Chakra: heart, throat, third eye
Correspondences: water, Venus, Jupiter, Sagittarius

Physical healing: dissolves tension and alleviates heat and inflammation; fortifies eyes, ears, and sinuses; treats respiratory conditions, such as asthma, allergies, coughing, and congestion; heals sore throat, thyroid ailments, and conditions affecting speech

Psychological healing: represents renewal, imparts deep sense of peace and hope, soothes frazzled nerves and relieves stress, improves communication, brings mental clarity

Spiritual healing: offers inspiration, relaxation, and faith; facilitates meditation, insight, and channeling; inspires and assists the pursuit of truth

Chalcedony, Chrome (Mtorolite)

Formula: SiO_2 with chromium (Cr) Hardness: 6.5–7
Crystal system: trigonal Formation process: igneous or
sedimentary Chakra: heart Correspondences: water,
Venus, Libra

Physical healing: promotes cardiac health, reduces pain and inflammation,
stimulates healing and repair of liver, helps body maintain healthy blood
sugar levels, gently detoxifies the body

Psychological healing: brings greater peace, harmony, and love; invokes heart-
centered courage during challenging times; inspires open-mindedness and
creativity; relieves anxiety, depression, and worry

Spiritual healing: facilitates awareness and understanding of unconditional love,
forgiveness, and compassion; helps you follow your bliss

Chalcedony, Grape (Grape Agate)

Formula: SiO_2 with iron (Fe) Hardness: 6.5–7
Crystal system: trigonal Formation process: igneous
Chakra: sacral, third eye Correspondences: water, Neptune,
Pisces, Sagittarius

Physical healing: promotes health of eyes, brain, and nervous system; eases
conditions affecting neurotransmitters; treats conditions of stomach, such as
ulcers and nausea; cleanses lymphatic system

Psychological healing: removes fear and old emotional programming, invites
serenity and peace, sparks wonder and joy by feeding the inner child,
stimulates emotional growth

Spiritual healing: heightens spiritual practice by facilitating meditation, ecstatic
states, and transmissions from higher planes; supports spiritual healing;
breaks karmic cycles; promotes global harmony

Note: Recent analysis reveals that grape chalcedony is a cryptocrystalline variety
of amethyst.

Chalcedony, Mushroom
(Moroccan Brown Chalcedony)

Formula: SiO_2 with impurities Hardness: 6.5–7 Crystal system: trigonal Formation process: igneous Chakra: root, sacral Correspondences: earth, Mercury, Venus, Taurus, Virgo

Physical healing: supports healthy digestion and relieves disorders affecting the stomach and colon; helpful for balancing the microbiome of the body and expelling parasites and infections (especially fungal ones); supports fertility, pregnancy, and childbirth

Psychological healing: a wonderful stone to ensure healthy growth and development for children; centers and protects; offers grounding, stability, and motivation; invites a joyful and playful attitude; stimulates creativity

Spiritual healing: helps with finding direction in life, attracts nourishing energies from Mother Earth, clears a connection to earth energies and nature spirits

Chalcedony, Pink

Formula: SiO_2 with manganese (Mn) Hardness: 6.5–7 Crystal system: trigonal Formation process: igneous or sedimentary Chakra: heart Correspondences: water, Venus, Libra

Physical healing: promotes health of circulatory system; treats diabetes, poor circulation, heart disease; warms extremities; promotes lactation in mothers; maintains health of spleen

Psychological healing: nurtures emotional body and provides calming, clarifying influence to emotions; boosts confidence; reveals inner and outer beauty; cultivates love and romance

Spiritual healing: stone of innocence, brings joy, heals inner child, initiates contact with divine love

Chalcedony, Purple

Formula: SiO_2 with iron (Fe) Hardness: 6.5–7 Crystal system: trigonal Formation process: igneous or sedimentary Chakra: heart, crown Correspondences: air, Jupiter, Sagittarius

Physical healing: nourishes the brain and nervous system, helpful for conditions affecting sleep

Psychological healing: calms the mind; invites peace and tranquility, even in the midst of turmoil; excellent for reconciliation; promotes understanding and empathy, thereby improving relationships

Spiritual healing: gently opens and protects the third eye chakra, facilitates psychic development while filtering out unhelpful energy and information, enhances dream recall and lucid dreaming, cleanses the aura

Chalcedony, White

Formula: SiO_2 Hardness: 6.5–7 Crystal system: trigonal Formation process: igneous or sedimentary Chakra: heart Correspondences: water, Moon, Cancer

Physical healing: traditionally worn to promote lactation for new mothers, improves complexion and promotes healthy skin, reduces mucus buildup

Psychological healing: promotes fairness and impartiality; reconciles conflict between heart and mind; engenders nurturing, motherly qualities

Spiritual healing: facilitates attainment of hope, peace, and grace; wards off nightmares for restful sleep; enhances meditation and promotes stillness; expedites connection to the Divine

Chalcedony Rose

Formula: SiO_2 with impurities   Hardness: 6.5–7
Crystal system: trigonal   Formation process: igneous
Chakra: earth star, heart   Correspondences: earth, spirit,
Moon, Venus, Virgo, Aquarius

Physical healing: provides restful sleep and encourages relaxation; improves immune function; supports healthy digestion; promotes health of reproductive system, skin, mucous membranes, and eyes

Psychological healing: inspires confidence; soothes tension; invites a positive outlook; improves focus; facilitates open, easy, and honest communication

Spiritual healing: an extremely lucky stone that inspires hope and joy, improves meditation, draws out inner talents, protects and boosts efficacy of magic and spell craft, facilitates contact with nature spirits

Chalcopyrite

Formula: $FeCuS_2$ Hardness: 3.5–4   Crystal system: tetragonal
Formation process: sedimentary   Chakra: solar plexus
Correspondences: earth, fire, Venus, Libra

Physical healing: treats inflammation, neurological disorders, and weakened immune function; relieves pain; stimulates hair growth; cleanses liver, kidneys, and colon

Psychological healing: reveals psychological cause of illness, if there is one; helps monitor and direct the mind with purpose; empowers positive change; helps you to learn from mistakes; supports intellect and emotional intelligence

Spiritual healing: balances masculine and feminine energies, breaks up energy blockages, stimulates curiosity, helps overly rational people seeking spiritual experiences to shift their attention from brain to heart

Chalk

Formula: mostly calcite ($CaCO_3$) **Hardness:** 2–3 **Crystal system:** mostly trigonal **Formation process:** sedimentary **Chakra:** sacral, third eye **Correspondences:** water, Moon, Cancer

Physical healing: supports skeletal health, eases upset stomach, promotes detoxification, strengthens organs of elimination system, relieves fatigue

Psychological healing: softens rigid thoughts, beliefs, and emotions; unveils forgotten and repressed memories; diminishes restlessness; cultivates motivation

Spiritual healing: cleanses and protects aura, creates an invisible grid around the home for protection and cleansing, deepens connection to mystery and magic, strengthens focus for healing and channeling earth energies, facilitates clairvoyance and crystallomancy

Note: Chalk is a variety of limestone (p. 166).

Charoite

Formula: $K(Ca,Na)_2Si_4O_{10}(OH,F)\cdot H_2O$ with manganese (Mn) **Hardness:** 5–6 **Crystal system:** monoclinic **Formation process:** metamorphic **Chakra:** solar plexus, heart, third eye, crown, soul star **Correspondences:** air, Jupiter, Saturn, Sagittarius

Physical healing: helps body repair bone and cellular structures; relieves fluid retention and swelling; hastens recovery from sunburn, UV radiation, and electromagnetic pollution

Psychological healing: imparts mental and emotional stamina for sustaining positive changes, releases resistance and fear, helps identify and release negative behaviors, promotes objectivity

Spiritual healing: intensifies dreams; heightens psychic senses; filters out emotional bias that could taint incoming psychic information; helps in attaining spiritual purpose, creating joy, and acting in service to the greater good; releases and transmutes karma

Chiastolite

Formula: andalusite (Al_2SiO_5) with carbon (C)
Hardness: 6.5–7.5 Crystal system: orthorhombic
Formation process: metamorphic Chakra: root
Correspondences: earth, air, fire, water, spirit, Venus, Libra

Physical healing: provides balance for overtaxed nerves; counteracts excess acidity; promotes physical strength and flexibility; strengthens joints, liver, and immune system; traditionally used to heal wounds

Psychological healing: dispels fear, guilt, worry, and stress; promotes mental clarity and stability; reinforces better choices

Spiritual healing: confers powerful protection and returns negativity to sender; excellent ally in all manner of transitions; promotes balance in life; facilitates astral travel, shamanic journeying, and lucid dreaming

Chrysanthemum Stone

Formula: usually celestite ($SrSO_4$) in limestone (mostly $CaCO_3$) Hardness: 3–4 Crystal system: orthorhombic and trigonal Formation process: sedimentary or metamorphic Chakra: all, especially root Correspondences: earth, spirit, Taurus, Aquarius

Physical healing: supports health of bones, teeth, and gums; may reduce tumors, cysts, and other growths; promotes healthy skin; detoxifies body

Psychological healing: imparts integrity, honor, and sense of duty; strengthens familial and group bonds; brings harmony, peace, and beauty to any environment; promotes tidy, conscientious, and joyful lifestyle

Spiritual healing: deepens awareness of the present by releasing attachment to past and future, inspires you to slow down and see the bigger picture

Note: Composition and structure are highly variable, depending on source.

Chrysocolla

Formula: $(Cu,Al)_2H_2Si_2O_5(OH)_4 \cdot nH_2O$ Hardness: 2.3–3.5
Crystal system: orthorhombic Formation
process: igneous or sedimentary Chakra: throat
Correspondences: water, Venus, Taurus, Libra

Physical healing: soothes sore throat or tonsillitis; balances thyroid activity;
treats fever, muscle spasms, and asthma; relieves stress-related symptoms,
particularly of the stomach and respiratory system

Psychological healing: nurtures and soothes emotional imbalances; facilitates
heartfelt expression and improves communication; empowers the voice;
empowers speakers, writers, singers, performers, and anyone engaged in
other creative endeavors

Spiritual healing: floods mind and spirit with inspiration, enables you to better
perceive and pursue beauty, facilitates deeper connection to the Divine
Feminine

Chrysoprase

Formula: chalcedony (SiO_2) with nickel (Ni)
Hardness: 6.5–7 Crystal system: trigonal
Formation process: igneous Chakra: heart
Correspondences: water, Venus, Taurus, Libra

Physical healing: improves eye health and vision; treats conditions of skin, urinary
tract, and infections; detoxifies the body

Psychological healing: releases codependency, jealousy, and despair; heals
broken heart; fosters trust, security, and hope; rebuilds self-esteem after
rejection or loss; promotes forgiveness; lends strength to break free from
abusive relationships

Spiritual healing: awakens perception of the world through the heart, inspires
wonder and imagination, provides security and grace during transition

Note: see also chalcedony (p. 92)

Chrysotile

Formula: serpentine [$Mg_3Si_2O_5(OH)_4$] Hardness: 2.5–3
Crystal system: monoclinic Formation process: metamorphic
Chakra: earth star, root, third eye, causal Correspondences: earth,
Mercury, Gemini, Virgo, Capricorn

Physical healing: promotes health of blood vessels and respiratory system,
   improves digestion and nutrient absorption, reduces upset stomach caused
   by emotional imbalance
Psychological healing: cultivates honesty, integrity, and dedication; minimizes
   combative, argumentative, and irritable traits; assuages codependency and
   control issues; facilitates release, trust, and surrender
Spiritual healing: excellent for psychic development and visionary meditation,
   breaks up stagnant karma in the aura, eliminates outdated soul contracts
Note: Handle fibrous, unpolished specimens with care, as particles are dangerous
   if inhaled. See also serpentine (p. 232).

Cinnabar

Formula: HgS Hardness: 2–2.5 Crystal system: trigonal
Formation process: igneous or sedimentary Chakra: root,
sacral, third eye Correspondences: fire, Mercury, Saturn,
Gemini, Leo, Aquarius

Physical healing: assuages conditions of mucous
membranes, stomach, intestines; raises metabolism; may prevent or reverse
loss of cognitive abilities, such as from stroke or dementia; targets systemic
and chronic infections; detoxifies blood and lymph
Psychological healing: inspires confidence, dignity, and power; facilitates
   concentration; alleviates nervousness, restlessness, and low self-esteem
Spiritual healing: combats dogmatic belief and rigidity in spiritual practice;
   attunes to practices of alchemy, magic, and theurgy; transmutes negative
   energies, beliefs, and practices; boosts psychic vision; attracts wealth
Note: Cinnabar is extremely toxic. Handle with caution!

Citrine

Formula: quartz (SiO_2) with lithium (Li), aluminum (Al), and/or iron (Fe) **Hardness:** 6.5–7 **Crystal system:** trigonal
Formation process: igneous **Chakra:** solar plexus
Correspondences: fire, Sun, Leo

Physical healing: excellent for organs of elimination: skin, kidneys, bladder, liver, lungs, and large intestine; unwinds tension in the body; boosts metabolism; promotes stomach health

Psychological healing: represents letting go and empowerment, enables release of old beliefs and feelings, increases self-esteem and productivity, boosts personal power and mental acumen

Spiritual healing: guides you toward fulfilling your purpose; brings optimism and aligns the life path; encourages self-actualization, success, abundance, and prosperity

Colombianite (Pseudotektite)

Formula: mostly SiO_2 with traces of magnetite (Fe_3O_4)
Hardness: 5–6 **Crystal system:** amorphous
Formation process: igneous **Chakra:** all
Correspondences: fire, spirit, Jupiter, Sagittarius

Physical healing: stimulates brain function and decalcifies pineal gland, excellent palliative for nerve damage, supports healthy metabolism

Psychological healing: develops trust in your abilities and instincts; cultivates resilience, willpower, commitment, and follow-through; invites joy and creativity, no matter the situation; invites pride and joy in your progress and accomplishments

Spiritual healing: accelerates spiritual growth, personal development, and ascension; imparts compassion and wisdom; enhances manifestation and fulfills wishes; helps in finding direction and purpose; expands sense of self

Note: Colombianite and related stones saffordite and agnimanitite are classed as *pseudotektites* and are a form of obsidian (see p. 178).

Conglomerate (Puddingstone)

Formula: variable, mostly quartz (SiO_2)
Hardness: 6–7   Crystal system: mostly trigonal
Formation process: sedimentary   Chakra: root, sacral
Correspondences: earth, Mercury, Gemini

Physical healing: balances body pH; coordinates and harmonizes visceral organs; alleviates environmental allergies; soothes pain and inflammation; improves digestion, elimination, and circulation

Psychological healing: fortifies relationships (familial, professional, platonic, or romantic); stimulates self-reflection, self-critique, and personal development; reveals limiting beliefs and behaviors

Spiritual healing: enables recognition of bigger picture, cultivates sense of belonging, confers protection and peace, enhances connection to nature and the four elements

Copper

Formula: Cu   Hardness: 2.5–3   Crystal system: cubic
Formation process: igneous, sedimentary, or metamorphic
Chakra: sacral, solar plexus, heart   Correspondences: water, earth, Venus, Sun, Taurus, Libra, Virgo, Sagittarius

Physical healing: reduces pain and inflammation; eases and strengthens joints; supports circulatory system and cardiac health; nourishes female reproductive system, especially helpful for menstruation and pregnancy; alleviates exhaustion; balances over- or underactive libido

Psychological healing: brings emotional balance; boosts creativity; encourages harmony, cooperation, empathy, and understanding

Spiritual healing: deepens love, compassion, and connection to all life; offers a link to the Divine Feminine; inspires pursuit of beauty and love; may be used for abundance

Coquina

Formula: limestone (mostly calcite, $CaCO_3$) made almost entirely of broken shells Hardness: 3–3.5 Crystal system: trigonal Formation process: sedimentary Chakra: sacral, causal Correspondences: water, spirit, Neptune, Pisces

Physical healing: beneficial for skin, nails, and hair; strengthens bones and teeth; soothes respiratory conditions; improves circulation and digestion; promotes restful sleep

Psychological healing: brings joy and gratitude; has an uplifting and softening effect on gloom, despair, and depression; cultivates resilient boundaries; imparts confidence; helps in feeling safe, secure, and loved

Spiritual healing: cleanses aura, heals environmental and generational karma cycles, imparts pragmatism and levelheadedness to spiritual practice, encourages past-life recall, supports soul retrieval and shamanic healing

Note: also exhibits general properties of fossils (see p. 123) and limestone (p. 166)

Coral, Agatized

Formula: SiO_2 Hardness: 6.5–7 Crystal system: trigonal Formation process: sedimentary Chakra: sacral Correspondences: water, earth, spirit, Moon, Mercury, Neptune, Pisces

Physical healing: excellent fortifier for teeth, bones, and ligaments; supports cellular regeneration; excellent for assuaging a variety of hereditary conditions

Psychological healing: harmonizes right and left sides of brain and unites logic with intuition, helps resolve generational trauma and programming from childhood

Spiritual healing: facilitates communication with ancestors; knits together broken community and heals ancestral and communal karma; promotes oneness, unity, and spiritual strength; traditionally used to protect from storms

Note: see also agate (p. 42) and fossil (p. 123)

Coral, Red

Formula: mostly CaCO$_3$ Hardness: 3–4 Crystal system: trigonal and/or orthorhombic Formation process: organic (sedimentary) Chakra: root, sacral Correspondences: water, fire, spirit, Mars, Venus, Neptune, Aries

Physical healing: supports heart and circulatory system; regulates metabolism; excellent fortifier for skin, teeth, and bones; heals discrepancies in bone marrow; helps heal open wounds, cuts, and scrapes; supports healthy menstruation and health of the uterus

Psychological healing: invites joy, pleasure, and happiness; promotes assertive attitude; grants inspiration; fosters warm and caring disposition, emotional openness, and appreciation for beauty

Spiritual healing: traditionally used to protect against harm, connects to Divine Feminine, lends strength to stand in your power

Coral, White

Formula: mostly CaCO$_3$ Hardness: 3–4 Crystal system: trigonal and/or orthorhombic Formation process: organic (sedimentary) Chakra: root Correspondences: water, spirit, Moon, Neptune, Cancer, Pisces, Virgo

Physical healing: strengthens skin, teeth, and bones; soothes upset stomach and promotes healthy digestive system; promotes lactation in new mothers; may stimulate repair and regeneration of brain and sensory organs

Psychological healing: helps nourish and heal the inner child; releases childhood trauma; dissolves judgment, frustration, and feeling constrained or held back; encourages forgiveness

Spiritual healing: initiates purification, cleansing, and healing at all levels; gently protects; connects to the energies of the oceans and moon; attunes tides of life; facilitates strength-through-surrender

Covellite

Formula: CuS **Hardness:** 1.5–2 **Crystal system:** hexagonal **Formation process:** igneous or sedimentary **Chakra:** sacral, solar plexus, third eye **Correspondences:** air, fire, Venus, Jupiter, Sagittarius

Physical healing: promotes deep, regenerative sleep; protects against harmful radiation; supports healing from radiation-related conditions; discourages growth of unhealthy tissue; supports health of eyes, sinuses, throat, and stomach

Psychological healing: releases anxiety, unlocks creativity, boosts communication, excellent palliative for mental overstimulation or emotional exhaustion, invites self-love

Spiritual healing: stone of wisdom; facilitates dreaming, journeying, and after-death communication; promotes acceptance, tolerance, and harmony

Creedite

Formula: $Ca_3Al_2SO_4(F,OH)_{10} \cdot 2(H_2O)$ **Hardness:** 3.5–4 **Crystal system:** monoclinic **Formation process:** metamorphic **Chakra:** sacral, brow, crown, soul star **Correspondences:** fire, Sun, Leo

Physical healing: supports health of muscles and skeletal system, speeds recovery from injury, promotes assimilation of nutrients, encourages health of reproductive system, strengthening for the liver

Psychological healing: boosts mental faculties, learning, and personal development; mediates conflict and mitigates drama; sparks motivation, creativity, and expression; eases sexual trauma and shame; promotes healthy views of sexuality

Spiritual healing: expansive, enlightening, and evolutionary stone; balances masculine and feminine energies; enhances meditation, astral travel, ancestral healing, and access to the Akashic records; cultivates wisdom; activates kundalini

Cryolite

Formula: Na_3AlF_6 Hardness: 2.5–3.5
Crystal system: monoclinic Formation process: igneous
Chakra: all, especially higher heart, soul star
Correspondences: air, spirit, Mercury, Uranus, Gemini, Aquarius

Physical healing: supports health of skeletal and nervous systems, strengthens bone and teeth, improves cognitive function, regenerates after brain injury, may treat speech impediments

Psychological healing: promotes good humor, grace under pressure, and positivity; sharpens perception; dissolves avoidance, indecision, and procrastination; strengthens character; lends confidence for public speaking

Spiritual healing: incorporates spiritual practice into daily life; roots awareness and intelligence in the heart; connects to divine love and compassion; encourages surrender, psychic development, and communication with guides, spirits, and angels; protects by making your energy undetectable

Cuprite

Formula: Cu_2O Hardness: 3.5–4 Crystal system: cubic
Formation process: sedimentary Chakra: root, sacral
Correspondences: earth, Venus, Taurus, Virgo, Aquarius

Physical healing: supports health of female reproductive system, ameliorates sexual dysfunction, promotes health of heart and circulatory system

Psychological healing: helps to release old relationships, enhances creativity, engenders emotional balance, helps create sustainable and fulfilling romantic relationships, boosts confidence, reduces worry and fear

Spiritual healing: represents magic and alchemy, deeply grounds and nourishes, enhances receptive (yin) energies, heals shadow through introspection, emboldens you to conquer obstacles, facilitates connection to Divine Feminine

Dalmatian Stone (Aplite)

Formula: complex and variable Hardness: 6.5–7 Crystal system: trigonal Formation process: igneous Chakra: root
Correspondences: earth, Mercury, Virgo

Physical healing: initiates detoxification; supports immune health; excellent support for muscles, tendons, cartilage, aches, and pain; alleviates conditions affecting skin, colon, circulatory, and nervous systems; strengthens will to conquer addiction

Psychological healing: invites joy and humor; assuages skepticism, pessimism, fear, anxiety, and nightmares; brings psychological balance

Spiritual healing: confers protection, balance, and strength; facilitates animal communication; translates ideas into action; excellent for manifestation and abundance; invites group harmony and cohesion

Note: Dalmatian stone (often mislabeled as jasper) is a fine-grained igneous rock called aplite with properties similar to granite (see p. 136).

Danburite

Formula: $CaB_2Si_2O_8$ Hardness: 7–7.5
Crystal system: orthorhombic
Formation process: igneous, sedimentary, or metamorphic
Chakra: heart, crown, soul star Correspondences: air, Jupiter, Leo, Sagittarius, Aquarius

Physical healing: beneficial for respiratory system, especially lungs and sinuses; brings light into the physical body for overall healing; excellent palliative for stress-related illness

Psychological healing: soothing and balancing stone that mediates extreme emotions, soothes antagonistic relationships

Spiritual healing: dissolves dualistic worldviews, highlights interconnectedness of all life, unites heart and crown chakras, evokes heart-centered approach to life, strengthens psychic senses and facilitates spirit communication, enhances ability to channel messages from non-physical beings

Danburite, Blue

Formula: $CaB_2Si_2O_8$ Hardness: 7–7.5 Crystal system: orthorhombic Formation process: metamorphic Chakra: throat, third eye, crown Correspondences: air, Uranus, Sagittarius, Aquarius

Physical healing: soothes irritation of skin and mucous membranes, alleviates sore throat, detoxifies body, may relieve bloating and gas

Psychological healing: cools hot temper; reveals hidden pain and trauma while allowing you to maintain emotional detachment; illuminates links between intuition and logic; promotes clear communication, even when discussing emotionally charged or challenging topics

Spiritual healing: stone of wisdom and angelic support, enhances astral travel and lucid dreaming, potent karmic purifier

Danburite, Pink

Formula: $CaB_2Si_2O_8$ with manganese (Mn) Hardness: 7–7.5 Crystal system: orthorhombic Formation process: igneous, sedimentary, or metamorphic Chakra: heart, higher heart, crown, soul star Correspondences: air, Venus, Libra

Physical healing: helps to heal conditions of the heart and circulatory system, nerves, and brain; treats disorders of the liver and muscles; helps alleviate physical conditions that have an underlying emotional cause; relieves allergies

Psychological healing: powerful ally for releasing past relationships, brings emotional clarity, balancing to the heart and mind, lifts self-esteem and encourages self-love

Spiritual healing: instills charity, compassion, service, and empathy; evokes humanitarian views and actions; encourages loving-kindness

Danburite, Yellow

Formula: $CaB_2Si_2O_8$ with iron (Fe) Hardness: 7–7.5
Crystal system: orthorhombic Formation process: igneous or metamorphic Chakra: solar plexus, crown, soul star
Correspondences: fire, Sun, Leo, Sagittarius

Physical healing: especially salubrious for the digestive system, stimulates metabolism, encourages healthy eating habits

Psychological healing: represents optimism, hope, and positivity; brings clarity and stillness to overactive mind; sparks unbridled joy; promotes healthy restraint and self-control

Spiritual healing: stone of spiritual sovereignty; links solar plexus and crown chakras; conveys angelic fire for cleansing the body, mind, and spirit; excellent ally for spiritual teachers; heals karmic patterns related to power and authority

Datolite

Formula: $CaB(SiO_4)(OH)$ Hardness: 5–5.5
Crystal system: monoclinic Formation process: igneous or sedimentary Chakra: solar plexus, heart, third eye, crown, soul star Correspondences: water, air, Jupiter, Aries

Physical healing: benefits skeletal, nervous, and circulatory systems; improves coordination; excellent adjunct for recovery from injury; helps stabilize hereditary conditions and illnesses affecting DNA and RNA

Psychological healing: inspires dignity, respect, and tact; strengthens mind and memory; maintains calm during chaos and change; releases fear, anxiety, and grief; reveals hidden talents

Spiritual healing: teaches impermanence, nonattachment, and surrender; facilitates karmic and ancestral healing; cultivates inner peace; builds connection to natural world and nature spirits

Diamond

Formula: C Hardness: 10 Crystal system: cubic
Formation process: igneous Chakra: crown, soul star
Correspondences: earth, air, fire, water, spirit, Sun, Venus, Mars, Aries, Libra, Leo

Physical healing: encourages healthy growth and regeneration of cells and tissues; stabilizes and balances all processes within the body; engenders strength, stamina, fitness; eases dizziness and vertigo; strengthens skeletal system; effective for healing conditions of the thymus, as well as conditions affecting DNA

Psychological healing: increases order, logic, and mental balance; stimulates imagination; inspires courage, bravery, and fearlessness; dissipates jealousy, entitlement, and low self-esteem; excellent for encouraging love and trust

Spiritual healing: stone of unconditional love; alleviates egotism, greed, poverty consciousness, and pride; inspires gratitude, wisdom, communion with the Divine; powerfully protects; infuses body, mind, and spirit with light; symbolizes mastery, enlightenment, and attainment

Diaspore

Formula: AlO(OH) Hardness: 6.5–7 Crystal system: orthorhombic Formation process: igneous, sedimentary, or metamorphic Chakra: third eye, crown, soul star Correspondences: air, Mercury, Gemini, Aquarius

Physical healing: supports health of nervous and immune systems, improves balance and coordination, strengthens bones, balances body pH

Psychological healing: strengthens learning, communication, and language skills; excellent for motivating and inspiring writers; invites new perspectives; aids conflict resolution; promotes adaptability; releases judgment

Spiritual healing: strongly stimulating to the third eye; improves psychic ability; facilitates psychic readings, trances, journeying, and remote viewing; anchors higher energies into body and the planet

Diopside

Formula: CaMgSi$_2$O$_6$ **Hardness:** 5.5–6.5 **Crystal system:** monoclinic **Formation process:** igneous or metamorphic **Chakra:** heart **Correspondences:** air, earth, Mercury, Gemini, Virgo

Physical healing: relieves pain, especially headaches; regulates blood pressure and blood sugar levels; promotes overall healing and helps the body repair itself

Psychological healing: helps in overcoming fear, regret, and indecision; gently opens the heart to release anxiety, worry, and stress; energy stabilizing for overcoming obsession and addiction; facilitates learning and integration of new knowledge

Spiritual healing: balances yin and yang energies, helps evenly distribute life force through physical and subtle bodies, highlights connections to nature and the cosmos, provides optimal conditions to experience spiritual freedom

Diopside, Black Star

Formula: CaMgSi$_2$O$_6$ with magnetite (Fe$_3$O$_4$) **Hardness:** 5.5–6.5 **Crystal system:** monoclinic **Formation process:** igneous or metamorphic **Chakra:** earth star, root **Correspondences:** earth, Saturn, Capricorn

Physical healing: promotes health of circulatory system; strengthens walls of blood vessels; supports health of bones, muscles, and brain; helps realign spine

Psychological healing: balances and stabilizes emotions; promotes forgiveness; eases pain from emotional trauma; facilitates emotional release, especially through tears; enhances creativity; boosts logic

Spiritual healing: excellent accelerator for karmic healing and releasing past-life baggage, promotes a more spiritual worldview, reveals the spiritual cause beneath everyday phenomena, protects against harmful energies

Diopside, Chrome

Formula: $CaMgSi_2O_6$ with chromium (Cr) Hardness: 5.5–6.5
Crystal system: monoclinic Formation process: igneous
Chakra: earth star, heart, third eye
Correspondences: earth, fire, Saturn, Sagittarius, Capricorn

Physical healing: excellent for overall healing, cellular repair, and nourishing the body; helpful in alleviating conditions of gallbladder, bones, kidneys, and heart; may be used as an adjunct to medical treatment for bone cancer; promotes health of intestines and organs of elimination

Psychological healing: energizes inspiration, problem-solving, and creativity; strengthens the ability to overcome obstacles; boosts analytical skills; loosens writer's block; instills motivation and resiliency

Spiritual healing: lights spiritual flame within; protects energy field; invokes sense of guardianship for the planet; facilitates communication with nature spirits and devas, especially the devas of gemstones

Dioptase

Formula: $CuSiO_3 \cdot H_2O$ Hardness: 5 Crystal system: trigonal Formation process: sedimentary
Chakra: heart, higher heart Correspondences: water, Venus, Taurus

Physical healing: promotes eye health; helps regenerate damaged tissue, especially of the liver; supports health of the heart and immune system

Psychological healing: ultimate stone of forgiveness, opens the heart chakra and encourages self-love, reveals the heart's desires

Spiritual healing: activates the higher heart chakra and ushers in the power of unconditional love; taps into the transformative, alchemical power of love; awakens awareness of higher truth; fosters spiritual freedom

Diorite

Formula: variable **Hardness:** variable
Crystal system: variable **Formation process:** igneous
Chakra: solar plexus, throat **Correspondences:** earth, fire, Venus, Libra

Physical healing: eases tension; soothes sore muscles and strained tendons; supports respiratory health; helpful in alleviating troubling conditions of ears, nose, and throat; strengthens bones and teeth

Psychological healing: balances and calms intense, fiery, or out-of-control emotions; soothes anger, grief, worry, and anxiety; assuages feelings of fear and abandonment; reduces skepticism and stubbornness; opens a closed mind

Spiritual healing: harmonizes polar energies, such as yin and yang, masculine and feminine; shields against psychic attack and geopathic stress; excellent centering tool for meditation; draws impurities and attachments out of aura and chakras

Dolomite

Formula: $CaMg(CO_3)_2$ **Hardness:** 3.5–4 **Crystal system:** trigonal **Formation process:** sedimentary
Chakra: all **Correspondences:** earth, Saturn, Aries, Capricorn

Physical healing: detoxifies and strengthens; supports health of bones, teeth, hair, and nails; relieves pain and tension, especially headache and toothache; regulates metabolism and weight gain/loss

Psychological healing: calms and soothes; excellent palliative for stress, grief, and emotional pain; helps in finding more enjoyment from everyday tasks, thereby overcoming procrastination

Spiritual healing: helps in detaching from ego, promotes self-discovery, aids in recognizing the spiritual potential of each moment

Dumortierite

Formula: $Al_7BO_3(SiO_4)_3O_3$ Hardness: 7
Crystal system: orthorhombic   Formation process: igneous
Chakra: throat, third eye   Correspondences: air, Uranus,
Leo, Aquarius

Physical healing: mitigates pain, including headaches and cramps; relieves nausea and promotes health of digestive system; balances endocrine system

Psychological healing: offers resolve, commitment, and responsibility; encourages release from addiction and obsession; lessens fear and anxiety; promotes organization; helps release toxic relationships and enforce boundaries; brings clarity, focus, and discipline

Spiritual healing: premier stone of patience; helps embrace stillness, quiet, and nonattachment, thereby improving meditation; facilitates past-life recall and karmic healing; improves psychic development

Emerald

Formula: $Be_3Al_2SiO_6$ with chromium (Cr)   Hardness: 7.5–8
Crystal system: hexagonal   Formation process: igneous or
metamorphic   Chakra: heart   Correspondences: water, earth,
Venus, Mercury, Saturn, Taurus, Gemini

Physical healing: master physical healer that soothes and restores entire body; improves health of eyes, circulatory system, heart, and reproductive system

Psychological healing: instills virtue, attracts love, and nourishes the emotions; overrides unhappiness, despondency, and disconnection by infusing the entire being with love and light; brings solace for depression and isolation

Spiritual healing: stone of radical love that restores the world; encourages state of surrender and fills the body, mind, and spirit with unconditional love; cleanses guilt, shame, blame, and family karma; illuminates truth and animates pursuit of justice

Note: see also beryl (p. 76)

Eosphorite

Formula: $MnAl(PO_4)(OH)_2 \cdot H_2O$ Hardness: 5
Crystal system: orthorhombic   Formation
process: igneous   Chakra: heart   Correspondences: fire,
Sun, Venus, Leo

Physical healing: strengthens heart and circulatory system; balances hormones
and eases discomforts of puberty, menopause, and other physical transitions

Psychological healing: imparts hope and optimism; clears emotional baggage;
promotes authentic connection, communication, and relationships; dissolves
patterns of anger and resentment; alleviates homesickness; channels
rebellious feelings into productive change

Spiritual healing: symbolizes enlightenment and spiritual evolution; opens
and protects heart chakra; accelerates and strengthens magic, ritual, and
manifestation; facilitates past-life recall and karmic healing

Epidote

Formula: $Ca_2Al_2(Fe^{3+},Al)(SiO_4)(Si_2O_7)O(OH)$ Hardness: 6–7
Crystal system: monoclinic   Formation process: igneous
or metamorphic   Chakra: heart   Correspondences: earth,
water, Mercury, Virgo

Physical healing: excellent support for overall healing; targets conditions
affecting thyroid, adrenals, liver, gallbladder, and digestive system; enhances
recovery from long-term illness; breaks down tumors, cysts, lumps, and other
kinds of abnormal growths; stimulates regeneration of damaged tissues

Psychological healing: clarifies intentions; enhances focus and patience; assuages
anxiety, worry, and fear; softens rude, defensive, or overly sarcastic attitudes;
instills hope in troubled times

Spiritual healing: raises the physical body's vibration and lessens uncomfortable
effects of ascension process and spiritual growth, strongly boosts
manifestation process, imparts faith and trust, attracts prosperity

Euclase

Formula: $BeAlSiO_4(OH)$ **Hardness:** 7.5
Crystal system: monoclinic **Formation process:** igneous
Chakra: heart, higher heart, third eye, crown
Correspondences: air, Mercury, Virgo, Sagittarius

Physical healing: combats infection, inflammation, pain, and bruising; soothes eyes, vision, nervous system, and brain; may reduce speech impediments

Psychological healing: excellent for mental abilities, including learning, study, memory, and mental clarity; sparks efforts for excellence and poise; imparts diplomacy and tact; encourages truth and helps you to project honesty; invites self-forgiveness and better self-care

Spiritual healing: helps in understanding and releasing karmic cycles, ultimately aiming for complete release from the cycle of *samsara*—birth, life, death, and rebirth; transmutes heavy, dense, and stagnant energy in aura and environment; strongly stimulates psychic senses

Eudialyte

Formula: $Na_{15}Ca_6Fe_3Zr_3Si(Si_{25}O_{73})(O,OH,H_2O)_3(Cl,OH)_2$
Hardness: 5–6 **Crystal system:** trigonal
Formation process: igneous **Chakra:** root, heart
Correspondences: earth, water, Moon, Leo, Virgo

Physical healing: boosts vitality; calms overactive adrenal glands and reduces fight or flight (or freeze) response; excellent for recovering from fatigue, overexertion, and chronic low energy

Psychological healing: considered a stone of successful love; combats grief, fear, and terror; offers emotional fortitude; eases feelings of jealousy, regret, shame, separation, and bitterness; plants seeds of optimism and encourages self-love

Spiritual healing: supports moving outside comfort zone for meaningful growth, interrupts karmic patterns of self-denial and martyrdom, teaches lessons from mistakes

Flint

Formula: SiO$_2$ **Hardness:** 6.5–7 **Crystal system:** trigonal
Formation process: sedimentary **Chakra:** earth star, root, sacral **Correspondences:** earth, fire, Mars, Pluto, Aries, Gemini, Scorpio

Physical healing: improves strength and stamina; supports health of the skeletal system, particularly the jaw and other joints; increases collagen and improves skin health; soothes stiffness of arthritis

Psychological healing: facilitates release of unhealthy relationships; lends courage to overcome shyness; minimizes fear and offers solace, comfort, and emotional strength; improves communication and understanding

Spiritual healing: powerful ally for karmic healing, ancestral communication, and shamanic journeys; strongly protects; excellent aid in cutting cords; ally in earth-healing

Fluorite

Formula: CaF$_2$ **Hardness:** 4 **Crystal system:** cubic
Formation process: igneous, sedimentary, or metamorphic **Chakra:** all, especially third eye, crown
Correspondences: air, Mercury, Gemini, Capricorn

Physical healing: supports healthy skeletal system by nourishing bones, ligaments, teeth, and cartilage; promotes healthy joints and spinal alignment; excellent for the brain and nervous system; breaks down barriers to healing, which can be helpful for chronic conditions

Psychological healing: stabilizes and balances mind; improves focus, concentration, memory, and organization; fortifies self-discipline; draws out suppressed or latent emotions; expands awareness and opens the gateway to the subconscious mind; overcomes narrow-mindedness

Spiritual healing: facilitates meditation and psychic development, and clears the energy field of debris; breaks down patterns of injustice and oppression to facilitate global change; anchors positive change

Fluorite, Blue

Formula: CaF_2 with iron (Fe) or europium (Eu)   Hardness: 4
Crystal system: cubic   Formation process: igneous or
sedimentary   Chakra: all, especially throat, third eye
Correspondences: air, water, Mercury, Pisces

Physical healing: releases longstanding tension from body; supports health of eyes,
nose, throat, and ears; relieves joint pain; excellent for respiratory system, brain,
and spine; eliminates parasites; prevents and repairs damage to DNA

Psychological healing: reduces worry, fear, and anger; invites deep calm; redirects
the mind away from disappointment, resentment, and frustration and
channels this energy into more productive tasks; inspires clear, concise, and
mentally driven communication

Spiritual healing: deepens commitment to truth and justice, excellent for
focusing meditation, grants better understanding of karmic cycles, integrates
lost or broken soul fragments

Fluorite, Blue John

Formula: CaF_2 with hydrocarbons (chiefly C and H)
and iron (Fe)   Hardness: 4   Crystal system: cubic
Formation process: igneous   Chakra: all, especially
throat, third eye   Correspondences: air, spirit,
Mercury, Pluto, Scorpio

Physical healing: improves nutrient absorption; treats fatigue, fever, and chills;
supports overall health of respiratory system; helps overcome chronic illness

Psychological healing: stone of mental and manual dexterity; inspires creativity,
innovation, and adaptation; supports learning new skills, especially those
related to technology, language, and culture

Spiritual healing: excellent defense for empaths; helps detach from others'
emotions; offers support and clarity so we can be of service to others; reduces
atmospheric and environmental toxins; encourages altruism, generosity, and
service; attracts luck; promotes psychic development

Fluorite, Brown (Rootbeer Fluorite)

Formula: CaF_2 with hydrocarbons (chiefly C and H)   Hardness: 4
Crystal system: cubic   Formation process: igneous or
sedimentary   Chakra: root, solar plexus
Correspondences: earth, Sun, Leo, Virgo

Physical healing: promotes healthy skin; reduces scar tissue formation; supports the organs of elimination; helps the body recover from exposure to environmental toxins and radiation; may be used to treat cancer, as an adjunct to medical treatment

Psychological healing: helps in maintaining a level head; invites pragmatism; opens the mind, especially in cases of fixation and bias

Spiritual healing: simultaneously grounds and expands, helpful for bringing new projects to fruition, anchors higher consciousness into the material plane, supports starseeds and young souls, enhances communication with starbeings, helps release earthbound spirits

Fluorite, Clear

Formula: CaF_2 Hardness: 4   Crystal system: cubic
Formation process: igneous or sedimentary   Chakra: all,
especially third eye, crown   Correspondences: air, Moon,
Mercury, Gemini, Cancer

Physical healing: heals conditions of the respiratory system; relieves irritation of mucous membranes; strengthens skin, teeth, bones, eyes, and nervous system; dissolves pain; improves vision

Psychological healing: cleanses mind; counteracts feelings of shame, guilt, and being unclean; brings stillness to the mind; calms overthinkers and worrywarts

Spiritual healing: initiates purification, brings clarity and order to spiritual practice, clears obstructions in energy field

Fluorite, Green

Formula: CaF_2 with iron (Fe), chromium (Cr), or samarium (Sm)
Hardness: 4 **Crystal system:** cubic
Formation process: igneous or sedimentary   **Chakra:** all
Correspondences: air, Mercury, Gemini

Physical healing: targets all kinds of infections and stimulates immune response; treats conditions of eyes, ears, nose, tear ducts, throat, and sinuses; quells vomiting and diarrhea; very detoxifying and restorative

Psychological healing: bridges the heart and mind, may intensify emotional states to bring better understanding of them, opens the mind to new possibilities, helps replace unhealthy habits and behaviors by anchoring positive and healthy ones instead

Spiritual healing: removes blocks to overall well-being and growth; cleanses all chakras, but is most effective for the heart; helps in finding direction in life; supports the work of energy healers by enhancing the flow of healing and preventing practitioners from taking on their clients' energy

Fluorite, Pink

Formula: CaF_2 with yttrium (Y) **Hardness:** 4 **Crystal system:** cubic **Formation process:** igneous or sedimentary **Chakra:** all, especially heart **Correspondences:** air, Mercury, Venus, Libra, Pisces

Physical healing: good for migraines, injury, and body aches; helps to recover from brain injury; supports the skeletal and nervous systems; relieves seasonal allergies and other conditions affecting respiratory system and mucous membranes; regulates hormones; minimizes psychosomatic illness

Psychological healing: breaks down barriers to understanding and expressing repressed emotions, brings solace when facing despair, boosts confidence, provides order to and insight into emotions

Spiritual healing: imparts egalitarian and humanitarian worldview; promotes compassion, charity, and goodwill; facilitates soul retrieval

Fluorite, Purple

Formula: CaF_2 Hardness: 4   Crystal system: cubic
Formation process: igneous or sedimentary   Chakra: all, especially third eye   Correspondences: air, Jupiter, Sagittarius

Physical healing: alleviates headaches and insomnia; promotes overall health of skeletal system; often used to treat brain and nervous system, as well as conditions affecting DNA; reduces the growth of tumors and infections

Psychological healing: helps in breaking unwanted habits; assuages depression, bipolar disorder, and grief; purifies the mind; brings emotional stability; boosts memory

Spiritual healing: bridges the mind and spirit, expands consciousness, enhances intuition and psychic development, makes dreams more vivid, promotes liberation and determination on the path of the spiritual seeker, reduces feelings of overwhelm from responsibility

Fluorite, Rainbow

Formula: CaF_2 Hardness: 4   Crystal system: cubic
Formation process: igneous   Chakra: all
Correspondences: air, Mercury, Uranus, Gemini, Aquarius

Physical healing: remedies conditions of the chest, lungs, mucous membranes, and skin; strengthens bones; supports healthy skin; promotes flexibility in joints; stimulates healing of injuries; confers overall healing benefits

Psychological healing: expands the mind; helps in exploring full range of human emotion; helps maintain open-mindedness; offers creativity, inspiration, innovation; helps you follow your dreams

Spiritual healing: boosts intuition and aids psychic development; promotes freedom; enhances meditation; helps assimilate new energies and eases channels for energy healing and other holistic modalities; cleanses and restores energy field; repairs leaks and tears in aura; protects against cords, attachments, and psychic debris

Note: The properties of each color contained in rainbow fluorite also apply.

Fluorite, Yellow

Formula: CaF_2 with oxygen (O), yttrium (Y), or cerium (Ce)
Hardness: 4   Crystal system: cubic   Formation
process: igneous or sedimentary   Chakra: all, especially
solar plexus   Correspondences: air, Mercury, Sun, Gemini, Leo

Physical healing: promotes healthy skeletal system, liver, thyroid, and digestive system; discourages disordered eating habits; maintains healthy blood pressure and cholesterol levels

Psychological healing: facilitates learning, boosts intellect, dissolves worry, invites positive outlook, encourages learning to be less defensive or guarded

Spiritual healing: very centering; promotes understanding and assimilation of new information and energy; supports growth and expansion in pursuit of spiritual truth; bolsters cooperative efforts in community; cultivates practical, experiential wisdom

Fluorite, Yttrian

Formula: $(Ca,Y)F_2$ Hardness: 4   Crystal system: cubic
Formation process: igneous or sedimentary
Chakra: all, especially crown, soul star
Correspondences: air, fire, Jupiter, Sagittarius, Pisces

Physical healing: helpful for skeletal system; may be used to reduce growths, cysts, fibroids, and tumors; protects DNA from damage; dissolves psychosomatic conditions

Psychological healing: stone of higher learning; encourages self-discovery; ushers compassion and understanding to subconscious mind; releases feelings of inadequacy, imperfection; brings completion to periods of turmoil

Spiritual healing: stone of wonder, facilitates pursuit of truth and philosophy, helps integrate spiritual experience and new energies for evolution and spiritual growth, helps with accessing Akashic records

Fossil

Formula: variable   Hardness: variable
Crystal system: variable   Formation process: sedimentary
Chakra: variable   Correspondences: earth, water, spirit,
Saturn, Capricorn

Physical healing: supports health of skeletal system, moderates hereditary
conditions, imparts longevity and healthy aging

Psychological healing: supports memory; releases old mental and emotional
programming; helps to maintain calm in states of crisis; strengthens
impartiality and removes bias when reviewing past events; invites order,
reason, and punctuality

Spiritual healing: symbolizes tradition, destiny, and karma; connects to ancestral
energy; enhances past-life recall; promotes karmic and ancestral healing;
protects

Fossil, Belemnite

Formula: calcite or aragonite ($CaCO_3$)   Hardness: 3–4
Crystal system: trigonal or orthorhombic
Formation process: sedimentary   Chakra: sacral
Correspondences: water, spirit, Neptune, Pisces

Physical healing: traditionally used to heal rheumatism and conditions of the
eyes; strengthens skeletal system and joints, particularly hands and fingers;
enhances libido, fertility, and stamina

Psychological healing: sharpens focus; stabilizes emotions; brings light and hope;
helps to conquer fear, greed, and isolation; enhances creativity, imagination,
and motivation

Spiritual healing: protects against harm; ensures happy, safe home; strengthens
manifestation; clears cords and attachments from aura

Fossil, Dinosaur Bone

Formula: usually quartz (SiO_2)   **Hardness:** 6.5–7
Crystal system: trigonal   **Formation process:** sedimentary
Chakra: root, third eye   **Correspondences:** earth, spirit,
Saturn, Capricorn

Physical healing: strengthens skeletal system, joints, and muscle tissue; improves health of bone marrow and blood cells; balances sympathetic and parasympathetic nervous systems

Psychological healing: enhances empathy and understanding; helps in overcoming shyness and social awkwardness; enhances learning, expression, and self-expression; heightens awareness of instinctual reactions and promotes conscious response

Spiritual healing: connects to ancient wisdom, invokes power of dragons and dragon energies, encourages intentional relationship with the land and earth energies

Fossil, Sea Urchin

Formula: usually calcite ($CaCO_3$) or quartz (SiO_2)
Hardness: variable   **Crystal system:** trigonal   **Formation process:** sedimentary   **Chakra:** earth star, heart, third eye
Correspondences: earth, air, fire, water, spirit, Venus, Virgo

Physical healing: strengthens body; supports overall healing and regeneration; traditionally used to encourage fertility and for conditions affecting the head, such as congestion, headache, earache, and injuries of the head

Psychological healing: centers and clears the mind; highlights and releases old mental patterns; restores motion to frozen or stuck emotions; strengthens resolve for self-care and shadow work; imparts whimsy, lightheartedness, and good cheer

Spiritual healing: confers protection, blessings, and luck; averts envy, psychic attack, and harmful magic; nourishes and strengthens spirit; enhances meditation, astral travel, and trance states; facilitates ancestral communication

Fossil, Shark Tooth

Formula: variable   Hardness: variable
Crystal system: variable   Formation process: sedimentary
Chakra: throat   Correspondences: earth, spirit, Saturn,
Capricorn

Physical healing: strengthens teeth, nails, and bones; enhances body's defenses
in the skin and immune system

Psychological healing: dissolves timidity, shyness, and fear of expression;
improves communication; bolsters courage and assertiveness; reduces
tendency to take on too much responsibility

Spiritual healing: strongly protects, cuts through stagnant karmic patterns, cuts
psychic and karmic cords, encourages seizing of the moment

Note: Other fossilized teeth exhibit similar properties.

Fuchsite

Formula: K(Al,Cr)$_2$(AlSi$_3$O$_{10}$)(OH)$_2$ Hardness: 2.5   Crystal
system: monoclinic   Formation process: metamorphic
Chakra: heart   Correspondences: air, Mercury, Virgo

Physical healing: imparts flexibility and resiliency; good for metabolism,
circulatory system, and skin; treats rashes, itch, cough, allergies, and
hemorrhoids

Psychological healing: brings flexibility to the mind; inspires joy, playfulness, and
love; decreases mental chatter; offers inspiration, freedom, and innovation;
heals inner child; enhances expression and communication

Spiritual healing: encourages seeing the bigger picture, resonates with
unconditional love, enables acceptance and adaptation, promotes
understanding setbacks as spiritual lessons

Fulgurite

Formula: mostly SiO_2 Hardness: 5.5–6.5   Crystal system: amorphous   Formation process: metamorphic
Chakra: earth star, root, crown, soul star
Correspondences: earth, air, fire, water, spirit, Mars, Jupiter, Aries

Physical healing: promotes healthy eyes, ears, sinuses, and throat; eases symptoms of dizziness and vertigo; balances respiratory and circulatory systems

Psychological healing: supports breaking through obstacles to movement and self-development; ignites decisive and immediate action; bolsters courage, power, focus, and creativity; excellent aid for improving communication and relationships

Spiritual healing: a stone of prayer and communion with the higher realms; facilitates contact with and channeling of ancestors, guides, angels, spirits, and other beings; clears karma associated with relationships; clears and aligns central channel in the human energy field

Gabbro

Formula: variable   Hardness: variable
Crystal system: variable   Formation process: igneous
Chakra: root, causal   Correspondences: earth, fire, Saturn, Aquarius

Physical healing: strengthens the body; stimulates cellular regeneration and repair of tissues; counteracts exhaustion, fatigue, and overexertion; releases chronic and slow-moving illness; calming for stomach and kidneys

Psychological healing: promotes faith in self, encourages determination, helps in discerning needs from wants, emphasizes creativity rather than routine, sheds light on the subconscious mind, promotes emotional and mental equilibrium

Spiritual healing: stone of new beginnings, helps when you feel stuck, brings latent karma to the surface to be released, reveals the "why" behind current situations, helps in learning from the past, facilitates soul retrieval

Galena

Formula: PbS   Hardness: 2.5   Crystal system: cubic
Formation process: igneous, sedimentary, or metamorphic
Chakra: root   Correspondences: earth, Saturn, Capricorn

Physical healing: treats infection and systemic toxicity; neutralizes radiation; promotes cellular regeneration; alleviates stiffness, pain, and inflammation

Psychological healing: wards off melancholy, depression, and seriousness; teaches responsibility, patience, and independence

Spiritual healing: powerful grounding stone, fosters understanding of repeating cycles, great for karmic healing, stimulates past-life recall, reveals bigger picture, encourages positive changes

Note: Galena is toxic; handle with care.

Garnet

Formula: $X_3Y_2(SiO_4)_3$ Hardness: 6.5–7.5
Crystal system: cubic   Formation process: igneous or metamorphic   Chakra: root   Correspondences: earth, fire, Mars, Aries, Capricorn

Physical healing: grounds, fortifies, and enlivens the body; boosts energy and stamina; regulates homeostatic mechanisms; strengthens muscles and skeleton; helps regulate the endocrine system; regulates metabolism and hormone levels

Psychological healing: counteracts isolation; provides motivation, stamina, and resolve; enhances mental acuity; invokes passion, sensuality, creativity, and romance

Spiritual healing: symbolizes abundance and unconditional love, facilitates connection to the Divine, stabilizes lower chakras, facilitates manifestation

Garnet, Almandine (Red Garnet)

Formula: $Fe_3Al_2(SiO_4)_3$ Hardness: 7–7.5   Crystal system: cubic   Formation process: igneous or metamorphic   Chakra: root   Correspondences: earth, fire, Mars, Saturn, Aries, Capricorn, Aquarius

Physical healing: revitalizes and strengthens; facilitates recovery after illness and injury; promotes health of nervous and circulatory systems, especially blood cell production, heart, and blood vessels

Psychological healing: provides peace, serenity, and awareness of the present moment; conquers worry, stress, anxiety, and fear; stimulates positive thinking; supports organization, memory, and mental clarity

Spiritual healing: protects and empowers, initiates rise of kundalini energy, offers continual grounding to support spiritual growth, focuses for meditation

Garnet, Black (Melanite)

Formula: $Ca_3Fe_2(SiO_4)_3$ with titanium (Ti)   Hardness: 6.5–7   Crystal system: cubic   Formation process: metamorphic   Chakra: earth star, root   Correspondences: earth, Saturn, Pluto, Capricorn, Scorpio

Physical healing: fortifies skeletal system, encourages assimilation of calcium for bone health, helps release tension and elongate the spinal column, supports kidneys

Psychological healing: encourages reliability and trustworthiness, hones individual skills and talents, bolsters willpower and helps break bad or unhealthy habits, helps with overcoming anxiety and depression, lends courage to break free from cycles of abuse, dispels regret and grief

Spiritual healing: grounds and protects; facilitates psychic development and shamanic journeying; empowers empaths, as it helps identify and separate others' energy from your own

Garnet, Demantoid

Formula: $Ca_3Fe_2(SiO_4)_3$ with chromium (Cr)   Hardness: 6.5–7
Crystal system: cubic   Formation process: igneous or
metamorphic   Chakra: root, heart
Correspondences: earth, spirit, Venus, Aries, Taurus

Physical healing: excellent for cardiac health and repair of blood vessels, supports
health of liver and kidneys, reduces congestion, improves digestion, helpful
for asthma and food allergies, helps fight infection, relieves pain

Psychological healing: facilitates release of old beliefs, behavior, and possessions;
reduces stubbornness; offers reassurance and comfort; dissolves guilt, shame,
and trauma linked to sexuality and body image

Spiritual healing: cleanses aura and opens the heart chakra, invites new
beginnings and personal growth, strongly activates kundalini energy, helps in
attaining spiritual maturity

Garnet, Golden Andradite (Topazolite)

Formula: $Ca_3Fe_2(SiO_4)_3$ Hardness: 6.5–7
Crystal system: cubic   Formation process: igneous
Chakra: root, solar plexus   Correspondences: earth,
Mars, Pluto, Aries

Physical healing: promotes health of nervous system, particularly when there is
damage to the synapses; supports liver health; encourages production of blood
in bone marrow; excellent accelerant for overall health, strength, and vitality

Psychological healing: dissolves impatience, increases willpower, boosts
focus and mental endurance, promotes discernment, excellent support for
cultivating successful love

Spiritual healing: fosters feelings of *philia* (Ancient Greek: brotherly love) and
community, imparts selflessness and trust, gently increases intuition, helps
integrate higher energies

Garnet, Grossular

Formula: $Ca_3Al_2(SiO_4)_3$ Hardness: 7–7.5
Crystal system: cubic   Formation process: igneous
or metamorphic   Chakra: root, solar plexus, heart
Correspondences: earth, Venus, Taurus, Libra, Capricorn

Physical healing: stimulates growth and repair at cellular level; promotes recovery after injury, illness, and surgery; regenerates, soothes, and strengthens; draws out pain

Psychological healing: cultivates gratitude and creativity, enhances communication by putting you at ease with your audience, opens the mind to new ideas, promotes cooperation

Spiritual healing: powerful stone of prosperity and abundance, cultivates inner peace and strength, reveals inner currents of wisdom and unconditional love, deeply connects to nourishing energies of Mother Earth and the Divine Feminine

Garnet, Hessonite

Formula: $Ca_3Al_2(SiO_4)_3$ with manganese (Mn) and iron (Fe)
Hardness: 7–7.5   Crystal system: cubic   Formation
process: metamorphic   Chakra: root, sacral, heart
Correspondences: earth, fire, Moon, Venus, Mars, Taurus, Gemini

Physical healing: strengthens circulatory system; helps eliminate waste from body; nourishes and fortifies kidneys, liver, and endocrine system; may reduce uncomfortable symptoms of menopause; treats infertility and sexual dysfunction

Psychological healing: cultivates self-esteem and healthy body image; encourages self-respect; fosters empathy, appreciation, and better communication; increases confidence; helps maintain composure

Spiritual healing: offers clarity and reveals bigger picture, promotes spiritual growth, reduces burnout on spiritual path, helps bring forth your skills to serve the world, increases self-love and attracts love from all around you

130

Garnet, Rainbow Andradite

Formula: $Ca_3Fe_2(SiO_4)_3$ Hardness: 6.5–7
Crystal system: cubic   Formation process: metamorphic
Chakra: all, especially earth star, root, crown
Correspondences: earth, spirit, Saturn, Uranus, Capricorn, Aquarius

Physical healing: supports healthy liver; regulates production of blood cells; imparts vitality; purifies, protects, and uplifts physical body; restores mobility after injury; regulates menstrual cycles

Psychological healing: enhances creativity, sharpens intellect, increases mental flexibility, increases discernment and imparts shrewdness, helps you face your shadow self

Spiritual healing: reveals the mystical amid the mundane, aligns personal will with divine will, purifies the aura, balances masculine and feminine energies, nourishes the inner child, cultivates a sense of belonging and purpose, encourages state of wonder and awe

Garnet, Rhodolite (Pink Garnet)

Formula: $(Mg,Fe)_3Al_2(SiO_4)_3$ Hardness: 7–7.5
Crystal system: cubic   Formation process: igneous or metamorphic   Chakra: root, heart
Correspondences: earth, Venus, Libra

Physical healing: enhances circulation and metabolism, warms cold extremities, increases fertility, encourages reproductive and sexual health

Psychological healing: excellent stone for self-care; promotes optimism, self-worth, love, and trust; facilitates expressions of love, romance, and sexuality; dissolves inhibition and increases passion

Spiritual healing: increases zeal and joy; offers support and stability during periods of spiritual and emotional transformation; connects to unconditional love; grounds the consciousness in the here and now; protects and uplifts the home; attracts positivity, health, abundance, and happiness

Garnet, Spessartine

Formula: $Mn^{2+}_3Al_2(SiO_4)_3$ Hardness: 6.5–7.5   Crystal system: cubic   Formation process: igneous or metamorphic Chakra: root, sacral   Correspondences: earth, fire, Mars, Aries, Aquarius

Physical healing: promotes health of reproductive system, stimulates libido, may stimulate sluggish metabolism, regulates hormones, improves assimilation of nutrients, boosts immune system

Psychological healing: dispels feelings of despair, despondency, and overwhelm; promotes certainty and counteracts indecision and self-doubt; reveals heart's desire; facilitates connection, attraction, and romance; strongly boosts creativity and sensuality; overcomes arrogance

Spiritual healing: excellent manifestation stone, instills connection to inner divinity, aligns personal will with divine will

Garnet, Uvarovite

Formula: $Ca_3Cr_2(SiO_4)_3$ Hardness: 6.5–7.5 Crystal system: cubic   Formation process: metamorphic Chakra: solar plexus, heart   Correspondences: earth, Uranus, Aquarius

Physical healing: excellent support for heart and skeletal system, maintains healthy blood pressure, relieves pain

Psychological healing: promotes decisive, meaningful action; eliminates feelings of unworthiness, low self-esteem, and fears of scarcity; releases old emotional wounds; improves charisma, enthusiasm, imagination, and communication

Spiritual healing: soulmate stone; awakens the desire to find purpose and meaning in life; imparts faith, trust, and determination on a spiritual path; helps reconcile limiting beliefs about money and release patterns of poverty and martyrdom; connects to unconditional love

Garnierite

Formula: (Ni,Mg)$_3$(Si$_2$O$_5$)(OH)$_4$ Hardness: 2.5   Crystal
system: monoclinic   Formation process: sedimentary or
metamorphic   Chakra: solar plexus, heart
Correspondences: air, Mercury, Leo, Virgo, Capricorn

Physical healing: promotes healthy joints, helps alleviate discomfort from carpal
tunnel syndrome, cleanses the liver, regenerates and detoxifies the body
Psychological healing: elevates self-esteem and self-love; builds resistance to
gossip, bullying, and spite; helps you feel like a winner; invites friendship,
generosity, humor, honor, and compassion
Spiritual healing: stone of accumulation, acquisition, and achievement; among
the best stones for abundance and prosperity; improves luck (especially for
games of chance); opens the heart chakra
Note: It is erroneously referred to as green moonstone.

Gaspéite

Formula: NiCO$_3$ Hardness: 4.5–5   Crystal system: trigonal
Formation process: sedimentary   Chakra: solar plexus, heart
Correspondences: earth, Venus, Taurus

Physical healing: gently detoxifies; supports digestive, respiratory, lymphatic, and
cardiovascular health; reduces overly acidic conditions; improves coordination;
soothes skin
Psychological healing: provides emotional support and balance; imparts joy,
happiness, and openheartedness; lifts self-esteem; reduces sadness, fear, and
irritability; enhances friendship; releases need for external validation
Spiritual healing: induces sense of belonging; excellent for transitions, particularly
sudden ones; encourages ethical decisions and lifestyle; attracts success and
fulfillment; facilitates awareness of and connection to all life

Geode

Formula: variable, often quartz (SiO_2) **Hardness:** variable
Crystal system: variable **Formation process:** igneous
Chakra: earth star, sacral, third eye (varies with mineral content)
Correspondences: earth, water, Mercury, Gemini, Virgo

Physical healing: supports health of cranium, brain, eyes, and organs of the head; traditionally used for fertility and healthy pregnancy and childbirth; wonderful for boosting overall healing

Psychological healing: reveals inner world of thoughts, beliefs, and feelings; imparts patience, understanding, and focus; strengthens communication, resolve, and decision-making skills

Spiritual healing: represents transformation, creativity, inspiration, and renewal; excellent for planetary healing and connecting to earth energies; draws support from Mother Nature; protects; supports astral travel and manifestation

Note: Geodes also exhibit the properties of their specific mineral composition.

Gneiss

Formula: variable **Hardness:** variable
Crystal system: variable **Formation process:** metamorphic
Chakra: root, heart, crown **Correspondences:** earth, water, Jupiter, Uranus, Sagittarius, Pisces

Physical healing: combats low energy and burnout; strengthens circulatory, immune, and digestive systems; relieves sore, tired muscles; promotes physical strength and endurance

Psychological healing: represents change; improves organization; differentiates different tasks or roles; releases stagnant emotions; reduces stress, worry, and anxiety connected to change or transition; boosts self-esteem

Spiritual healing: improves visualization and imagination; imparts compassion, understanding, and equitable thinking; helps you reach to new heights while staying grounded; offers assurance and joy; encourages movement of energy through the chakras from root to crown

Goethite

Formula: $Fe^{3+}O(OH)$ **Hardness:** 5–5.5 **Crystal system:** orthorhombic **Formation process:** sedimentary **Chakra:** earth star, root, third eye **Correspondences:** earth, Mars, Aries

Physical healing: helps to alleviate disorders affecting the ears and hearing, strengthens and grounds the body, reduces symptoms of anemia, improves circulatory system and bone marrow

Psychological healing: assuages grief and fear, soothes discomfort resulting from gender dysphoria, prompts self-discovery and exploration of the subconscious mind, supports creative expression, offers solace if you are filled with longing

Spiritual healing: boosts psychic senses, especially clairaudience and clairsentience; inspires prophetic dreams; improves accuracy of psychic information; facilitates past-life recall, reveals access to Akashic records and communion with the heart of Mother Earth; powerfully aids manifestation

Gold

Formula: Au **Hardness:** 2.5–3 **Crystal system:** cubic **Formation process:** igneous, sedimentary, or metamorphic **Chakra:** solar plexus, heart, crown **Correspondences:** fire, Sun, Leo

Physical healing: a master healer of body, mind, and spirit; exerts warming effect on body; energizes and revitalizes; soothes nerves; enhances digestion; excellent support for joint, brain, and sexual health

Psychological healing: boosts integrity, character, and sense of identity; enhances learning; reduces egotism, greed, and jealousy; overcomes shyness, melancholy, and low self-worth; conquers fear and indecision; offers motivation, determination, willpower, and optimism

Spiritual healing: clears harmful and stagnant energy from aura and chakras; strongly protects; facilitates attainment of wealth, success, and sovereignty; enhances all forms of manifestation; transmutes negativity into positivity

Golden Labradorite (Bytownite)

Formula: (Ca,Na)[Al(Al,Si)Si$_2$O$_8$]   Hardness: 6–6.5
Crystal system: triclinic   Formation process: igneous
Chakra: solar plexus   Correspondences: fire, Sun, Leo

Physical healing: supports health of digestive and elimination systems, excellent for cleansing the body, supports healthy metabolism

Psychological healing: excellent stone for leaders, bolsters confidence and motivation, dissolves tendency to procrastinate, helps exercise willpower constructively

Spiritual healing: offers bright, solar energy for success, abundance, and joy; reveals and releases past-life memories related to power and authority

Note: It is not a variety of labradorite, despite its common name.

Granite

Formula: variable   Hardness: variable   Crystal system: variable
Formation process: igneous   Chakra: all, especially root
Correspondences: earth, fire, Pluto, Scorpio

Physical healing: offers physical vitality, stamina, and endurance; strengthens bones, hair, and nails; stimulates healthy cell growth and discourages abnormal growth

Psychological healing: improves focus, encourages practicality and pragmatism while reducing skepticism, promotes cooperation and harmony

Spiritual healing: strongly protects and stabilizes, builds firm foundation for spiritual growth, supports direct and express experiences of the Divine, helps to safely close connections after channeling or psychic work, neutralizes geopathic stress

Hackmanite

Formula: $Na_8Al_6Si_6O_{24}(Cl_2,S)$ Hardness: 5.5–6
Crystal system: cubic   Formation process: igneous
Chakra: higher heart, third eye, causal
Correspondences: air, Uranus, Scorpio, Aquarius

Physical healing: strengthens bones, teeth, ligaments, and cartilage; balances endocrine system; supports immune and lymphatic systems; counteracts fever

Psychological healing: unites logic and intuition; promotes greater understanding of psychological patterns; softens defensive traits; eases feelings of overwhelm; encourages acceptance and raises self-esteem; dissolves fear, guilt, and tension; encourages open-mindedness

Spiritual healing: stone of truth and virtue, cultivates inner peace and nonduality, releases attachments, dissolves cords, excellent for counterbalancing electromagnetic and psychic pollution, helps reveal the bigger picture, breaks down dogmatic views

Halite

Formula: NaCl   Hardness: 2–2.5
Crystal system: cubic   Formation process: sedimentary
Chakra: all, especially crown
Correspondences: earth, Venus, Saturn, Cancer, Pisces

Physical healing: promotes healthy metabolism, fluid balance, and elimination of waste; promotes respiratory health; alleviates seasonal allergies and congestion; excellent aid for skin health and vitality; promotes health of small intestine

Psychological healing: strongly stimulates and purifies the mind, clears hyper-emotive states to promote clarity and reasoning, breaks down harmful subconscious beliefs and thoughts

Spiritual healing: deeply purifies and protects; releases attachments, cords, entities, and other harmful patterns from the aura; facilitates psychic development; draws light into aura and chakras

Heliodor (Golden Beryl)

Formula: $Be_3Al_2(SiO_3)_6$ with iron (Fe)   Hardness: 7.5–8
Crystal system: hexagonal   Formation process: igneous
Chakra: solar plexus, crown, soul star   Correspondences: fire, Sun, Leo

Physical healing: supports health of digestive system, eyes, and immune system; improves vitality; curbs cravings for unhealthy food

Psychological healing: elevates mood; helps in maintaining calm, positive outlook during stressful times; reduces aggression and channels anger into positive outlets; amplifies self-worth, courage, commitment, and joy

Spiritual healing: nourishes and strengthens causal body in aura, facilitates past-life recall, helps in overcoming karmic patterns, aligns personal power with divine will, improves focus in meditation, encourages perseverance

Note: see also beryl (p. 76)

Hematite

Formula: Fe_2O_3 Hardness: 5.5–6.5   Crystal system: trigonal   Formation process: igneous or sedimentary   Chakra: earth star, root
Correspondences: earth, Mars, Aries

Physical healing: tones and strengthens; promotes regeneration; powerful ally for health of blood and circulatory system; draws out pain, stanches bleeding, and reduces inflammation; alleviates headaches; improves iron absorption; may help remedy insomnia; promotes healing after injury and surgery

Psychological healing: encourages drive, ambition, and resolve; strongly grounds and calms; promotes mental mastery; enhances memory; confers mental discipline

Spiritual healing: promotes awareness; activates earth star chakra; provides strength to review old experiences, habits, and situations to better understand your role in them; highlights inner strengths and weaknesses to help growth on every level

Hematite, Rainbow (Turgite)

Formula: hematite (Fe_2O_3) with goethite [$FeO(OH)$]
Hardness: 5.5–6.5   Crystal system: trigonal   Formation process: sedimentary   Chakra: earth star, root, causal
Correspondences: earth, spirit, Mars, Uranus, Aries, Aquarius

Physical healing: strengthens body; enhances circulatory, immune, and reproductive health; balances libido; reduces chronic fatigue; harmonizes metabolism and homeostatic processes; regulates all functions of timing; reduces jet lag

Psychological healing: cultivates joy, happiness, and optimism; reduces guilt and shame; deepens appreciation for beauty and pleasure; reduces feelings of isolation, darkness, and hopelessness

Spiritual healing: initiates alignment of the subtle bodies, chakras, and meridians; gently and joyfully grounds high-frequency energies into the body, aura, and the planet; stimulates movement of kundalini; excellent support for manifestation

Hematite, Specular

Formula: Fe_2O_3 Hardness: 5.5–6.5   Crystal system: trigonal
Formation process: sedimentary   Chakra: earth star, root, crown, soul star   Correspondences: earth, Mars, Aries, Sagittarius, Aquarius

Physical healing: strongly stimulates immune system; soothes irritation of the eyes and promotes strong vision; improves cardiovascular health; strengthens lungs, liver, and bone marrow

Psychological healing: draws forth inner skills and talents, boosts confidence, enhances insight and critical thinking skills, promotes self-reflection

Spiritual healing: facilitates scrying, clairvoyance, and intuition; grounds and expands simultaneously; enhances manifestation; encourages exploration and attainment of life purpose; unites energies of heaven and earth

Hemimorphite

Formula: $Zn_4(Si_2O_7)(OH)_2 \cdot H_2O$ Hardness: 4.5–5   Crystal system: orthorhombic   Formation process: sedimentary
Chakra: sacral, heart, throat, third eye
Correspondences: water, air, spirit, Venus, Libra

Physical healing: balances metabolism, alleviates conditions of the skin, exerts cooling effect that reduces fevers and relieves burns and sunburns, expedites wound healing, promotes health of brain, relieves restless leg syndrome

Psychological healing: breaks down anger, hatred, aggravation, and frustration; promotes courteous, gracious, and service-oriented attitude; eliminates conceit, self-centeredness, and greed; instills honesty; helps in maintaining composure

Spiritual healing: stone of peace, service, and humility; promotes spiritual development; invites patience, luck, and deep peace; inspires creativity at every level of life; attracts opportunity and success

Herderite

Formula: $CaBe(PO_4)(F,OH)$ Hardness: 5–5.5
Crystal system: monoclinic   Formation process: igneous
Chakra: third eye, crown, soul star   Correspondences: air, spirit, Uranus, Aries, Aquarius

Physical healing: mostly affects health of the brain; alleviates headaches, migraines, and symptoms of brain injury; may also regulate health of pancreas, spleen, and gallbladder

Psychological healing: uplifts, inspires, and gives hope; initiates both directness and passion, thereby drawing out leadership qualities; maintains calm in emotionally tense situations; helps change harmful behavior by replacing with healthier habits

Spiritual healing: boosts psychic skills; enhances spirit communication; aligns all chakras; expands awareness of the self; instills sense of duty, service, and empathy; accelerates spiritual evolution, initiatory experiences, and expanded consciousness

Herkimer Diamond

Formula: quartz (SiO_2) with carbon (C)   Hardness: 7
Crystal system: trigonal   Formation process: sedimentary
Chakra: all, especially crown, soul star
Correspondences: earth, air, fire, water, spirit, all planets, all signs

Physical healing: promotes overall healing, especially at cellular level; relieves pain, headaches, inflammation; protects against radiation; regulates rhythm of the body and supports homeostasis

Psychological healing: provides clarity, discernment, and focus; relieves stress

Spiritual healing: activates chakras; cleanses aura; enhances spiritual awareness, inner vision, meditation, psychic development, astral travel, soul retrieval, and communication with guides and angels; catalyzes spiritual development; excellent for encouraging lucid dreams; engenders sense of spiritual responsibility; enhances and harmonizes other crystals

Note: see also quartz (p. 198)

Heulandite

Formula: 3.5–4   Hardness: $(Ca,Na)_{2-3}Al_3(Al,Si)_2Si_{13}O_{36}\cdot12H_2O$
Crystal system: monoclinic   Formation process: igneous, sedimentary, or metamorphic   Chakra: heart, third eye, crown
Correspondences: air, Mercury, Jupiter, Virgo, Sagittarius

Physical healing: supports organs of elimination, especially kidneys and liver; may relieve aches and pains; promotes healthy joints; helps to alleviate viral infections

Psychological healing: seeks emotional balance; releases jealousy, bitterness, resentment; helps examine and transform bias, judgment, privilege, and rigid adherence to dogma and tradition; aids decision making; centers for successful study and learning

Spiritual healing: helps with relearning skills and wisdom from past lives; offers connection to Atlantis and Lemuria; replaces skepticism with practical wisdom; encourages dreams and astral travel; invites loving-kindness, forgiveness, and empathy

141

Hiddenite

Formula: LiAl(SiO$_3$)$_2$ with chromium (Cr) or iron (Fe)
Hardness: 6.5–7   Crystal system: monoclinic   Formation
process: igneous   Chakra: heart, higher heart, third eye
Correspondences: water, Venus, Neptune

Physical healing: calms, cools, and soothes the body; reduces inflammation, pain,
   and toothache; promotes health of liver, nervous system, heart, and thymus;
   boosts immune system
Psychological healing: transforms psychological imbalances; releases anger,
   anxiety, irritability, melancholy, and fear; dissolves unworthiness; induces
   state of joy and gratitude; improves decision-making skills; alleviates sense of
   overwork and too much responsibility
Spiritual healing: inspires gratitude; attracts prosperity and abundance;
   represents new beginnings; invites serenity and devotion to the heart, mind,
   and spirit; dissolves ego and attachment; boosts intuition; invites blissful,
   ecstatic states in meditation

Howlite

Formula: Ca$_2$B$_5$SiO$_9$(OH)$_5$ Hardness: 3.5   Crystal
system: monoclinic   Formation process: sedimentary
Chakra: third eye, crown   Correspondences: air,
Mercury, Gemini

Physical healing: breaks up stagnant energies and fluids, expels toxins, corrects
   irregularities in DNA, counteracts effects of dehydration
Psychological healing: among the best stones for stress, induces deep relaxation,
   filters anxious and nervous thoughts from mind, improves concentration,
   strengthens reasoning skills, helps you slow down when life is moving too
   quickly
Spiritual healing: encourages manifestation and co-creation via the mind and
   reasoning skills, invites action to complement and fulfill daydreams

142

Hypersthene

Formula: $(Mg,Fe)SiO_3$ Hardness: 5.5–6
Crystal system: orthorhombic   Formation process: igneous or metamorphic   Chakra: root, solar plexus
Correspondences: earth, Pluto, Scorpio, Sagittarius, Capricorn

Physical healing: reduces pain, inflammation, and tension; supports pituitary function; neutralizes overly acidic states; improves blood and circulatory system; excellent palliative for exhaustion

Psychological healing: clears away confusion and misunderstanding; promotes critical thinking and boosts problem-solving skills; assuages fear; calms sensitive people, especially in crowds; helps find balance between activity and rest or work and play; excellent palliative for trauma

Spiritual healing: promotes balance, excellent support for shadow work, integrates lost soul fragments, facilitates astral travel, encourages you to stand up for what is right, inspires faith, helps in reclaiming personal power

Ilvaite

Formula: $CaFe^{2+}_2Fe^{3+}Si_2O_7O(OH)$ Hardness: 5.5–6
Crystal system: monoclinic   Formation process: igneous
Chakra: earth star, root   Correspondences: earth, Mars, Pluto, Aries, Scorpio

Physical healing: excellent support for conditions of blood and circulatory system, reduces hemorrhage and ulcers, lowers fever, promotes health of liver, may initiate state of rapid detox and purging, encourages healthy appetite

Psychological healing: strongly stabilizing to the mind and emotions, calms a quick temper, promotes patience and emotional clarity

Spiritual healing: helps in maintaining practical, grounded approach to spirituality; heightens imagination; promotes connection to higher self; inspires search for truth; strongly protects, especially for empaths and sensitive people; prevents psychic vampirism

Iolite

Formula: $(Mg,Fe)_2Al_4Si_5)_{18}$ Hardness: 7–7.5 Crystal system: orthorhombic Formation process: metamorphic Chakra: third eye Correspondences: air, Jupiter, Neptune, Libra, Sagittarius, Pisces

Physical healing: targets nervous system and sensory organs; relieves nerve pain and numbness; prevents memory loss and boosts cognitive function; detoxifies; reduces blockages and swelling; alleviates sinus pressure

Psychological healing: invites hope amid adversity and stress; promotes psychological balance and endurance; helps further changes to create positive and lasting change; offers reassurance, especially in the face of fear of the unknown; softens spite; releases need for control

Spiritual healing: supports meditation, dreaming, visualization, and astral travel; facilitates soul retrieval and past-life recall; stimulates psychic development

Jade, Black

Formula: nephrite $[Ca_2(Mg, Fe)_5Si_8O_{22}(OH)_2]$ with iron (Fe), magnetite (Fe_3O_4) Hardness: 6–6.5 Crystal system: monoclinic Formation process: metamorphic Chakra: root Correspondences: earth, water, Saturn, Pluto, Scorpio, Capricorn

Physical healing: excellent for regulating body fluids, good support for kidneys, eliminates toxins from blood, regulates blood pressure, promotes healthy bile production, eases symptoms of irritable bowel syndrome

Psychological healing: among the best stones for psychological trauma; stone of survival; helps reclaim personal power; eases insecurity, fear, and lack of self-worth; invites clarity and independence

Spiritual healing: offers inspiration and insight from dreams, helps in finding direction in life, deeply protects and nurtures, prompts action to improve life, brings forth light during dark times, imparts wisdom

Jade, Blue

Formula: nephrite [$Ca_2(Mg, Fe)_5Si_8O_{22}(OH)_2$] or jadeite ($NaAlSi_2O_6$)   **Hardness:** 6–6.5   **Crystal system:** monoclinic   **Formation process:** metamorphic   **Chakra:** heart, throat   **Correspondences:** earth, air, Uranus, Aquarius

Physical healing: promotes regeneration of damaged or diseased tissue, reduces inflammation, promotes fertility, balances overactive libido, reduces hypertension and rapid heart rate

Psychological healing: encourages smooth communication, boosts mental faculties and imparts objectivity and impartiality, cools anger and rage, eases grief, promotes balanced emotions and reduces overreaction

Spiritual healing: stone of harmony, abundance, and balance; mediates between intellect and intuition; balances masculine and feminine energies; eases all forms of transition

Jade, Green

Formula: nephrite [$Ca_2(Mg, Fe)_5Si_8O_{22}(OH)_2$] or jadeite ($NaAlSi_2O_6$)   **Hardness:** 6–6.5   **Crystal system:** monoclinic   **Formation process:** metamorphic   **Chakra:** sacral, heart   **Correspondences:** earth, water, Venus, Taurus, Libra

Physical healing: supports kidneys, bladder, and urinary tract; treats urinary infections, allergies, hearing loss; boosts vitality and fertility; excellent support for skin, collagen, and connective tissues; encourages longevity and restful sleep

Psychological healing: induces peace, harmony, and successful relationships; overcomes poverty mentality and heals relationship with money and prosperity

Spiritual healing: facilitates karmic and ancestral healing; stimulates past-life recall; enhances shamanic journeys, lucid dreaming, astral travel; cultivates refinement of spirit; guides the way to enlightenment

Jade, Lavender

Formula: jadeite ($NaAlSi_2O_6$)   Hardness: 6.5–7
Crystal system: monoclinic
Formation process: metamorphic   Chakra: heart, third eye
Correspondences: air, spirit, Jupiter, Sagittarius

Physical healing: supports health of the heart and circulatory system; alleviates conditions of the nerves, especially when painful; calms rashes, hives, and inflammation; ameliorates stress-related illness

Psychological healing: soothing to the emotions; resolves trauma, emotional pain, and anguish; cultivates self-worth and trust in self; enables you to feel safe; inspires happiness and joy

Spiritual healing: enhances meditation, psychic development, and lucid dreaming; sparks courage to share your truth with the world; expands compassion for all living things; excellent facilitator of angelic communication; confers spiritual protection

Jade, Red

Formula: nephrite [$Ca_2(Mg, Fe)_5Si_8O_{22}(OH)_2$] or jadeite ($NaAlSi_2O_6$) with iron (Fe) or manganese (Mn)   Hardness: 6.5–7
Crystal system: monoclinic   Formation process: metamorphic
Chakra: earth star, root, sacral   Correspondences: water, fire, Mars, Aries

Physical healing: stimulates, strengthens, and restores physical tissue, particularly muscles; enhances physical strength, endurance, and libido; excellent fortifier for the blood; supports overall health and well-being; may support recovery from addiction

Psychological healing: instills drive, motivation, courage, and passion; reduces gullibility and naivete; supports creativity

Spiritual healing: couples resolve and determination with spiritual devotion, protects and grounds, helps prevent stagnation on spiritual path

Jade, White

Formula: nephrite [$Ca_2(Mg, Fe)_5Si_8O_{22}(OH)_2$] or jadeite ($NaAlSi_2O_6$)
Hardness: 6.5–7   Crystal system: monoclinic
Formation process: metamorphic   Chakra: sacral
Correspondences: water, Moon, Cancer

Physical healing: confers anti-aging benefits for skin and joints, supports health of the kidneys and organs of elimination, lessens thirst and fever, promotes health of the reproductive system, alleviates cramps

Psychological healing: instills harmony, kindness, and peace; assuages worry and anger; improves family unity and harmony

Spiritual healing: stone of justice and equitable action; imparts benevolence, respect, devotion, and purity; cleanses causal body of stale karmic patterns, especially ancestral karma

Jade, Yellow

Formula: nephrite [$Ca_2(Mg, Fe)_5Si_8O_{22}(OH)_2$] or jadeite ($NaAlSi_2O_6$)   Hardness: 6.5–7   Crystal system: monoclinic
Formation process: metamorphic   Chakra: sacral, solar plexus   Correspondences: earth, air, Sun, Mercury, Gemini

Physical healing: supports health of stomach and digestive system, helps bladder and skin, nourishes and strengthens the body

Psychological healing: invites happiness, gratitude, friendship, and loyalty; raises self-worth and loyalty to self; stabilizes professional environments; neutralizes peer pressure; helps regulate balance between individuals and relationships/group consciousness

Spiritual healing: stone of luck, success, and joy; excellent for manifesting new opportunity; helps you stay true to your own heart

Jasper

Formula: SiO_2 Hardness: 6.5–7   Crystal system: trigonal
Formation process: igneous or sedimentary   Chakra: root,
sacral (varies by type)   Correspondences: earth, Mars, Aries,
Taurus

Physical healing: fortifies and nourishes the body, promotes overall healing,
energizes, relieves imbalance of intestines and reproductive system, supports
connection with nature to revitalize and heal

Psychological healing: eliminates distraction and strengthens focus; curbs
anxiety, insecurity, escapism, and procrastination; heightens courage and
determination; promotes emotional resilience; spurs recovery from rejection
and failure

Spiritual healing: excellent grounding stone that promotes communion with
nature; offers protection, success, and happiness; often used to attract wealth

Note: Jaspers are generally composed of chalcedony (see p. 92). Some "jaspers" are
not jasper but other kinds of rocks.

Jasper, Brecciated

Formula: SiO_2 Hardness: 6.5–7   Crystal system: trigonal
Formation process: sedimentary
Chakra: root   Correspondences: earth, Mars, Pluto, Virgo,
Scorpio

Physical healing: helps knit together broken bone and damaged tissue, energizes
the body, encourages health of circulatory system, warms cold extremities,
alleviates allergies, improves complexion and reduces scar tissue

Psychological healing: counteracts guilt, shame, and self-doubt; improves self-
esteem; supports conflict resolution; helps with extrication from manipulative,
narcissistic relationships

Spiritual healing: grounds, restores, and nourishes the spirit; initiates
remembrance of innate perfection and wholeness; supports all processes of
self-healing of body, mind, and spirit

"Jasper," Bumblebee

Formula: calcite ($CaCO_3$) with realgar (As_4S_4), orpiment (As_2S_3), and pyrite (FeS_2) Hardness: 3 Crystal system: trigonal, monoclinic, cubic Formation process: igneous Chakra: root, sacral, solar plexus Correspondences: fire, Neptune, Pluto, Leo, Scorpio

Physical healing: improves metabolism, supports nervous system and sensory organs, improves muscle strength, excellent for pacifying food allergies and sensitivities

Psychological healing: stimulates the mind; brings fresh perspective; confers joy; nourishes inner child; sparks creativity, charisma, and transformation; raises productivity and seeds industrious habits; helps spark joy in everyday work

Spiritual healing: brings momentum to spiritual growth, replenishes and transmutes vital energy, coordinates and harmonizes groups, encourages victory and success in all endeavors, removes obstacles

Note: not a true jasper; also called eclipse jasper

Jasper, Calligraphy Stone (Elephant Skin Jasper, Cobra Jasper)

Formula: SiO_2 with fossils and clay Hardness: 6.5
Crystal system: trigonal, monoclinic
Formation process: sedimentary Chakra: root, sacral, causal
Correspondences: earth, Saturn, Capricorn

Physical healing: supports digestive system, especially the stomach and intestines; helpful for pancreas and liver; targets hereditary conditions; relieves conditions of the skin and scalp

Psychological healing: lends courage to overly shy and introverted people; facilitates cautious optimism; helps identify and release unhealthy, harmful, or disingenuous people and situations; stimulates the mind and learning

Spiritual healing: assists you in slowing down and being present, helps eliminate distractions from spiritual practice, protects home and family, said to bring luck and prosperity

Jasper, Cherry Creek

Formula: SiO_2 with dolomite ($CaMgCO$) and hematite (Fe_2O_3)
Hardness: 6.5–7   Crystal system: trigonal
Formation process: sedimentary   Chakra: root, crown
Correspondences: earth, Venus, Mars, Taurus

Physical healing: excellent for inflammation, pain, and stiffness; improves strength and flexibility; warms cold extremities; offers support for chronic illness

Psychological healing: soothes out-of-control emotions; helps process grief; brings peace, calm, and clarity; reveals hidden or latent emotions; sparks passion and creativity; counteracts despair, depression, and stress; lends dignity and poise in challenging situations

Spiritual healing: protects and cleanses energy field, offers stamina and resilience, promotes justice and supports those who seek it, offers stability and grounding to ensure continuous spiritual growth, draws out inner talents

Jasper, Dragon's Blood

Formula: SiO_2 with epidote $[Ca_2Al_2(Fe^{3+},Al)(SiO_4)(Si_2O_7)O(OH)]$ and piemontite $[Ca_2(Al,Mn^{3+},Fe^{3+})_3(SiO_4)(Si_2O_7)O(OH)]$
Hardness: 6.5–7   Crystal system: trigonal and monoclinic
Formation process: igneous or sedimentary   Chakra: all, especially earth star, heart   Correspondences: earth, fire, Mars, Aries

Physical healing: supports immune system; catalyzes regenerative and detoxifying processes; promotes health of brain, nervous system, gallbladder, liver, thyroid, and intestines; strengthens hair and nails

Psychological healing: confers strength, courage, resiliency; counteracts patterns of doubt and self-pity; heightens discernment, patience, and reasoning skills; enhances studies

Spiritual healing: offers connection to nature and earth energies, grounds and protects, assists quest for wisdom, initiates rise of kundalini energy, nourishes inner child, removes obstacles on spiritual path

Jasper, Fascia

Formula: SiO_2 Hardness: 6.5–7 Crystal system: trigonal
Formation process: igneous Chakra: root, sacral, third eye
Correspondences: earth, water, air, Moon, Saturn, Cancer,
Capricorn

Physical healing: promotes healing and repair of connective tissue, ligaments, tendons, and joints; detoxifies the body; supports health of lymphatic system; reduces pain, inflammation, and scar tissue formation

Psychological healing: ameliorates feelings of despondency, loneliness, and sadness; gently lifts buried trauma to the surface for integration and healing; absorbs unhealthy emotions; engenders tolerance, acceptance, and understanding

Spiritual healing: gently grounds and balances the entire energy field, facilitates psychic development, releases attachment and egotism, repairs holes and tears in the aura, highlights interconnectedness of all life, transmutes and heals collective consciousness of humankind, cultivates wonder and awe

Jasper, Ibis

Formula: SiO_2 Hardness: 6.5–7
Crystal system: trigonal Formation process: sedimentary
Chakra: root, third eye Correspondences: earth, air, Mercury,
Gemini

Physical healing: assists healing of broken bones, open wounds, and damaged tissue; supports healthy hair and nails

Psychological healing: excellent support for recovery from addiction, trauma, PTSD, and abuse; enables feeling whole after breakups or rejection; boosts reading comprehension; enhances learning

Spiritual healing: stone of wisdom, truth, and perception; grounds intelligence into action to further spiritual path; facilitates access to Akashic records, ancestral wisdom, and past-life memories

Note: Ibis jasper is a variety of brecciated jasper (see p. 148).

"Jasper," Leopardskin

Formula: complex and variable   Hardness: 6.5–7
Crystal system: trigonal, monoclinic, triclinic
Formation process: igneous   Chakra: root, solar plexus
Correspondences: earth, Mercury, Virgo, Capricorn

Physical healing: supports metabolism and all rhythmic processes of the body; reduces effects of aging; alleviates stress-related illness; supports healthy skin, digestion, and elimination; helps carpal tunnel syndrome

Psychological healing: offers clarity, flexibility, and understanding; represents adaptation; strengthens memory; creates momentum when you feel stuck or unwilling to change

Spiritual healing: supports health of causal or karmic body; attracts positive influences; aligns with purpose, abundance, and divine timing; helps in staying grounded, centered, protected, and present in everyday reality

Note: Leopardskin "jasper" is not a true jasper; it is a variety of rhyolite (see p. 213).

Jasper, Maligano

Formula: SiO_2 Hardness: 6.5–7
Crystal system: trigonal   Formation process: sedimentary
Chakra: root, sacral, solar plexus
Correspondences: earth, fire, Sun, Leo

Physical healing: helps knit together broken bone, open wounds, and damaged tissue; balances microbiome of skin and intestines; beneficial for thyroid, spleen, kidneys, immune system, and connective tissue

Psychological healing: boosts mental faculties, especially related to study and learning; promotes flexibility and adaptability amid change, helps heal inner child

Spiritual healing: stone of inspiration and new beginnings, removes obstacles from path, attracts opportunity and aligns with synchronicity and divine timing, enhances intuition, broadcasts alerts to oncoming danger or misfortune

Note: Maligano jasper is a variety of brecciated jasper (see p. 148).

Jasper, Mookaite

Formula: SiO_2 with amorphous silica   Hardness: 6.5–7
Crystal system: trigonal and amorphous   Formation
process: sedimentary   Chakra: root, sacral, solar plexus,
third eye   Correspondences: earth, Sun, Leo

Physical healing: regulates blood pressure, reduces scar tissue, knits together
open wounds, hydrates skin and reduces lines and wrinkles (as an elixir),
strengthens hair and nails

Psychological healing: stimulates memory and recall; promotes emotional
flexibility, creativity, motivation; fosters emotional warmth; mitigates
loneliness and grief

Spiritual healing: nourishes and uplifts, connects to earth energies, helps sift
through karmic patterns to resolve ancestral karma

Jasper, Ocean

Formula: SiO_2 Hardness: 6.5–7   Crystal system: trigonal
Formation process: igneous   Chakra: root, solar plexus,
heart, throat   Correspondences: earth, water, Neptune,
Pisces

Physical healing: promotes cellular regeneration, supports thyroid and adrenal
health, synchronizes body's natural rhythms and processes

Psychological healing: helps examine emotions and their cycles; soothes
turbulent emotions; inspires stillness and peace; helps in expressing repressed
emotions; promotes understanding, cooperation, kindness, and empathy

Spiritual healing: prompts state of surrender, facilitates meditation, attunes
to tides of life, connects to Divine Feminine, brings healing and balance to
groups and communities

Note: Ocean jasper is a spherulitic variety of chalcedony (see p. 92).

Jasper, Picture

Formula: SiO_2 Hardness: 6.5–7   Crystal system: trigonal
Formation process: sedimentary   Chakra: root
Correspondences: earth, Mars, Aries, Taurus

Physical healing: combats fatigue, offers strength during chronic illness, stimulates bone growth, promotes healthy digestion, alleviates symptoms of allergies, supports healthy connective tissue

Psychological healing: inspires resilience and soothes after rejection and loss, boosts problem-solving skills, helps in maintaining level head during stressful times, invites emotional renewal

Spiritual healing: helps you stay the course on a spiritual path, encourages small changes to ensure your life's purpose is fulfilled, initiates communion with the planet and nature, helps you to access energy from sacred sites, stimulates past-life recall

Jasper, Polychrome (Desert Jasper)

Formula: SiO_2 Hardness: 6.5–7   Crystal system: trigonal
Formation process: sedimentary
Chakra: all, especially root   Correspondences: earth, Mars, Aries, Virgo

Physical healing: stimulates metabolism and immune function, promotes health of feet and ankles, gently detoxifies, lessens symptoms of seasonal allergies

Psychological healing: encourages creativity, expression, and passion; helps you to see the richness of life's experiences; midwifes new ideas and fresh attitudes; curbs feelings of resentment and jealousy; protects against others' envy

Spiritual healing: inspires joy in everyday activities; deeply grounds and nourishes; teaches versatility, authenticity, and passion on the spiritual path

Jasper, Poppy

Formula: SiO_2 with hematite (Fe_2O_3)
Hardness: 6.5–7   Crystal system: trigonal
Formation process: sedimentary   Chakra: root
Correspondences: earth, Mars, Aries

Physical healing: uplifts, energizes, and stimulates entire body; overcomes low energy and exhaustion; stimulates metabolism; increases strength and endurance; especially helps in labor and childbirth

Psychological healing: invites greater joy and creativity, combats limiting beliefs, ameliorates depression, reduces tendency to procrastinate, enlivens body and mind to break through creative blocks

Spiritual healing: makes space for action to bring solace when faced with turmoil, overwhelm, and disconnection; inspires feelings of service; sparks compassionate action

Jasper, Porcelain

Formula: SiO_2 Hardness: 6.5–7   Crystal system: trigonal
Formation process: igneous or sedimentary
Chakra: solar plexus, heart, higher heart
Correspondences: earth, air, Venus, Neptune, Taurus, Pisces

Physical healing: promotes overall healing and repair of soft tissues; excellent support for heart, kidney, liver, and digestive system; brings balance to female reproductive system

Psychological healing: brings mental and emotional clarity rooted in love and compassion; brings dynamic balance to relationships (especially romantic ones); clears old emotional wounds; reduces anger, resentment, and fear

Spiritual healing: powerfully protects and shields; invites compassion, empathy, and responsibility for spiritual development; deeply soothes and enhances meditation; aids in release of karmic baggage

Jasper, Red

Formula: SiO_2 with hematite (Fe_2O_3)   **Hardness:** 6.5–7
Crystal system: trigonal   **Formation process:** igneous or
sedimentary   **Chakra:** root   **Correspondences:** earth, Mars, Aries,
Taurus

Physical healing: brings strength and energy to the body, breaks up stagnation,
promotes cardiac health, regulates blood pressure, improves virility and sexual
performance

Psychological healing: improves concentration, willpower, and passion; reduces
irritability; boosts creativity; alleviates shame, guilt, and low self-esteem

Spiritual healing: powerfully activates the root chakra; awakens kundalini energy;
strongly protects, as it drives away nightmares and unwelcome entities

Jasper, Silver Leaf

Formula: SiO_2 **Hardness:** 6.5–7   **Crystal system:** trigonal
Formation process: sedimentary   **Chakra:** root,
solar plexus, third eye   **Correspondences:** earth, Mercury,
Gemini

Physical healing: treats imbalance and dysfunction in sensory organs, improves
liver function, offers support and overall healing to entire body

Psychological healing: instills confidence and clarity; combats uncertainty, doubt,
and despair; invites self-reflection to help you better assess your psychological
health and release unwanted patterns; imparts serenity; fosters independence;
encourages discipline and follow-through

Spiritual healing: helps you trust your instincts and intuition, makes spiritual
truths more tangible via contemplation and meditation, may resolve ancestral
patterns and karmic cycles, invites new beginnings

Jasper, Yellow

Formula: SiO_2 with limonite [$FeO(OH) \cdot nH_2O$]   Hardness: 6.5–7
Crystal system: trigonal   Formation process: igneous or
sedimentary   Chakra: root, solar plexus
Correspondences: earth, Mercury, Gemini, Capricorn

Physical healing: supports health of skin, connective tissue, liver, spleen, kidneys,
intestines, and immune system; excellent for jump-starting weight loss;
relieves symptoms of fibromyalgia; reduces excess phlegm; promotes healthy
digestion and elimination

Psychological healing: inspires endurance, tenacity, and resilience; helps you
digest and process experiences, emotions, and old programming; eliminates
patterns that no longer serve

Spiritual healing: a protective stone, particularly for all forms of travel; helps you
to fulfill your purpose in life; promotes discipline and pragmatism as needed
for continuous spiritual development

Jet

Formula: complex and variable, rich in carbon (C)
Hardness: 2.5–4   Crystal system: amorphous
Formation process: organic (sedimentary)   Chakra: root
Correspondences: earth, spirit, Saturn, Pluto, Capricorn

Physical healing: draws out pain; relieves headaches and inflamed joints;
treats conditions of epithelial tissue, especially mouth and gums; stimulates
digestion; supports detoxification

Psychological healing: a soothing, empowering stone for standing up to
oppression, abuse, and loss of willpower; releases grief and sadness; promotes
peaceful sleep and dispels nightmares

Spiritual healing: strongly protects; grounds, centers, and cleanses; removes
cords, entities, and foreign energies; awakens past-life memories; facilitates
spirit communication; supports expression of spiritual identity

Note: Jet is fossilized wood, a variety of lignite. See also fossil (p. 123).

Kambaba Stone
(Eldarite, Crocodile "Jasper")
Formula: complex and variable   Hardness: 6.5
Crystal system: mostly trigonal and triclinic
Formation process: igneous   Chakra: root, heart
Correspondences: earth, water, Venus, Libra, Pisces

Physical healing: balances body's rhythmic processes; promotes healthy pregnancy and childbirth; heals and balances at cellular level; nourishing for skin, mucous membranes, glands, and immune system

Psychological healing: imparts good judgment, boosts courage and confidence, eliminates doubt and fear, enables you to rise above abuse

Spiritual healing: helps synchronize natural cycles with the earth; connects to ancient wisdom, astrology, and the Divine Feminine; strongly grounds and nourishes; develops sense of purpose

Note: an orbicular form of rhyolite (see p. 213)

Kämmererite
Formula: $Mg_5(Al,Cr)_2Si_3O_{10}(OH)_8$ Hardness: 2–2.5
Crystal system: monoclinic   Formation process: metamorphic
Chakra: higher heart, third eye, crown
Correspondences: water, air, Neptune, Virgo, Pisces

Physical healing: reduces stiffness and pain, combats infection, helps conditions of nervous and reproductive systems, strongly detoxifies, coordinates left and right hemispheres of brain

Psychological healing: promotes mental flexibility; eliminates rigid, dogmatic beliefs; reduces bias, narrow-mindedness, and prejudice; helps in conquering indecision; softens and releases anger, guilt, shame, and fear; purges stale emotional patterns

Spiritual healing: cleanses aura and removes attachments, stagnation, and unwanted entities; expands and raises consciousness; aids pursuit of truth; links to higher self and spirit guides; draws forth inner Buddha-nature

Kimberlite

Formula: complex and variable   **Hardness:** variable
Crystal system: variable   **Formation process:** igneous
Chakra: earth star   **Correspondences:** earth, fire, spirit,
Pluto, Aries, Scorpio

Physical healing: activates immune system, strengthens eyes and vision, balances hormones, improves nutrient absorption, facilitates childbirth

Psychological healing: helpful for those who bottle emotions; reveals hidden thoughts, beliefs, and feelings; facilitates emotional release; brings balance to emotional extremes; excellent for transcending and transforming trauma

Spiritual healing: catalyzes sudden, rapid spiritual growth; protects against and purges unwanted energies and attachments; grounds and nourishes; strongly boosts psychic senses; facilitates astral travel, shamanic healing, and visionary experiences; connects to inner earth energies

Kornerupine

Formula: $(Mg,Fe^{2+})_4(Al,Fe^{3+})_6(SiO_4,BO_4)_5(O,OH)_2$
Hardness: 6–7   **Crystal system:** orthorhombic   **Formation process:** metamorphic   **Chakra:** all, particularly heart, throat
Correspondences: earth, Pluto, Gemini, Scorpio

Physical healing: powerful physical healer; regenerates at every level; excellent support for connective tissue, circulatory system, and immune function; helps in overcoming infections and parasites; eases death and dying processes

Psychological healing: a powerful stone for overcoming self-destructive behavior; unites daydreaming with action; ends procrastination, denial, darkness, despair, and gloom; helps you find joy in everyday living; improves your communication

Spiritual healing: stone of endings and new beginnings, helps you to recognize the sacredness of each moment, represents mystery and initiation, transforms fear and darkness into hope and unconditional love

Kunzite

Formula: $LiAlSi_2O_6$ with manganese (Mn)   **Hardness:** 6–7
Crystal system: monoclinic   **Formation process:** igneous
Chakra: heart, higher heart   **Correspondences:** water,
Venus, Neptune, Libra, Pisces

Physical healing: soothes and heals heart and nervous system, alleviates hypertension, relieves joint pain, supports immune system

Psychological healing: invites joy, peace, and gratitude; profoundly relaxing; combats anxiety, nervousness, depression, and other psychological conditions; promotes healthy relationships; encourages forgiveness and emotional healing

Spiritual healing: taps into awareness and expression of divine, unconditional love; awakens loving, compassionate thought and action; fosters greater tolerance

Kyanite, Black

Formula: Al_2SiO_5 with iron oxide (Fe_2O_3)
Hardness: 4.5–6.5   **Crystal system:** triclinic
Formation process: metamorphic   **Chakra:** all,
especially third eye   **Correspondences:** earth, spirit,
Mercury, Aries, Taurus, Libra

Physical healing: addresses cellular imbalance, alleviates pain, lowers blood pressure, increases dexterity, coordinates all systems of the body, supports brain health

Psychological healing: improves mental clarity, logic, and memory; untangles emotional baggage; reveals patterns stored deep within subconscious; releases feelings of victimhood; imparts agency and feeling in control of life

Spiritual healing: excellent for clearing and aligning aura and chakras; removes unwanted energies, entities, and other attachments; breaks up and releases blockages in aura; facilitates past-life recall; initiates sense of compassion and responsibility

Kyanite, Blue

Formula: Al_2SiO_5 **Hardness:** 4.5–6.5   **Crystal system:** triclinic
Formation process: metamorphic   **Chakra:** all, especially
third eye and causal   **Correspondences:** earth, air, fire,
water, spirit, Mercury, Libra, Sagittarius

Physical healing: promotes better alignment of joints, especially those in the spine; balances nervous system, brain, and cerebrospinal fluid; improves coordination; treats conditions of sensory organs

Psychological healing: facilitates clear thinking and analysis, awakens higher mind, develops objectivity and reasoning skills, expands perspective, improves connection between conscious and subconscious

Spiritual healing: gently aligns and balances chakras, aura, meridians; clears energy pathways; supports understanding of karmic patterns; facilitates meditation; excellent centering for travel, both physical and psychic

Kyanite, Green

Formula: Al_2SiO_5 with iron (Fe) and vanadium (V)
Hardness: 4.5–6.5   **Crystal system:** triclinic   **Formation
process:** metamorphic   **Chakra:** all, especially heart, throat
Correspondences: earth, spirit, Venus, Aries, Taurus, Libra

Physical healing: supports immune health by balancing body's ecosystem, protects myelin sheaths on nerves, neutralizes overly acidic conditions, improves manual dexterity

Psychological healing: inspires honesty, truthfulness, and heart-centered communication; links higher mind to the heart; brings clarity to confusing or conflicting emotions; releases victimhood, failure, and defeat

Spiritual healing: aligns all chakras and layers of the aura and links them with the heart, facilitates connection with intelligence of devas and the natural world, facilitates exploration of sense of identity, supports karmic healing and shamanic journeying

Kyanite, Orange

Formula: Al_2SiO_5 with manganese (Mn)
Hardness: 4.5–6.5   Crystal system: triclinic
Formation process: metamorphic   Chakra: all,
especially sacral   Correspondences: fire, spirit, Mars,
Aries, Sagittarius

Physical healing: alleviates problems of lymphatic system, bone marrow, and adrenals; helps overcome eating disorders; regulates blood sugar levels; eliminates sciatic pain; integrates and releases energetic and karmic underpinnings of physical illness or injury

Psychological healing: stimulates memory; energizes and enlivens the mind; promotes creativity; improves relationships, both platonic and romantic; facilitates connection; improves understanding of karmic nature of relationships

Spiritual healing: strengthens instincts, intuition, and psychic impulses; initiates sense of timelessness; helps in breaking free from karmic ruts; helps you find pleasure in all areas of life

Labradorite

Formula: $(Na,Ca)(Al,Si)_4O_8$ Hardness: 6–6.5
Crystal system: triclinic   Formation process: igneous
Chakra: all, especially crown   Correspondences: earth, air,
fire, water, spirit, Jupiter, Neptune, Leo, Scorpio, Sagittarius

Physical healing: relieves imbalances resulting in pain, alleviates colds and flu, supports kidneys, provides insight into the root cause of disease or imbalance

Psychological healing: enhances mental faculties, particularly imagination and problem-solving skills; counteracts escapism and daydreaming; channels creativity into concrete goals; overcomes depression and emotional sensitivity

Spiritual healing: strengthens and brightens the aura; repairs damage to aura and chakras; improves ability to set boundaries, provides protection, and averts psychic attack; supports meditation, manifestation, and spiritual development; helps connect to spiritual purpose

Lapis Lazuli

Formula: lazurite [$(Na,Ca)_8(Al,Si)_{12}O_{24}(S,SO_4)$] with pyrite
(FeS_2) and calcite ($CaCO_3$)   **Hardness:** 5.5
Crystal system: cubic, trigonal   **Formation
process:** metamorphic   **Chakra:** heart, throat, third eye
Correspondences: air, Venus, Jupiter, Saturn, Taurus,
Sagittarius

Physical healing: promotes healthy eyes and strong vision; relieves inflammation
and indigestion; supports health of circulatory system, especially the heart;
good for the skeletal system

Psychological healing: harmonizes heart and mind; removes inner conflict;
stimulates mental capacity; prompts clear, heartfelt communication; fosters
insight and hope; nurtures friendship; links logic with intuition

Spiritual healing: traditionally used for protection, awakens intuition, encourages
self-mastery, facilitates meditation, enhances psychic perception, helps master
karmic lessons

Larimar

Formula: pectolite [$NaCa,2,Si_3O_8(OH)$] with traces of copper (Cu)
Hardness: 4.5   **Crystal system:** triclinic
Formation process: igneous   **Chakra:** heart, throat
Correspondences: water, Neptune, Pisces

Physical healing: dissipates congestion, stagnation, and poor circulation; helps
urinary tract infections, headache, and menstrual pain; excellent for restoring
stasis in cases of childhood illness

Psychological healing: deeply nurtures; relieves emotional pain, grief, loss, and
rejection; reduces indecision; initiates healthy communication; teaches us to
be more loving

Spiritual healing: invites release and surrender, connects to currents of
unconditional love, heals the inner child, deepens meditation, invites
profound stillness and inner peace

Larvikite

Formula: plagioclase feldspar [$NaAlSi_3O_8$—$CaAl_2Si_2O_8$] with augite [$(Ca_xMg_yFe_z)(Mg_{y1}Fe_{z1})Si_2O_6$] and other minerals **Hardness:** 6–6.5 **Crystal system:** mostly triclinic and monoclinic **Formation process:** igneous **Chakra:** root, throat, third eye, crown **Correspondences:** air, Moon, Cancer, Leo, Scorpio, Sagittarius

Physical healing: balances nervous system, dispels excess energy and curbs lethargy, supports lungs and respiratory system, relieves insomnia, reduces blood pressure, cools and soothes irritated tissue

Psychological healing: balances daydreaming and procrastination; encourages responsibility; excellent aid for teachers, parents, and guardians; prompts unbiased decisions based on facts, not feelings; reduces mood swings

Spiritual healing: protects and shields; neutralizes psychic attack, harmful magic; facilitates contact with ancestors, fairies, and spirits of the land; facilitates astral travel and shapeshifting

Lazulite

Formula: $(Mg,Fe^{2+})Al_2(PO_4)_2(OH)_2$ **Hardness:** 5.5–6 **Crystal system:** monoclinic **Formation process:** igneous, sedimentary, or metamorphic **Chakra:** third eye **Correspondences:** air, Jupiter, Gemini, Sagittarius, Aquarius

Physical healing: promotes health of brain, larynx, nerves, bones, and teeth; soothes eye strain, particularly from screens; hastens tissue repair

Psychological healing: grants emotional clarity and honesty; sparks confidence to face fear, doubt, and shadow self; improves communication, especially by imbuing courage to speak up about needs

Spiritual healing: facilitates insight, meditation, psychic development, and past-life recall; enhances dream state and increases frequency of lucid and prophetic dreams; promotes feelings of bliss, euphoria, and transcendence

Lepidolite

Formula: $K(Li,Al,Rb)_2(Al,Si)_4O_{10}(F,OH)_2$ Hardness: 2.5–3
Crystal system: monoclinic   Formation process: igneous
Chakra: heart, higher heart   Correspondences: water,
Neptune, Uranus, Pisces, Aquarius

Physical healing: imparts flexibility and relieves joint pain, amplifies conventional cancer treatments, facilitates childbirth, treats conditions affecting DNA and RNA

Psychological healing: extremely soothing and centering; promotes calm awareness; excellent stone for alleviating anxiety, depression, and bipolar disorder; helps in overcoming emotional trauma, nervousness, anger, and worry; initiates impulse of forgiveness; imparts joy

Spiritual healing: encourages independence and spiritual freedom; releases beliefs, behaviors, and attitudes that inhibit perception of love and goodness; promotes surrender, acceptance, and loving-kindness

Libyan Desert Glass

Formula: mostly SiO_2 Hardness: 6
Crystal system: amorphous   Formation process: igneous
Chakra: solar plexus, heart, crown, soul star
Correspondences: fire, spirit, Sun, Aries, Leo

Physical healing: excellent adjunct in overall healing; supports nervous, digestive, and immune systems; excellent for stress-related and psychosomatic illness; may reduce tumors and growths; promotes health of eyes

Psychological healing: releases emotional trauma, especially when rooted in childhood experience; brings confidence, joy, exuberance, and spontaneity; dissolves doubt and cognitive dissonance

Spiritual healing: supports dynamic, immediate manifestation; powerful ally for abundance, prosperity, and success; facilitates connection to ancient wisdom, interstellar communication, and spiritual evolution

Limestone

Formula: mostly calcite ($CaCO_3$) Hardness: 2–4 Crystal system: mostly trigonal Formation process: sedimentary Chakra: root, sacral Correspondences: water, earth, Saturn, Neptune, Pisces

Physical healing: supports health of bones, teeth, cartilage, and ligaments; settles upset stomach; may alleviate conditions of the skin; releases tension; boosts energy; purifies and detoxifies

Psychological healing: improves overall emotional well-being; uplifts and stabilizes mood; sparks creativity; releases fear, worry, frustration, and oversensitivity; facilitates changes in thoughts and behavior to support overall well-being

Spiritual healing: aligns all the layers of the aura; excellent for ancestral and karmic healing; taps into ancient memories, emotions, and energies—both personal and planetary; scrubs aura of unwanted energies; supports breaking free from old cycles; helps transcend periods of stagnancy in spiritual practice

Limonite

Formula: $FeO(OH) \cdot nH_2O$ Hardness: 4–4.5 Crystal system: orthorhombic Formation process: sedimentary Chakra: root, solar plexus Correspondences: earth, Mars, Virgo

Physical healing: combats dehydration, fever, and physical weakness; strengthens skeletal, digestive, and circulatory systems; supports liver function; promotes virility and healthy libido

Psychological healing: soothes when you are feeling down or glum for no apparent reason; combats feelings of isolation, selfishness, and indifference; supports sense of belonging; infuses dignity and empathy to help you face personal attacks; helps when you feel scattered

Spiritual healing: protects against psychic attack; grounds you, makes your home feel more welcoming, offers sense of kinship with spirits of nature, promotes focus for psychic development

Magnesite

Formula: $MgCO_3$ Hardness: 3.5–4.5   Crystal system: trigonal   Formation process: sedimentary or metamorphic   Chakra: crown   Correspondences: water, earth, Moon, Cancer, Libra

Physical healing: assuages digestive issues; ameliorates acid reflux and ulcers; balances cholesterol; alleviates pain, including headaches and migraines; excellent support for bones and teeth; improves sleep

Psychological healing: calms and pacifies; assuages irritation, impatience, and intolerance; promotes conflict resolution, mental flexibility, and multitasking skills; improves communication by supporting better listening

Spiritual healing: assists meditation, psychic development (especially clairaudience), and perception of subtle energy; teaches surrender and patience in spiritual development; inspires discipline necessary for revolutionary transformation

Magnetite

Formula: Fe_2O_4 Hardness: 5.5–6.5   Crystal system: cubic   Formation process: igneous or metamorphic   Chakra: earth star, root, third eye   Correspondences: earth, Mars, Aries, Sagittarius

Physical healing: supports brain and pineal health; regulates all rhythmic process of the body; alleviates dizziness and pain; strengthens circulatory system; treats conditions of liver, bone marrow, gallbladder, and endocrine system

Psychological healing: fortifies you to dig into your subconscious to resolve imbalances; stabilizes rapid mood changes; improves charisma and personal magnetism

Spiritual healing: helps you align with higher purpose; guides you to find direction in life; grounds and aligns subtle bodies; balances polar energies, including inner masculine and feminine forces; protects; activates higher awareness; improves manifestation

Malachite

Formula: $Cu_2CO_3(OH)_2$ **Hardness:** 3.5–4 **Crystal system:** monoclinic **Formation process:** sedimentary **Chakra:** solar plexus, heart **Correspondences:** earth, fire, Venus, Taurus, Libra

Physical healing: draws out pain; harmonizes internal organs; corrects irregular cycles and rhythms, such as heartbeat, sleep and menstrual cycles, elimination; regulates blood pressure; relieves congestion; strengthens eyes and vision

Psychological healing: encourages emotional release, relieves psychological pain and distress, heals old emotional wounds, calms anxiety and PTSD, strengthens willpower, improves relationships

Spiritual healing: circumvents egotism and fosters alignment with divine will, supports inner vision and creative visualization, identifies and releases foreign energies in aura, aids manifestation and abundance

Marble

Formula: mostly calcite ($CaCO_3$) **Hardness:** 3–4 **Crystal system:** trigonal **Formation process:** metamorphic **Chakra:** sacral, crown **Correspondences:** water, Moon, Cancer, Gemini, Virgo

Physical healing: normalizes respiratory system, eyes, and hormonal imbalances; combats seasonal allergies; supports kidney function; strengthens bones and teeth; relieves pain; promotes healthy childhood development

Psychological healing: invites inspiration, creativity, and new perspectives; strengthens problem-solving skills and common sense; helps in overcoming feelings of disappointment, disenchantment, bitterness, or resentment; dissolves apathy

Spiritual healing: stabilizes and eases growth, transformation, and transitions; facilitates dream recall; invites sense of sacred in the everyday; facilitates connection to higher self

Marble, Picasso (Picasso "Jasper")

Formula: mostly calcite ($CaCO_3$)   **Hardness:** 3–4
Crystal system: trigonal   **Formation process:** metamorphic
Chakra: sacral   **Correspondences:** earth, fire, Jupiter, Taurus, Cancer, Sagittarius

Physical healing: supports healthy digestive and nervous systems, balances metabolism, ameliorates carpal tunnel syndrome, alleviates pain, boosts immune function

Psychological healing: excellent for sparking creativity and motivation; calms overactive thoughts, especially helpful in ameliorating anxiety; instills focus, joy, and drive; helps you find pleasure and satisfaction in your work

Spiritual healing: offers steady and continuous grounding to support processes of growth or change; promotes awareness of inner self; facilitates contact with guides and teachers, particularly those from the stars

Marble, Zebra (Zebra "Jasper")

Formula: mostly calcite ($CaCO_3$) and dolomite ($CaMg(CO_3)_2$) with manganese (Mn)   **Hardness:** 3–4
Crystal system: trigonal   **Formation process:** metamorphic
Chakra: root   **Correspondences:** earth, air, Mercury, Gemini, Virgo

Physical healing: promotes health of kidneys, gallbladder, skin, teeth, bones, and heart; initiates body's natural cleansing and detoxification processes; mitigates effects of environmental toxins; soothes allergies; may help resolve vitamin deficiencies

Psychological healing: excellent stress reducer; promotes optimism, creativity, ingenuity, and problem-solving skills; balances cycles of work and rest and helps prevent burnout; counteracts shallowness and self-absorption

Spiritual healing: promotes balance in all aspects of life, cultivates sense of inner freedom, cultivates compassion and empathy

Marcasite

Formula: FeS$_2$ Hardness: 6–6.5 Crystal system: orthorhombic
Formation process: sedimentary Chakra: root, solar plexus
Correspondences: fire, Sun, Aries, Leo

Physical healing: detoxifies and tones skin; reduces blemishes, bruises, scars, and warts; promotes health of organs of elimination

Psychological healing: improves self-esteem, confidence, and motivation; reveals repressed needs and desires; facilitates self-acceptance and combats perfectionism; helps eliminate bad habits and unwanted personality traits

Spiritual healing: represents success and sovereignty, addresses past-life patterns of martyrdom and poverty, attracts abundance and prosperity

Note: Marcasite is seldom used in jewelry because it is too brittle; most stones labeled marcasite are pyrite or hematite.

Meteorite (Nickel-Iron Meteorite)

Formula: mostly nickel (Ni) and iron (Fe) Hardness: 4–7
Crystal system: cubic Formation process: igneous
Chakra: root, solar plexus, crown Correspondences: earth, spirit, Mars, Uranus, Pluto, Scorpio, Aquarius

Physical healing: helpful for circulatory system, muscles, neck, and brain; may improve conditions of the eyes

Psychological healing: strengthens cognitive ability, inspires independence, stimulates emotional detachment and removes bias during turbulent or challenging life experiences

Spiritual healing: bridges heaven and earth; strongly activates upper chakras; enhances psychic development, astral travel, spirit communication, and ancestral healing; helpful for starseeds, walk-ins, and other beings newly incarnated in human bodies

Meteorite, Chondrite (Stony Meteorite)

Formula: complex and variable   Hardness: 4–6
Crystal system: variable   Formation process: igneous
Chakra: earth star, third eye, crown, soul star
Correspondences: earth, spirit, Uranus, Pluto, Scorpio, Aquarius

Physical healing: supports overall strength and structure of the body; promotes cellular regeneration; improves health of brain, nervous system, and memory

Psychological healing: subtly stabilizes emotions, opens mind, enhances imagination and creative problem-solving

Spiritual healing: stimulates connections to past lives on other worlds; strongly boosts psychic ability; facilitates meditations and astral travel, particularly through the cosmos; deepens communication with extraterrestrial and cosmic beings

Meteorite, Pallasite

Formula: mostly nickel (Ni) and iron (Fe) with olivine/peridot [$(Mg,Fe)_2SiO_4$]   Hardness: 4–7   Crystal system: cubic and orthorhombic   Formation process: igneous   Chakra: root, heart, third eye, soul star   Correspondences: earth, fire, spirit, Mars, Venus, Uranus, Aquarius

Physical healing: strengthens, tones, and balances entire body; supports liver, gallbladder, stomach, and intestines; excellent for improving function of muscles and tendons; supports cardiac health

Psychological healing: reveals hidden mental and emotional patterns; brings emotional insight, clarity, and understanding; eliminates fear

Spiritual healing: releases soul contracts; highlights original causes of all conditions, patterns, and experiences; increases abundance and prosperity; connects the heavens to the earth; grounds, energizes, and empowers

Note: see also nickel-iron meteorite (p. 170) and peridot (p. 190)

Moldavite

Formula: mostly SiO_2 Hardness: 5–6
Crystal system: amorphous   Formation process: igneous
Chakra: heart, higher heart, third eye, crown, soul star
Correspondences: earth, air, fire, water, spirit, Venus, Mercury

Physical healing: prompts healing via attainment of better understanding of physical illness or injury, combats fungal infections and parasites, accelerates symptoms of healing crisis to initiate resolution of health issue

Psychological healing: activates intelligence of heart; transcends boundaries of rational intellect; awakens long-held emotional and spiritual wounds to embrace and release them; promotes new ways of thinking, problem-solving, and heightened creativity

Spiritual healing: invites transformation and rapid change; accelerates learning of karmic lessons; integrates psychic abilities; supports channeling, clairvoyance, manifestation, astral travel, meditation, lucid dreaming, and other spiritual pursuits

Molybdenite

Formula: MoS_2 Hardness: 1–1.5   Crystal system: hexagonal
Formation process: igneous   Chakra: all, especially third eye
Correspondences: earth, water, Saturn, Pluto, Scorpio, Capricorn

Physical healing: imparts restful sleep; supports repair and regeneration at cellular and subcellular levels; promotes health of mouth, jaw, teeth, and esophagus

Psychological healing: encourages self-reflection; boosts focus, willpower, and follow-through; dissolves fear, hesitation, and indecision; catalyzes shadow work; induces forgiveness and surrender; releases judgment; increases dependability, responsibility, and conviction

Spiritual healing: repairs damage to etheric body (especially helpful after psychic attack); promotes vivid dreams and sharpens clairvoyance; enhances astral travel, manifestation, and spirit communication

Note: Molybdenite is toxic, and it should be handled with care.

Moonstone, Black

Formula: orthoclase ($KAlSi_3O_8$) with carbon (C) or iron (Fe)
Hardness: 6–6.5   Crystal system: monoclinic
Formation process: igneous   Chakra: root, sacral, third eye
Correspondences: water, Moon, Saturn, Pluto, Cancer, Scorpio

Physical healing: encourages rest and regeneration, promotes reproductive health and menstrual cycle, good for convalescence, supports end-of-life care and the dying process

Psychological healing: supports emotional healing through release, provides a window to the subconscious, helps sustain hope in darkest moments

Spiritual healing: symbolizes endings and new beginnings; confers strong protection; excellent for meditation, psychic development, and prophetic dreams

Moonstone, Peach

Formula: orthoclase ($KAlSi_3O_8$) with iron oxide (Fe_2O_3)
Hardness: 6–6.5   Crystal system: monoclinic
Formation process: igneous   Chakra: sacral, heart
Correspondences: water, fire, Moon, Virgo

Physical healing: reduces chronic tension and pain; alleviates conditions of nervous system; improves skin; regulates hormonal balance; excellent for reproductive system, fertility, and balancing libido; improves sleep by balancing work and rest cycles; balances fluids of body

Psychological healing: improves self-esteem; catalyzes inner and outer beauty; alleviates tension, worry, and anxiety; helps heal unresolved childhood patterns; inspires hope, optimism, and enthusiasm; ignites love and romance

Spiritual healing: gently protects, improves manifestation, helps attain deeply seated peace and tranquility

Moonstone, Rainbow

Formula: labradorite $[(Na,Ca)(Al,Si)_4O_8]$ Hardness: 6–6.5
Crystal system: triclinic Formation process: igneous
Chakra: all, particularly third eye, crown, causal
Correspondences: earth, air, fire, water, spirit, Moon, Cancer

Physical healing: rejuvenates, strengthens, and promotes flexibility of physical body; heals conditions of throat and sinuses, such as seasonal allergies; ameliorates ulcers, acid reflux, and other stomach conditions; improves hearing

Psychological healing: enhances emotional well-being, clears vestiges of emotional trauma from aura, inspires hope and optimism, uplifts the heart

Spiritual healing: protects the aura and seals against leaks, tears, and holes; strengthens intuition and psychic senses; taps into inner feminine energy and connects to Divine Feminine; purifies aura and chakras

Moonstone, Silver (Gray Moonstone)

Formula: orthoclase $(KAlSi_3O_8)$ with iron (Fe)
Hardness: 6–6.5 Crystal system: monoclinic
Formation process: igneous Chakra: sacral, crown
Correspondences: water, Moon, Cancer

Physical healing: supports health of skin, hair, connective tissue, hormonal cycles, reproductive system, and brain; eases symptoms of menopause and dementia; helps for embracing aging with joy; cools fever; slows overactive processes

Psychological healing: offers mental clarity and insight into emotional patterns; helps for remaining unbiased, discerning, and level-headed; balances critical thinking skills with intuition; excellent propellant for fresh starts and inspiration

Spiritual healing: excellent stone for manifestation; protects and shields; helps avert psychic attack and magical harm; facilitates intuition, psychic development, and lucid dreaming; deepens connection to Divine Feminine

Moonstone, White

Formula: orthoclase ($KAlSi_3O_8$) Hardness: 6–6.5
Crystal system: monoclinic Formation process: igneous
Chakra: crown Correspondences: water, air, Moon, Cancer, Libra

Physical healing: balances rhythms and cycles of body; excellent support for ovaries and uterus; treats infertility, painful menstruation; improves lactation; promotes healthy pregnancy and childbirth; enhances youthfulness and healthy skin; improves sleep

Psychological healing: assists in setting healthy boundaries; resolves childhood baggage and trauma; invites wonder and imagination; provides encouragement, validation, and emotional honesty; encourages breaking through deception and illusion

Spiritual healing: stone of safe travel, strengthens intuition, heightens dreams, connects to Divine Feminine, purifies and protects aura

Moqui Marble (Ironstone Concretion)

Formula: hematite (Fe_2O_3) and goethite (FeOOH) encapsulating sandstone (SiO_2) Hardness: 5–6 Crystal system: mostly trigonal and orthorhombic Formation process: sedimentary
Chakra: earth star, root Correspondences: earth, Mars, Aries, Aquarius, Libra

Physical healing: strengthens body, bolsters immune response, alleviates uneasy conditions stemming from spiritual causes

Psychological healing: transmutes fear and discomfort; improves discernment, empathy, and listening skills; encourages sense of belonging and connection; calms overactive mind

Spiritual healing: provides connection to ancestors; strongly grounds and protects; harmonizes yin/yang; stimulates clairvoyance; offers protection during meditation, astral travel, and ritual; powerfully activates earth energies

Note: Also called mochi marble or shaman stone. Also exhibits properties of goethite (p. 135), hematite (p. 138), and sandstone (p. 220).

Morganite

Formula: beryl ($Be_3Al_2Si_6O_{18}$) with manganese (Mn)
Hardness: 7.5–8   **Crystal system:** hexagonal
Formation process: igneous   **Chakra:** heart
Correspondences: water, Venus, Taurus, Libra

Physical healing: eases physical conditions exacerbated by emotional states; helpful for heart, nerves, and reproductive organs

Psychological healing: releases patterns of anger, greed, fear, hatred, confusion, impatience, and resentment; adjusts excessive or diminished emotional energy; alleviates feelings of isolation and loneliness; transforms fear into love; imparts self-love, acceptance, and self-esteem; offers excellent support for all relationships

Spiritual healing: carries energy of divine love, facilitates angelic connection, unites love with wisdom, enables love to transform your entire life, dissolves ego

Note: see also beryl (p. 76)

Muscovite

Formula: $KAl_2(AlSi_3O_{10})(F,OH)_2$ **Hardness:** 2–4
Crystal system: monoclinic   **Formation process:** igneous or metamorphic   **Chakra:** throat, third eye
Correspondences: air, Mercury, Cancer, Virgo

Physical healing: supports nerve, joint, kidney, and stomach health; promotes flexibility; helps curb stress-related illness; regulates sleep cycles and blood sugar

Psychological healing: boosts mental prowess; supports self-reflection, optimism, and mental flexibility; helps in maintaining calm under pressure; helps for seeing bigger picture; invokes feeling seen by others; promotes introspection

Spiritual healing: cultivates compassion, loving-kindness, and spiritual clarity; dissolves separation and imparts unity consciousness; deflects psychic attack; illuminates and crystallizes plans for future

Natrolite

Formula: $Na_2Al_2Si_3O_{10} \cdot 2H_2O$ **Hardness:** 5–6 **Crystal system:** orthorhombic **Formation process:** igneous, sedimentary, or metamorphic **Chakra:** third eye, crown, soul star **Correspondences:** water, air, spirit, Saturn, Neptune, Cancer, Scorpio, Pisces

Physical healing: excellent for brain and nerves; strengthens muscle, skin, small intestine, and connective tissue; balances kidneys, thyroid, and endocrine system; stimulates expulsion of excess fluid; treats conditions of feet

Psychological healing: helps in facing fear, reduces excessive mental and emotional tension, reduces tendency for self-sabotage, gently boosts confidence

Spiritual healing: powerful catalyst for developing psychic and spiritual gifts; facilitates channeling, astral travel, lucid dreaming, shamanic journeying, and contact with angels, spirits, and extraterrestrial intelligence

Nuummite

Formula: gedrite $[Mg_2(Mg_3Al_2)(Si_6Al_2)O_{22}(OH)_2]$, anthophyllite $[Mg_2Mg_5Si_8O_{22}(OH)_2]$, and other minerals **Hardness:** 5.5–6 **Crystal system:** mostly orthorhombic **Formation process:** metamorphic **Chakra:** earth star, root, solar plexus, third eye, causal **Correspondences:** earth, air, fire, water, spirit, Mercury, Jupiter, Sagittarius

Physical healing: soothes disorders of brain, nervous system, and heart; supports kidney function; promotes health of ears

Psychological healing: purges suppressed emotions, especially shame, guilt, and trauma; helps in integrating shadow self; cultivates respect, confidence, and dynamic balance; helps you to reclaim personal power

Spiritual healing: powerful shamanic ally for healing, journeying, and soul retrieval; taps into past-life memories, ancestral patterns, and ancient wisdom; dissolves past-life agreements and harmful karmic patterns; awakens true purpose and helps manifest true will and power

Obsidian, Apache Tears

Formula: mostly SiO_2 Hardness: 5–6 Crystal system: amorphous Formation process: igneous
Chakra: root Correspondences: earth, fire, Saturn, Pluto, Scorpio, Sagittarius, Capricorn

Physical healing: promotes health of eyes, tear ducts, ovaries, and uterus; resolves pain and tightness, especially in lower back; rectifies disorders of circulatory and immune systems, as well as nutrient deficiencies; strengthens hair and nails

Psychological healing: clarifies mind and emotions, prompts healthy emotional release, dissolves conditioning from childhood and old traumas, excellent for assuaging grief, expands experience of greater joy

Spiritual healing: attracts luck and fortune, protects against harmful energies and others' emotions, enhances communication with devas and nature spirits, gently cleanses and grounds the aura

Obsidian, Black

Formula: mostly SiO_2 Hardness: 5–6
Crystal system: amorphous Formation process: igneous
Chakra: root Correspondences: earth, fire, Saturn, Scorpio

Physical healing: promotes cardiovascular health; dissolves tightness, pain, constriction, and blockages; promotes healthy digestion and metabolism

Psychological healing: catalyzes self-awareness; reveals subconscious mind; assists in overcoming grief, fear, addiction, and depression; releases trauma; highlights origin of imbalance or unhealthy emotional states

Spiritual healing: represents death, rebirth, and initiation; prepares the self for spiritual growth by illuminating subconscious mind; cuts cords and removes negative attachments; strongly protects; useful for scrying and psychic awareness

Obsidian, Gold Sheen

Formula: mostly SiO_2 Hardness: 5–6
Crystal system: amorphous Formation process: igneous
Chakra: root, solar plexus Correspondences: earth, fire, Sun,
Pluto, Leo, Sagittarius

Physical healing: promotes healthy eyes, stomach, and esophagus; promotes healing the root of disease and imbalance; supports attaining healthy or ideal weight; excellent for healing wounds; improves endurance and strength

Psychological healing: promotes patience; addresses tendencies toward egotism, selfishness, and arrogance; improves body image; sparks optimism, charisma, and friendliness

Spiritual healing: helps reclaim personal power and aids discovery and fulfillment of purpose; boosts abilities in healing arts; guides through dark night of the soul; attunes to Divine Masculine

Obsidian, Mahogany

Formula: mostly SiO_2 with iron (Fe) and magnesium (Mg)
Hardness: 5–6 Crystal system: amorphous
Formation process: igneous Chakra: root, sacral, solar plexus
Correspondences: earth, fire, Mars, Aries, Leo, Sagittarius

Physical healing: strengthens physical tissue; relieves inflammation; improves circulation; lowers fever; alleviates sinus pressure; treats physical and emotional components of shock, PTSD, and hyperactivity

Psychological healing: cultivates healthy body image; improves confidence and self-esteem; releases core feelings of inadequacy; dissolves poor concentration, depression, irritability, short temper, and fear of intimacy

Spiritual healing: grounds and protects, helps focus for meditation, stabilizes and protects processes of change and transformation

Obsidian, Midnight Lace

Formula: mostly SiO_2 **Hardness:** 5–6
Crystal system: amorphous   **Formation process:** igneous
Chakra: root   **Correspondences:** earth, air, fire, water, spirit, Pluto, Scorpio

Physical healing: alleviates pain, inflammation, and bruising; supports health of connective tissue and mucous membranes; improves circulation

Psychological healing: inspires quiet strength, resilience, and creativity; releases painful memories and emotional burdens

Spiritual healing: induces trance-like states for meditation, astral travel, dream work, channeling, and visualization; excellent aid for all forms of journeying and spirit contact; supports ancestral healing; strongly protective against a wide range of harmful energies and situations

Obsidian, Rainbow

Formula: mostly SiO_2 **Hardness:** 5–6
Crystal system: amorphous   **Formation process:** igneous
Chakra: root, heart   **Correspondences:** earth, air, fire, water, spirit, Sagittarius

Physical healing: promotes health of endocrine system and glands; regulates hormones; improves circulation; reduces inflammation, bruising, and pain; shortens recovery time after medical treatments such as surgery, chemotherapy, and radiation; promotes bone health

Psychological healing: provides breakthrough for addiction, depression, disappointment, anger, confusion, and fear; helps those who are stuck in the past; releases trapped memories that lead to physical imbalance

Spiritual healing: stone of surrender, guides toward wisdom and transformation, offers hope, reveals inner workings of spiritual path, heightens intuition, confers protection, excellent ally for soul retrieval and shamanic journeys

Obsidian, Silver Sheen

Formula: mostly SiO_2 Hardness: 5–6
Crystal system: amorphous   Formation process: igneous
Chakra: root   Correspondences: earth, Moon, Saturn, Sagittarius

Physical healing: promotes healthy eyes, nose, and ears; supports menstrual health; assuages shock, toxicity, and injury

Psychological healing: excellent support for facing fears, reconciles inner conflict, highlights hidden emotional and mental patterns

Spiritual healing: balances polar energies and reconciles dualities, prevents psychic attack, attunes to the rhythm of the moon's cycle, excellent ally for psychic development and astral travel, attunes to Divine Feminine

Obsidian, Snowflake

Formula: mostly SiO_2 with cristobalite (SiO_2)   Hardness: 5–6
Crystal system: amorphous and tetragonal
Formation process: igneous   Chakra: root
Correspondences: earth, fire, Pluto, Gemini, Virgo, Scorpio

Physical healing: resolves low blood pressure, poor circulation, and joint pain; locates hidden pockets of infection (pair it with other stones to eliminate infection)

Psychological healing: reveals hidden fears buried in subconscious, draws out sources of inspiration from deep within, promotes overall balance of psyche

Spiritual healing: represents movement and illumination; breaks up stagnant energies; provides understanding, awareness, and momentum for spiritual growth; initiates insight and clarity; protects against harmful and invasive energies

Obsidian, Spiderweb
Formula: mostly SiO_2 Hardness: 5–6
Crystal system: amorphous   Formation process: igneous
Chakra: earth star, root, third eye, soul star
Correspondences: earth, Saturn, Capricorn

Physical healing: promotes health of cartilage, ligaments, tendons, muscle, and joints; alleviates hip and knee pain; good for nervous system; reduces scar tissue

Psychological healing: facilitates emotional release, reduces stress; helps in locating and trusting support systems for emotional healing, reminds you to rest and practice self-care to prevent burnout

Spiritual healing: promotes attaining greater wisdom and discernment; offers protection from harmful energies, entities, and psychic attack; deepens relationships with spirits, guides, and helpers; offers protection; filters out unnecessary or unhelpful psychic information

Obsidian, Velvet (Peacock Obsidian)
Formula: mostly SiO_2 Hardness: 5–6
Crystal system: amorphous   Formation process: igneous
Chakra: root, third eye   Correspondences: earth, fire, spirit, Leo

Physical healing: promotes cardiac and endocrine health; improves circulation; reduces inflammation, bruising, and pain; supports recovery after medical treatments such as surgery, chemotherapy, and radiation

Psychological healing: releases stale, painful memories; helps in maintaining dignity even in challenging situations; empowers to overcome spite, anger, and hatred; brings hope and insight; stabilizes mood

Spiritual healing: excellent for healing of ancestral wounds, soul retrieval, shamanic journeys, and astral projection; improves discernment of psychic information; integrates feelings of being interconnected with the earth and every aspect of creation

Opal

Formula: $SiO_2 \cdot n(H_2O)$ **Hardness:** 5.5–6   **Crystal system:** amorphous   **Formation process:** igneous or sedimentary   **Chakra:** all   **Correspondences:** water, spirit, Moon, Mercury, Venus, Neptune, Cancer, Libra, Scorpio

Physical healing: treats skin, respiratory system, and kidneys; rejuvenates body; balances fluid levels; promotes health of reproductive system

Psychological healing: brings emotional balance by magnifying and clarifying emotions, clears confusion and doubt, promotes responsibility, facilitates emotional release

Spiritual healing: confers luck, faith, love, and hope; transforms rigid energy patterns and releases blockages; grants wisdom; helps in embracing change; facilitates rebirth; connects to higher consciousness

Opal, Black

Formula: $SiO_2 \cdot n(H_2O)$ **Hardness:** 5.5–6   **Crystal system:** amorphous   **Formation process:** igneous or sedimentary   **Chakra:** all, especially root, crown   **Correspondences:** water, spirit, Moon, Pluto, Cancer, Scorpio

Physical healing: breaks down blockages, growths, and cysts; stimulates body's natural cleansing processes

Psychological healing: draws light and awareness to the subconscious; promotes greater emotional understanding; promotes acceptance, tolerance, and courage; transmutes fear

Spiritual healing: clears and expands aura; accelerates manifestation and magic; improves psychic abilities; initiates out-of-body experiences, astral travel, and shamanic journeys; inspires hope; strengthens will to live and grow

Opal, Blue

Formula: $SiO_2 \cdot n(H_2O)$ with copper (Cu)   Hardness: 5.5–6
Crystal system: amorphous   Formation process: igneous or
sedimentary   Chakra: heart, throat
Correspondences: water, Venus, Neptune, Taurus, Pisces

Physical healing: soothes respiratory system, reduces irritation and inflammation
of airways and mucous membranes, diminishes allergies, combats fatigue and
improves sleep, lowers blood pressure, supports lymph nodes and kidneys

Psychological healing: calms the mind, opens the heart, encourages communication, strengthens memory, improves heart-mind balance

Spiritual healing: invites healthy detachment and circumvents ego, enhances
perception, deepens intuition, encourages surrender, promotes compassion
and integrity

Opal, Dendritic (Merlinite)

Formula: $SiO_2 \cdot n(H_2O)$ with manganese oxides (MnO_x)
Hardness: 5.5–6   Crystal system: amorphous
Formation process: igneous or sedimentary
Chakra: root, heart, crown
Correspondences: water, earth, Mercury, Venus, Gemini,
Virgo

Physical healing: supports immune, circulatory, and nervous systems; cleanses
lymph; fights off colds and flu; improves equilibrium and reduces symptoms
of vertigo

Psychological healing: balances intellect and emotions, reduces stress, boosts
memory, enhances learning and is a wonderful ally for students

Spiritual healing: symbolizes growth and expansion; guides toward spiritual
balance and self-mastery; enhances meditation, contemplation, and inner
stillness

Opal, Ethiopian (Welo Opal)

Formula: $SiO_2 \cdot n(H_2O)$ Hardness: 5.5–6   Crystal system: amorphous   Formation process: igneous or sedimentary   Chakra: all, especially root, heart, crown   Correspondences: earth, air, fire, water, spirit, Moon, Mercury, Gemini, Cancer

Physical healing: promotes overall healing, balance, and clarity at physical level; balances sympathetic and parasympathetic nervous systems; helps in attaining healthy weight and may be useful for treatment of eating disorders

Psychological healing: imparts joy and elegance, ameliorates psychosomatic illness and treats a broad range of mental disorders

Spiritual healing: excellent karmic healing stone; transmutes stale energies, especially karma; promotes spiritual expansion and evolution; facilitates higher states of consciousness, psychic development, and contact with Divine; shields the aura from hostile energies

Opal, Fire

Formula: $SiO_2 \cdot n(H_2O)$ with iron (Fe)   Hardness: 5.5–6   Crystal system: amorphous   Formation process: igneous or sedimentary   Chakra: sacral, heart   Correspondences: water, fire, Mars, Aries

Physical healing: invigorates body and dispels fatigue, neutralizes overstimulation; balances hormones; stimulates sex drive; supports reproductive health and heals conditions of gonads

Psychological healing: invokes passion, creativity, and pleasure; helps with overcoming shyness; breaks down limiting beliefs; encourages assertiveness; releases fear; sparks sensuality; reduces anxiety drawn from intimacy, while promoting greater fulfillment from sex and intimacy

Spiritual healing: accelerates spiritual growth, channels the heart chakra's energy into lower chakras to promote unity and strength among the chakras, activates kundalini, inspires ecstatic spiritual practice

185

Opal, Green

Formula: $SiO_2 \cdot n(H_2O)$ with iron-rich clay (Fe), copper (Cu), or nickel (Ni)   Hardness: 5.5–6   Crystal system: amorphous
Formation process: igneous or sedimentary   Chakra: solar plexus, heart   Correspondences: earth, water, Jupiter, Aries, Sagittarius

Physical healing: relieves colds, flu, and sinus conditions; stimulates detoxification, especially via lymph and kidneys; promotes nutrient absorption; offers insight into karmic origins of recurring or chronic illness; combats exhaustion

Psychological healing: invites joy and freshness, promotes state of perpetual gratitude

Spiritual healing: allows you to see with a new perspective; encourages exploration of new directions; invites gratitude for karmic lessons unfolding, and helps surmount or offset karmic patterns via gratitude

Opal, Hyaline (Water Opal)

Formula: $SiO_2 \cdot n(H_2O)$ Hardness: 5.5–6
Crystal system: amorphous   Formation process: igneous
Chakra: all   Correspondences: water, Sun, Moon, Leo, Sagittarius

Physical healing: balances body's fluids; excellent help in dispelling conditions of eyes, tear ducts, and mucous membranes; supports health of sensory organs; reduces symptoms of dementia and brain injury; detoxifies

Psychological healing: fosters greater emotional clarity and insight; enhances communication of emotional needs; transforms and purifies confusing, conflicting, or harmful emotions

Spiritual healing: magnifies instinctive, intuitive knowing; enhances divine timing and increases synchronicities; facilitates clairvoyance, creative visualization, and prophetic dreams

Opal, Pink

Formula: $SiO_2 \cdot n(H_2O)$ with manganese (Mn)   Hardness: 5.5–6
Crystal system: amorphous   Formation process: igneous
Chakra: heart   Correspondences: water, Venus, Jupiter, Leo, Virgo, Libra, Sagittarius

Physical healing: nourishes the heart, skin, and circulatory system; regulates blood sugar; ameliorates imbalance of lungs and spleen

Psychological healing: gentle and effective emotional healer overall; dissolves worry, shame, shyness, and dissatisfaction; invites warmth, affection, compassion, and love; reduces tendencies toward aggression and violence

Spiritual healing: releases memory of trauma, softens karmic memories and patterns (especially those playing out emotionally and romantically), equalizes karmic debts, promotes angelic communication, inspires generosity and equanimity

Opal, Purple
(Morado Opal, Violet Flame Opal)

Formula: $SiO_2 \cdot n(H_2O)$ with manganese (Mn) or fluorite (CaF_2)   Hardness: 5.5–6   Crystal system: amorphous
Formation process: igneous or sedimentary
Chakra: heart, third eye, crown   Correspondences: water, air, Mercury, Jupiter, Gemini, Virgo, Sagittarius

Physical healing: excellent for muscles; enhances nutrient assimilation; helps regulate blood sugar; supports eyes and vision, and may improve color vision; decalcifies pineal gland

Psychological healing: transforms and releases old emotional patterns, particularly grief and sorrow; helps release psychological burdens; enhances rational thinking and objectivity; boosts intellect; instills emotional and intellectual boundaries

Spiritual healing: promotes insight, psychic development, meditation, and clarity; activates third eye chakra; reveals true meaning of wealth; transmutes negative and disharmonious energies with the power of the violet flame

Opal, White

Formula: $SiO_2 \cdot n(H_2O)$ Hardness: 5.5–6
Crystal system: amorphous
Formation process: igneous or sedimentary   Chakra: all
Correspondences: water, spirit, Moon, Cancer

Physical healing: supports healthy skin, hair, nails, and lymphatic system; treats conditions of respiratory and reproductive systems; alleviates painful menstruation; encourages lactation; de-escalates allergies and asthma

Psychological healing: brings emotions into conscious awareness, amplifies emotions, facilitates emotional release

Spiritual healing: clears and protects aura; brings movement to emotional body; releases stagnant emotional energies and attachments; inspires beauty, grace, and purity

Opal, Yellow

Formula: $SiO_2 \cdot n(H_2O)$ with iron (Fe)   Hardness: 5.5–6
Crystal system: amorphous   Formation process: igneous or sedimentary   Chakra: solar plexus
Correspondences: water, Uranus, Leo, Aquarius

Physical healing: improves health of circulatory, digestive, and nervous systems; eliminates calcifications, cysts, and tumors; strengthens process of elimination; fights infection; gently energizes

Psychological healing: represents joy and happiness; unites emotions with will; reduces internal conflict; creates inner and outer strength; strengthens dedication and commitment; eliminates limiting beliefs and behaviors; stimulates learning, creativity, and problem-solving skills; releases regret

Spiritual healing: inspires freedom and creativity in spiritual practice, aligns personal will with higher self and divine will, opens and aligns solar plexus chakra

Orpiment

Formula: As_2S_3 Hardness: 1.5–2
Crystal system: monoclinic   Formation process: igneous,
sedimentary, or metamorphic   Chakra: sacral, solar plexus
Correspondences: fire, earth, Sun, Leo

Physical healing: increases vitality, strengthens libido, assists recovery from chronic and/or debilitating conditions, supports health of ears, reduces damage to DNA, regulates cholesterol

Psychological healing: stone of joy, enjoyment, and pleasure; stimulates desire as a result of feeling emotionally fulfilled and connected; helps your needs and wants feel fulfilled; boosts mental powers

Spiritual healing: strongly alchemical stone, links to angelic realm, helps in planning for and enacting change, invites courage for profound self-transformation

Note: Orpiment is toxic; handle with care.

Orthoclase

Formula: $KAlSi_3O_8$ Hardness: 6   Crystal
system: monoclinic   Formation process: igneous
Chakra: throat, third eye   Correspondences: water,
air, Moon, Cancer

Physical healing: strengthens and supports bones, ligaments, cartilage, and connective tissue; deepens heart-brain coherence; promotes health of nervous system

Psychological healing: soothes racing thoughts and overactive mind; links emotions and intellect; invites critical thinking tempered by emotion and intuition; helps in processing tragedy, trauma, and grief; facilitates cooperation

Spiritual healing: spiritually expands, stimulates, and protects; boosts psychic senses; balances masculine and feminine energies; invokes compassion; brings clarity of purpose

Peridot

Formula: $(Mg,Fe)_2SiO_4$ **Hardness:** 6.5–7 **Crystal system:** orthorhombic **Formation process:** igneous
Chakra: heart **Correspondences:** fire, earth, Sun, Leo, Virgo

Physical healing: nourishes and detoxifies body, accelerates all healing processes, alleviates symptoms of cold and flu, stimulates appetite, promotes healthy liver and gallbladder function, reduces skin blemishes and warts

Psychological healing: engenders optimism, warmth, and loving thoughts; brings mental clarity; increases feelings of self-worth; helps you to receive with grace

Spiritual healing: grants wisdom and gratitude; promotes prosperity; reduces thoughts related to poverty, scarcity, and being undeserving of wealth and success; releases familial patterns and karmic lessons surrounding money; inspires prophetic dreams

Petalite

Formula: $LiAlSi_4O_{10}$ **Hardness:** 6–6.5
Crystal system: monoclinic **Formation process:** igneous
Chakra: higher heart, third eye, crown
Correspondences: air, Neptune, Pisces

Physical healing: reduces pain and inflammation, particularly associated with chronic conditions; supports health of sensory organs, heart, and nervous system

Psychological healing: one of the best stones for soothing emotions and promoting psychological balance; eases anxiety, fear, apathy, depression, and all kinds of trauma; assists recovery from abuse; calms, uplifts, and nourishes

Spiritual healing: inspires mindfulness; helps dissolve ego; supports meditation, psychic development, angelic communication, and spiritual growth

Petrified Wood

Formula: usually quartz (SiO_2)   Hardness: 6.5–7
Crystal system: trigonal   Formation process: sedimentary
Chakra: earth star, root   Correspondences: earth, spirit,
Saturn, Capricorn

Physical healing: stabilizes metabolism, promotes general healing, supports weight loss

Psychological healing: highlights and eliminates rigid beliefs and behaviors, releases bad habits, breaks longstanding patterns, softens controlling personality, eases stress and transition

Spiritual healing: balances relationship with, and between, mundane and spiritual worlds; combats materialism; invites you to be more fully present; teaches how to surrender to process of personal development; invites new beginnings; awakens past-life memories; resolves personal and ancestral karma

Note: see also fossil (p. 123)

Phenakite

Formula: Be_2SiO_4 Hardness: 7.5–8
Crystal system: trigonal   Formation process: igneous
or metamorphic   Chakra: third eye, crown, soul star
Correspondences: air, spirit, Uranus, Gemini, Aquarius

Physical healing: helpful for brain and nervous system, helps repair damaged DNA, resolves imbalances of aura and chakras that result in physical illness

Psychological healing: strongly enhances focus and clarity, promotes overall psychological balance, sparks courage, strengthens resolve, clears confusion, promotes understanding

Spiritual healing: stone of initiation and evolution; clears and activates energy field, energy pathways, and chakras; enhances meditation, creative visualization, psychic abilities; facilitates contact with spirit guides, angels, ancestors, and devas; raises consciousness; connects to Akashic records

Phosphosiderite

Formula: $FePO_4 \cdot 2H_2O$ Hardness: 3.5–4
Crystal system: monoclinic Formation process: igneous or sedimentary Chakra: solar plexus, crown, causal, soul star
Correspondences: earth, Mars, Uranus, Aquarius

Physical healing: supports health of skin, connective tissue, and hair; eases physical tension; detoxifies liver; strengthens legs and reduces pain in shins, calves, and ankles

Psychological healing: cools anger, mania, anxiety, panic, irritability, and rage; may be useful in treating addiction; improves relationships by encouraging disengagement from drama; promotes objectivity; invokes optimism

Spiritual healing: reduces spiritual bypassing; channels rage and anger into righteous, transformative action and justice; helps you tap into sense of purpose; promotes past-life recall and karmic healing; cultivates joy in spiritual practice; links spirituality with activism

Pietersite

Formula: quartz (SiO_2) with riebeckite [$Na_2(Fe^{2+}_3Fe^{3+}_2)$ $Si_8O_{22}(OH)_2$] Hardness: 6.5–7 Crystal system: trigonal
Formation process: sedimentary Chakra: solar plexus, third eye Correspondences: earth, air, fire, water, spirit, Pluto, Scorpio

Physical healing: regulates endocrine system and blood pressure; tones and repairs nervous system; improves circulation of blood, lymph, and other fluids; sharpens senses; combats fatigue

Psychological healing: purges old patterns from mind and spirit; boosts insight, confidence, and willpower; helps to embrace change; clears outdated programming; confronts fear, especially related to loss and vulnerability

Spiritual healing: supports quest for personal truth, stimulates clairvoyance and astral travel, highlights connection to Divine, supports karmic healing, clears ancestral karma from DNA, helps in weathering the storms of life

Pollucite

Formula: $(Cs,Na)_2(Al_2Si_4O_{12}) \cdot 2H_2O$ Hardness: 6.5
Crystal system: cubic   Formation process: igneous
Chakra: crown, soul star   Correspondences: air, Mercury,
Gemini, Aquarius

Physical healing: supports lungs, sinuses, and respiratory system; excellent for sinus infection, allergies, asthma, and other respiratory conditions; promotes regeneration; eases pain and tightness in chest; discourages growth of calcifications, cysts, and tumors

Psychological healing: combats mental restlessness; presents inner stillness that enhances learning; invites fresh perspectives; confers excellent soothing for anxiety, stress, and overactive mind

Spiritual healing: invokes healing with every breath, attunes to natural rhythms and cycles, cultivates deep peace, enhances intuition, supports other healing modalities, eases end-of-life transition

Prasiolite

Formula: quartz (SiO_2) with iron (Fe)   Hardness: 6.5
Crystal system: trigonal   Formation process: igneous
Chakra: solar plexus, heart, third eye, crown
Correspondences: earth, Saturn, Pluto, Scorpio, Capricorn

Physical healing: excellent support for heart, lungs, and digestive system; treats ulcers, acid reflux, and bloating; stimulates nutrient absorption and metabolism; may help treat eating disorders

Psychological healing: invites love, compassion, and acceptance; encourages you to honor yourself; promotes authenticity, honesty, and conviction; releases unhealthy need for attention or approval

Spiritual healing: links heart and crown chakras; cultivates conviction; connects to nature, the Earth Mother, and the Green Man, a personification of nature who symbolizes rebirth; helps in seeing money as vehicle of spirit; boosts manifestation and prosperity; enhances inner vision

Prehnite

Formula: $Ca_2Al(AlSi_3O_{10})(OH)_2$ Hardness: 6–6.5
Crystal system: orthorhombic
Formation process: igneous or metamorphic
Chakra: solar plexus, heart, third eye
Correspondences: earth, Mercury, Cancer, Virgo

Physical healing: treats conditions of kidneys, bladder, connective tissue, and circulatory system; supports health of lymphatic and digestive systems; heals bruises and varicose veins; improves metabolism; improves flexibility

Psychological healing: improves sleep and dreams; wards off nightmares; fosters healthy connection between heart and mind; excellent for forgiveness; invites acceptance; curbs avoidance, anxiety, and worry; offers excellent support for caregivers

Spiritual healing: helps you prioritize your needs and commit to self-care, integrates hidden lessons in life, promotes sense of connection to the universe

Preseli Bluestone (Dolerite, Diabase)

Formula: complex and variable   Hardness: 5.5–7
Crystal system: complex and variable
Formation process: igneous   Chakra: earth star, root
Correspondences: earth, air, fire, water, spirit, Saturn, Capricorn

Physical healing: releases tightness, pain, blockage, and constriction; deeply nourishes and heals the whole body; treats exhaustion, burnout, and stress

Psychological healing: promotes understanding; enhances reflection; helps in recognizing repeating behaviors; reduces absent-mindedness, anger, anxiety, fear, sadness, grief; stimulates memory and recall

Spiritual healing: deeply grounds and protects; activates psychic senses; excellent ally for past-life recall and healing personal, ancestral, and planetary karma; facilitates meditation, trance, shamanic journey, and prophecy; expands sense of self; balances and increases energy flow in entire energy field

Psilomelane

Formula: $(Ba,H_2O)_2(Mn^{+4},Mn^{+3})_5O_{10}$ Hardness: 5–6
Crystal system: orthorhombic Formation process: igneous or sedimentary Chakra: root Correspondences: earth, fire, Jupiter, Sagittarius

Physical healing: improves skin, lungs, intestines, heart, and circulatory system; helps body regulate blood sugar; prevents burnout and exhaustion

Psychological healing: helps in coming to terms with negative or painful experiences; teaches patience and counteracts feeling rushed, hasty, or brash; reminds you to think things through before acting; promotes frugality and curbs excessive spending

Spiritual healing: deeply grounds; helps in letting go of ego mind, especially during spiritual experiences; enhances trance, meditation, scrying, and psychic development

Pumice

Formula: mostly SiO_2 and other silica minerals Hardness: 6.5
Crystal system: amorphous Formation process: igneous
Chakra: solar plexus, heart, higher heart
Correspondences: air, Mercury, Jupiter, Gemini, Sagittarius, Aquarius

Physical healing: may alleviate dizziness, nausea, and insomnia; promotes healthy pregnancy and childbirth; stimulates detoxification, especially colon and skin; improves oxygenation and regeneration of cells

Psychological healing: diminishes defensiveness, irritability, and abrasive qualities; scrubs away emotional scars and trauma; releases negative attitudes; helps in letting go of fear and embracing vulnerability; imparts tenderness and kindness; encourages intimacy

Spiritual healing: absorbs negativity (cleanse this stone often), useful for protection and banishing, helps you to rise above circumstances, excellent ally for removing karmic burdens, offers lightness of spirit

Purpurite

Formula: $Mn^{3+}(PO_4)$ Hardness: 4–4.5
Crystal system: orthorhombic   Formation process: sedimentary
Chakra: third eye, crown   Correspondences: earth, air, Jupiter, Virgo

Physical healing: supports health of heart, circulatory system, and sensory organs, especially ears; speeds up healing of bruises, sores, open wounds, and stops bleeding; treats burnout and exhaustion

Psychological healing: boosts alertness and focus, assuages despondency and despair, helps enforce emotional boundaries and curb excess emotional labor, dissolves shyness and aloofness, promotes confident speech and action

Spiritual healing: invites inspiration, sparks psychic impulses, initiates purification, helps in maintaining and upholding personal ideals, lends strength to break free from egotism and materialism, protects against outside interference and psychic attack

Pyrite

Formula: Fe_2S_3 Hardness: 6–6.5   Crystal system: cubic
Formation process: igneous, sedimentary, or metamorphic
Chakra: root, solar plexus   Correspondences: earth, fire, Mars, Aries

Physical healing: strengthens and detoxifies, helps mitigate infection, treats conditions of the male reproductive system, promotes circulation and warms extremities

Psychological healing: promotes mental order, clarity, and memory; strengthens willpower; assuages fear, low self-esteem, depression, and apathy; enhances self-confidence, creativity, and assertiveness; helps you see inherent worth of yourself and your resources

Spiritual healing: protects, grounds, and stabilizes; increases ability to anchor higher energies on material plane; boosts manifestation; inspires action; magnetizes wealth

Pyrite, Rainbow

Formula: Fe_2S_3 Hardness: 6–6.5   Crystal system: cubic
Formation process: sedimentary   Chakra: root,
solar plexus   Correspondences: earth, fire, Mars, Aries,
Leo

Physical healing: supports healthy joints, nerves, and heart; boosts immune and circulatory systems; nourishes and strengthens sensory organs; promotes regeneration, especially after exposure to radiation

Psychological healing: encourages self-care, healthy boundaries, and awareness of present moment; encourages understanding and empathy in all relationships; sharpens business acumen

Spiritual healing: invites dynamic, evolutionary grounding; overcomes geopathic stress; provides protection during astral travel, trance states, meditation, and visionary journeys; enhances intuition; prevents psychic attack

Pyromorphite

Formula: $Pb_5(PO_4)_3Cl$ Hardness: 3.5–4   Crystal
system: hexagonal   Formation process: sedimentary
Chakra: solar plexus, heart   Correspondences: earth,
Saturn, Aries, Leo, Sagittarius, Capricorn

Physical healing: improves digestion and nutrient absorption; detoxifies body, especially liver, gallbladder, and spleen; diminishes growth of malignant cells (as an adjunct to medical treatment); reduces sensitivity to electromagnetic fields

Psychological healing: promotes acceptance, tolerance, and compassion; invites better compassion and appreciation for oneself; improves self-image; boosts confidence and motivation; reveals sources of negative thoughts

Spiritual healing: inspires connection to all life on earth; encourages better communication with devas, nature spirits, and guides; enhances intuition; dispels toxic energy; promotes adaptation, evolution, and personal development; ends repetitive karmic cycles

Note: Pyromorphite may be toxic if mishandled.

Quartz

Formula: SiO_2 **Hardness:** 7 **Crystal system:** trigonal
Formation process: igneous, sedimentary, or metamorphic
Chakra: all **Correspondences:** all elements, all planets,
all signs

Physical healing: versatile tool for overall health; increases vitality; reduces pain, infection, fever, injury, and blockage; strengthens lungs and respiratory system

Psychological healing: invites mental and emotional clarity; bolsters willpower, resolve, and responsibility; clears worry, confusion, anger, bitterness, fear, grief, detachment, anxiety, and depression

Spiritual healing: can be programmed for virtually any intent; provides clarity, inspiration, discipline, and illumination; facilitates meditation, psychic development, manifestation, and spiritual healing; strengthens human energy field; balances chakras; provides overall protection

Quartz, Actinolite in

Formula: SiO_2 with actinolite $[Ca_2(Mg,Fe)_5Si_8O_{22}(OH)_2]$
Hardness: 7 **Crystal system:** trigonal
Formation process: igneous **Chakra:** root, heart
Correspondences: earth, Venus, Pluto, Leo,
Scorpio

Physical healing: aids recovery from injuries caused by repetitive motion; improves respiratory health; excellent ally for overall healing, especially after injury, surgery; promotes cellular regeneration

Psychological healing: reduces stress; eliminates trauma, toxic people, and destructive behaviors; imparts creativity; helps release the past; eases restlessness, wanderlust, and distraction

Spiritual healing: stone of new beginnings; strongly protects; clears and activates root chakra; helps you find direction in life; improves meditation, visualization, and manifestation; promotes past-life recall

Note: see also actinolite (p. 41)

Quartz, Amphibole

Formula: SiO_2 with amphibole [$AX_2Z_5(Si,Al,Ti)_8O_{22}(OH,F,Cl,O)_2$] and other minerals   Hardness: 7
Crystal system: trigonal (quartz), monoclinic or orthorhombic (amphibole)   Formation process: igneous
Chakra: third eye, crown, soul star
Correspondences: fire, spirit, Jupiter, Sagittarius

Physical healing: works more closely with mind and spirit than physical body, repairs etheric body to assist recovery from injury and illness, releases psychological and spiritual imbalances related to illness

Psychological healing: promotes introspection; helps in processing trauma; brings lightheartedness, peace, and joy

Spiritual healing: facilitates angelic communication, highlights connections to spiritual planes, purifies causal body and burns off stale karma, helps with cutting cords, aligns subtle bodies, channels efforts into acts of service to one another and Source

Quartz, Beta

Formula: SiO_2 Hardness: 7   Crystal system: hexagonal
Formation process: igneous or metamorphic   Chakra: all
Correspondences: earth, air, fire, water, spirit, Sun, Leo, Virgo

Physical healing: strengthens and calibrates homeostatic and metabolic processes, supports health of nervous system, reduces tension and headaches, sometimes used to calm genetic disorders and cancer (as an adjunct to medical treatment)

Psychological healing: invites strength, clarity, and grace during transition, chaos, or turmoil; instills confidence; helps you to live life fully, intentionally, and responsibly; sparks wonder, curiosity, and enthusiasm

Spiritual healing: strongly stimulates energy flow in aura and chakras, breaks down energetic blockages, enhances all forms of intuition and psychic senses, aligns humanity with the natural world

Quartz, Blue Mist (Veil of Isis Quartz)

Formula: SiO_2 with hollow inclusions   Hardness: 7
Crystal system: trigonal   Formation process: igneous
Chakra: all, especially solar plexus, heart, third eye
Correspondences: earth, air, fire, water, spirit, Moon, Cancer

Physical healing: reduces pain; supports health of respiratory, circulatory, and reproductive systems; balances hormones; improves fertility and libido

Psychological healing: promotes state of calm focus; heals and nourishes inner child; guides a journey deep into the psyche for healing; initiates state of connection and communion with others; aids recovery from abuse, trauma, and loss

Spiritual healing: represents mystery and self-mastery; connects to spiritual planes, spirits, elementals, fairies, and ancient gods; supports planetary healing, evolution, and raising consciousness; empowers inner Divine Feminine

Quartz, Candle

Formula: SiO_2 Hardness: 7   Crystal system: trigonal
Formation process: igneous   Chakra: all, especially crown
Correspondences: earth, air, fire, water, spirit, Neptune, Gemini, Aquarius, Pisces

Physical healing: activates body's natural healing processes; supports health of DNA and RNA; promotes health of central nervous system, heart, and pericardium; alleviates headaches

Psychological healing: dissolves despondency, depression, and despair; awakens feelings of connection and support within family and community; improves self-esteem and body image; supports authentic connection, trust, and hope

Spiritual healing: illuminates spiritual path; contains storehouse of wisdom; attunes to changes in seasonal tides and astrological transits; connects to Akashic records, past-life memories, and angelic realm; releases ancestral karma; transmutes negativity

Note: Candle quartz is also known as pineapple quartz and celestial quartz.

Quartz, Dumortierite in

Formula: SiO_2 with dumortierite $[Al_7BO_3(SiO_4)_3O_3]$
Hardness: 7   Crystal system: trigonal
Formation process: igneous   Chakra: throat
Correspondences: air, Uranus, Aquarius

Physical healing: provides stamina and strength; mitigates chronic conditions; supports immune health; heals conditions affecting digestive and elimination organs, especially inflammatory bowel disease, diarrhea, and constipation

Psychological healing: gently clears and focuses mind; instills patience, peace, and even temper; assuages anger, frustration, and intolerance; inspires spiritual love and improves romantic relationships; improves communication

Spiritual healing: cultivates inner stillness and quiet to enhance meditation, psychic and spiritual pursuits, and ecstatic states; excellent for spirit communication; activates higher mind and latent spiritual abilities

Note: see also dumortierite (p. 114)

Quartz, Elestial

Formula: SiO_2 Hardness: 7   Crystal system: trigonal
Formation process: igneous   Chakra: all, especially earth star, solar plexus   Correspondences: earth, air, fire, water, spirit, Moon, Gemini

Physical healing: sheds light on causes of physical (and psychological, spiritual) imbalances, strengthens healing sessions overall, reduces burnout, improves symptoms of withdrawal, may treat conditions of skeleton and some forms of cancer (as an adjunct to medical treatment)

Psychological healing: purges repressed, stagnant, and unhealthy emotional patterns; facilitates shadow work and exploration of subconscious mind; aids emotional release

Spiritual healing: supports all alchemical, transformational, and evolutionary processes; reveals past-life memories; assists communication with angelic realm; heals, aligns, and restructures aura and chakras; brings healing to the soul level

Quartz, Faden

Formula: SiO_2 **Hardness:** 7 **Crystal system:** trigonal
Formation process: metamorphic **Chakra:** all
Correspondences: earth, air, fire, water, spirit, Moon, Pluto, Scorpio

Physical healing: activates body's natural healing ability; helps knit together open wounds, torn tissues, and broken bones; reduces pain

Psychological healing: helps identify and nurture psychological wounds, reduces internal conflict, facilitates genuine connection and communication in all relationships

Spiritual healing: repairs tears, holes, and leaks in aura; removes cords, implants, attachments, and entities from energy field; facilitates astral travel, lucid dreaming, and soul retrieval; promotes healing of ancestral and karmic patterns

Quartz, Garden (Lodolite)

Formula: SiO_2 with mineral inclusions, such as chlorite $[(Mg,Fe)_3(Si, Al)_4O_{10}(OH)_2 \cdot (Mg,Fe)_3(OH)_6]$ **Hardness:** 7 **Crystal system:** trigonal
Formation process: igneous **Chakra:** all **Correspondences:** earth, air, fire, water, spirit, Mercury, Virgo

Physical healing: cleanses and tones body, strengthens thymus and immune system, alleviates congestion and allergies

Psychological healing: magnifies imagination; overcomes boredom, disappointment, rejection, and heartbreak; relaxes and refreshes mind and spirit; promotes vulnerability and open-heartedness without fear or worry

Spiritual healing: grounds and centers; facilitates shamanic travel, dreamwork, visualization, past-life recall; eliminates negative energy and toxins from environment; promotes communication with nature spirits; enhances planetary healing, karmic and ancestral healing, and extraction of entities, cords, and foreign energies from human energy field and environment

Note: also called shaman quartz, dream quartz (a name shared with other varieties of quartz), and lodolite

Quartz, Girasol
(Moon Quartz, Metamorphosis Quartz)
Formula: SiO_2 with transparent, fibrous inclusions   Hardness: 7
Crystal system: trigonal   Formation process: igneous
Chakra: all   Correspondences: water, Moon, Cancer

Physical healing: excellent for chronic and latent conditions, cleanses and strengthens respiratory system, supports health of brain and nervous system

Psychological healing: bolsters perception, discernment, assertiveness, and compassion; promotes overall emotional healing; improves problem-solving skills; boosts creativity

Spiritual healing: strengthens psychic senses; enhances spirit communication; initiates surrender; awakens Divine Feminine within; transcends duality and polarity; supports change, transition, and transformation; enhances manifestation; strengthens aura

Quartz, Golden Healer
Formula: SiO_2 with limonite [$FeO(OH) \cdot nH_2O$]   Hardness: 7
Crystal system: trigonal   Formation process: igneous
Chakra: all   Correspondences: fire, Sun, Leo

Physical healing: master healing stone, supports recovery from all conditions, releases physical trauma linked to emotional and spiritual causes, excellent for immune system, supports healthy skin

Psychological healing: improves memory and recall; enhances confidence, clarity, and communication; supports changes in belief, behavior, and lifestyle; restores optimism, hope, and self-esteem after loss and rejection

Spiritual healing: stone of rebirth and enlightenment; strengthens connection to the spiritual amid the everyday; strongly activates psychic senses, telepathic communication, and visualization skills; awakens inner Christ-consciousness; transmutes negative energy from environment

Quartz, Growth Interference

Formula: SiO_2 with etchings left by calcite ($CaCO_3$) or other minerals   Hardness: 7   Crystal system: trigonal
Formation process: igneous   Chakra: all
Correspondences: earth, air, fire, water, spirit, Saturn, Uranus, Capricorn, Aquarius

Physical healing: aids recovery after injury, especially sprains and broken bones; imparts strength and resilience when facing chronic or terminal illness

Psychological healing: helps in confronting obstacles and setbacks with confidence and grace, expedites healing after trauma, imparts objectivity and peace in remembering past pain, improves self-image, releases adherence to unrealistic ideals and illusions, dissolves self-judgment

Spiritual healing: grants access to Akashic records; enhances astral travel, karmic healing, and psychic development; dissolves blockages in aura and life path; assists personal and planetary evolution

Quartz, Harlequin (Fire Quartz)

Formula: SiO_2 with hematite (Fe_2O_3)   Hardness: 7
Crystal system: trigonal   Formation process: igneous
Chakra: root   Correspondences: fire, Mars, Jupiter, Aries, Libra, Sagittarius

Physical healing: supports health of thymus, blood vessels, thyroid, metabolism, and nervous system; alleviates rashes and redness of skin; treats allergies; excellent support for immune system

Psychological healing: inspires playfulness, whimsy, and creativity; nourishes inner child; softens grave, over-serious, and overcritical personalities; heightens enjoyment, pleasure, and confidence; balances career and social life

Spiritual healing: activates kundalini energy, clears blockage and stagnation in meridians and energy pathways, renews engagement with spiritual practice, kindles inner fire of transformation, purifies environmental energies

Note: Many sources incorrectly label the inclusions as lepidocrocite. See also hematite (p. 138).

Quartz, Lemurian Seed Crystal

Formula: SiO_2 often with hematite (Fe_2O_3)   Hardness: 7
Crystal system: trigonal   Formation process: igneous
Chakra: all, especially heart, higher heart, crown,
soul star   Correspondences: earth, air, fire, water, spirit

Physical healing: promotes overall healing; has special affinity for brain, nervous system, and heart

Psychological healing: reduces feelings of isolation and separation; highlights support from family, community, and friends; builds feelings of being nurtured and loved

Spiritual healing: offers healing, ancient wisdom, and light for personal and planetary evolution; facilitates connection with the natural world; enhances communication with higher self, guides, and angelic beings; promotes karmic healing; connects to Divine Feminine; removes attachments, seals the aura, and creates sacred space

Quartz, Lithium

Formula: SiO_2 with traces of lithium (Li) and other minerals
Hardness: 7   Crystal system: trigonal   Formation
process: igneous   Chakra: all, especially higher heart
Correspondences: earth, air, fire, water, Neptune, Pisces

Physical healing: promotes overall healing of body, mind, and spirit; relieves pain, tension, and inflammation; excellent for stress-related illness; eases end-of-life transitions

Psychological healing: promotes mental and emotional balance; supports recovery from depression, bipolar disorder, anxiety, panic disorders, nervousness, anger, shyness, unrest, grief, and abandonment; relieves interpersonal tension

Spiritual healing: balances spirit on every level, including inner yin-yang, masculine-feminine energies; helps reveal past-life memories and unhealthy attachments; purifies and balances aura and chakras; enhances meditation, surrender, and attunement to higher consciousness

Quartz, Phantom

Formula: SiO_2 with various minerals   Hardness: 7
Crystal system: trigonal   Formation
process: igneous, sedimentary, or metamorphic
Chakra: all   Correspondences: all elements, all
planets, all signs (varies according to composition)

Physical healing: supports overall health and development, provides insight into disorders rooted in childhood, treats lung congestion and seizures

Psychological healing: excellent tool for sifting through subconscious mind, facilitates exploring shadow self and inner child, highlights aspects of the self that need more love and support, helps enforce healthy boundaries

Spiritual healing: facilitates past-life recall, karmic healing, and access to the Akashic records; supports meditation, psychic development, spiritual growth

Quartz, Prase (Green Quartz)

Formula: SiO_2 with actinolite [$Ca_2(Mg,Fe)_5Si_8O_{22}(OH)_2$], hedenbergite ($CaFeSi_2O_6$), or other minerals
Hardness: 7   Crystal system: trigonal
Formation process: igneous or metamorphic
Chakra: solar plexus, heart
Correspondences: earth, fire, Venus, Taurus, Libra

Physical healing: reduces pain, inflammation, and bruising; excellent for hair, nails, skin, and teeth; helpful for conditions of the heart, bladder, and immune system

Psychological healing: helps release the past and resolve grudges; dissolves bitterness, grief, anguish, and loneliness; promotes compassion, forgiveness, kindness, and gentleness

Spiritual healing: powerfully activates kundalini energy; eases karmic burdens; magnifies abundance and prosperity; enhances communication with angels, nature spirits, dragons, and guides; activates heart-centered intuition

Quartz, Record Keeper

Formula: SiO_2 Hardness: 7   Crystal system: trigonal
Formation process: igneous   Chakra: all
Correspondences: all elements, all planets, all signs

Physical healing: helps resolve physical conditions rooted in past lives, repairs damage to DNA, activates cellular memory

Psychological healing: encourages self-reflection, insight, and mental mastery; improves focus and recall; reduces fear related to future events; encourages sense of fulfillment; helps you draw on happy memories for enduring challenging times

Spiritual healing: helps in accessing past-life memories and ancient wisdom; awakens latent spiritual, intuitive, and healing skills; excellent ally for teachers; connects to wisdom of Atlantis, Lemuria, and extraterrestrial civilizations; facilitates karmic and ancestral healing

Quartz, Red (Hematoid Quartz)

Formula: SiO_2 with hematite (Fe_2O_3)   Hardness: 7
Crystal system: trigonal   Formation process: igneous
Chakra: root   Correspondences: fire, Mars, Aries

Physical healing: excellent support for circulatory and nervous systems; enhances vitality, stamina, and strength; balances body's pH; improves immune response; stanches bleeding and speeds wound healing; relieves pain and swelling, especially in feet

Psychological healing: increases mental focus and stability; imparts emotional strength, courage, optimism, and motivation; improves confidence, self-esteem, and contentment; releases guilt, shame, despair, and pessimism

Spiritual healing: strongly protects; removes negative attachments, cords, and entities from aura; activates kundalini; awakens inner warrior; excellent ally for planetary healing; stabilizes finances

Quartz, Rutilated

Formula: SiO_2 with rutile (TiO_2)   Hardness: 7   Crystal system: trigonal (quartz), tetragonal (rutile)   Formation process: igneous   Chakra: all   Correspondences: water, fire, spirit, Venus, Taurus, Gemini, Scorpio

Physical healing: energizes, restores, and regenerates; helps achieve healing breakthroughs; stimulates hair growth; encourages wound healing; counteracts side effects of radiation therapy; alleviates numbness, pain, and carpal tunnel syndrome

Psychological healing: enhances communication, encourages better listening skills, improves relationships, boosts confidence and creativity

Spiritual healing: greatly enhances personal magnetism, expands the aura, strengthens manifestation and healing on all levels, acts as a beacon of inspiration from the higher realms

Note: see also rutile (p. 219)

Quartz, Scepter

Formula: SiO_2 Hardness: 7   Crystal system: trigonal
Formation process: igneous   Chakra: all, especially solar plexus, heart   Correspondences: earth, air, fire, water, spirit, Jupiter, Sagittarius

Physical healing: breaks up blockages, stagnation, and inflammation; improves strength and stamina; regulates hormonal balance; treats sexual dysfunction

Psychological healing: helps you to stand firm and take responsibility; boosts confidence, respect, and wisdom; inspires good leadership skills; ignites action; targets misalignment of the will

Spiritual healing: represents spiritual power, wisdom, and sovereignty; helps identify root of any condition (physical, psychological, or spiritual); helpful in cases where cause of imbalance is unknown; fosters greater connection between therapist and client

Quartz, Spirit (Cactus Quartz)

Formula: SiO_2 with iron (Fe)   Hardness: 7
Crystal system: trigonal   Formation process: igneous
Chakra: third eye, crown, soul star   Correspondences: earth, air, fire, water, spirit, Jupiter, Uranus, Sagittarius, Aquarius

Physical healing: harmonizes systems of the body; excellent for skin, brain, and nervous system; helpful for allergies, colon health, and removing toxins

Psychological healing: uplifts mood; invites cooperation and harmony; sweeps away fear, pain, obsession, and anxiety; promotes generosity and compassion; improves sense of self-worth

Spiritual healing: transmutes old karma, especially associated with families, groups, and communities; initiates past-life recall; facilitates connection to soul family; instills group harmony; promotes planetary healing; attracts abundance; activates psychic abilities

Note: see also amethyst (p. 53)

Quartz, Tangerine

Formula: SiO_2 with hematite (Fe_2O_3)   Hardness: 7
Crystal system: trigonal   Formation process: igneous
Chakra: sacral   Correspondences: water, fire, Mars, Aries, Leo, Libra

Physical healing: enlivens and stimulates endocrine system, supports liver health, treats conditions of reproductive system, improves immune response

Psychological healing: invites optimism, warmth, and zeal; raises confidence; dissolves feelings of fear, inadequacy, and stagnation; nurtures inner child; inspires joy, creativity, playfulness, and spontaneity; facilitates introspection and self-inventory

Spiritual healing: aligns and synchronizes subtle bodies, enhances clairvoyance, spurs you to act on psychic information, forges strong link to higher self, encourages commitment to daily spiritual practice

Quartz, Tibetan

Formula: SiO_2 with carbon-rich (C) inclusions   Hardness: 7
Crystal system: trigonal   Formation process: igneous
Chakra: all, especially crown, soul star
Correspondences: all elements, all planets, all signs

Physical healing: supports nervous system health, regenerates and repairs physical body, promotes overall well-being, discourages disordered eating habits

Psychological healing: improves relationships; decreases codependency; imparts sympathy, compassion, and generosity; breaks limiting habits and emotions

Spiritual healing: cultivates healthy detachment and eliminates suffering; reduces ego-identification; accelerates spiritual growth; magnifies psychic ability; facilitates communication with spirits, guides, angels, and other celestial beings; clears, protects, and strengthens human energy field; instills greater sense of justice, responsibility, and equity; promotes planetary healing

Quartz, Tourmalinated

Formula: SiO_2 with black tourmaline $[Na(Fe,Mn)_3Al_6B_3Si_6O_{27}(OH)_3(OH,F)]$ Hardness: 7   Crystal system: trigonal
Formation process: igneous   Chakra: all, especially earth star, soul star   Correspondences: earth, air, Mercury, Gemini

Physical healing: reduces pain, tension, and blood pressure; helpful for asthma, allergies, and bronchitis; strengthens elimination system; ally for dieting, fasting, and cleanses

Psychological healing: harmonizes mind and emotions; reduces depression, sadness, and inner conflict; clears confusion; identifies and releases disharmonious mental and emotional energies

Spiritual healing: strongly purifies body, mind, and spirit; removes negativity, blockages, stagnation, and attachments from aura and chakras; balances yin and yang energies; repairs damage to aura

Note: Tourmalinated quartz may contain blue, green, or other tourmalines; in these cases the properties more closely reflect the type of tourmaline it contains.

Quartz, Trigonic

Formula: SiO_2 Hardness: 7   Crystal system: trigonal
Formation process: igneous   Chakra: all, especially soul
star   Correspondences: all elements, all planets, all signs

Physical healing: awakens spiritual blueprint for overall health and healing, induces deep relaxation to support repair and regeneration of body, works more closely with spiritual anatomy than physical

Psychological healing: helps eliminate conflict, discord, and separation; increases awareness and understanding of psychological patterns

Spiritual healing: stone of initiation, transcendence, and awakening; facilitates soul journeys, including birth, death, and astral travel; links personal consciousness with superconscious; initiates soul-level healing; helps you to manifest your purpose; assists transformation

Quartz, White
(Snow Quartz, Quartzite)

Formula: SiO_2 Hardness: 7   Crystal system: trigonal
Formation process: igneous, sedimentary, or metamorphic
Chakra: all   Correspondences: earth, water, Moon, Cancer

Physical healing: stabilizing, slowing effect on body; good for overall healing; helps maintain the effects of other gemstones and healing modalities; treats conditions of the lungs; decreases overactive metabolism

Psychological healing: cools, stabilizes, and softens emotions; calms temper; quiets overactive mind; improves focus, discipline, and imagination; reduces attachment and possessiveness

Spiritual healing: anchors and maintains positive changes in all aspects of life, calibrates when life appears to move too quickly, slows and stabilizes rate of change and development, gently grounds and protects

Rhodizite

Formula: $(K,Cs)Al_4Be_4(B,Be)_{12}O_{28}$ Hardness: 8
Crystal system: cubic   Formation process: igneous
Chakra: all, especially solar plexus, third eye
Correspondences: all elements, all planets, all signs

Physical healing: strengthens immune system; promotes repair of damaged DNA; alleviates pain, especially headaches and migraines; beneficial for eyes and brain; increases vitality

Psychological healing: alleviates depression, pessimism, low self-worth; invites optimism, assertiveness, passion, creativity, enthusiasm, and confidence

Spiritual healing: immediately clears, activates, and strengthens chakras; initiates flow of kundalini; strongly amplifies other crystals, healing energies, and thoughts; powerfully activates psychic activity; boosts manifestation skills; facilitates remote viewing, astral travel, and lucid dreaming

Rhodochrosite

Formula: $MnCO_3$ Hardness: 3.5–4
Crystal system: trigonal   Formation process: sedimentary
Chakra: solar plexus, heart
Correspondences: fire, Venus, Taurus, Libra

Physical healing: improves flow of circulatory system, promotes elasticity of blood vessels, regulates blood pressure, restores libido, assuages acute hearing loss, counteracts overall lethargy and weakness

Psychological healing: heals inner child; encourages forgiveness, spontaneity, and joy; clears emotional debris from the aura and chakras; brings clarity to and understanding of emotions; reveals old wounds, particularly those from childhood and from past lives; facilitates emotional expression

Spiritual healing: develops freedom; sweeps away old patterns, karmic ties, and ancestral curses; teaches compassion, creativity, confidence, and humanitarianism; renews passion for life

212

Rhodonite

Formula: CaMn$_3$Mn(Si$_5$O$_{15}$)   Hardness: 5.5–6.5
Crystal system: triclinic   Formation process: metamorphic
Chakra: root, heart   Correspondences: fire, earth, Venus,
Pluto, Taurus

Physical healing: mends open wounds, broken bones, bruises, and inflammation; facilitates weight loss; alleviates symptoms of menopause; dissipates blood clots; reduces burnout; promotes health of lungs and digestive system

Psychological healing: promotes emotional balance; grounds out-of-balance and overactive emotions; boosts mental stamina and emotional fortitude; resolves anxiety, nervousness, mania, anger, fear, grief, phobias, and low self-esteem; deepens bonds in romantic relationships

Spiritual healing: facilitates understanding and awareness of current life scenarios and life purpose; encourages altruism and generosity; draws out innate skills and talents, especially for healing, spiritual growth, and transformation

Rhyolite

Formula: variable   Hardness: 6–7   Crystal system: variable
Formation process: igneous   Chakra: sacral
Correspondences: earth, Jupiter, Sagittarius

Physical healing: supports health of elimination system, urinary tract, and reproductive organs; treats conditions of blood vessels and skin; promotes electrolyte balance and nutrient assimilation

Psychological healing: helps in viewing the past with healthy detachment; detoxifies and releases harmful or toxic emotions, relationships, and situations; activates moving on when you're stuck in the past

Spiritual healing: improves focus during meditation, identifies and releases unwanted or harmful energies from the aura and chakras, facilitates karmic healing by identifying karmic patterns and past-life energies playing out in the present, serves as a useful adjunct to cord-cutting

Rhyolite, Rainforest

Formula: variable **Hardness:** 6–7 **Crystal system:** variable
Formation process: igneous **Chakra:** sacral, heart
Correspondences: earth, Venus, Taurus, Leo, Sagittarius

Physical healing: relieves pain and inflammation, fights infection, good for seasonal allergies, stimulates tissue regeneration, helps regulate blood sugar, stimulates circulatory system

Psychological healing: invites joy, contentment, hope, and harmony; helps you to see bigger picture; promotes creativity and problem-solving skills

Spiritual healing: fosters connection, kinship, and compassion with the planet and all hereon; excellent for healing animals and plants; awakens past-life memories, especially those related to magic

Rose Quartz

Formula: SiO_2 with trace minerals **Hardness:** 7
Crystal system: trigonal **Formation process:** igneous
Chakra: heart **Correspondences:** water, Venus,
Taurus, Cancer, Libra, Sagittarius

Physical healing: helpful for skin, heart, muscles, and joints; promotes healthy complexion; slows rapid pulse; improves circulation; treats conditions of reproductive organs; clears emotional patterns that collect in the physical body

Psychological healing: releases stagnant emotional patterns; invites self-love, forgiveness, compassion, and tenderness; helps you to express emotions; promotes sensitivity and empathy; helps enforce emotional boundaries; attracts love and romance; resolves grief, loneliness, emotional pain, fear, and anxiety

Spiritual healing: invites greater love, appreciation, and compassion; instills strength through service; cleanses, sorts, and releases emotional energy stored in all chakras and bodies of the aura

Note: The inclusions responsible for rose quartz's color have been hotly debated but appear to be a form of dumortierite (see p. 114).

Rose Quartz, Blue

Formula: SiO_2 with trace minerals   Hardness: 6.5–7
Crystal system: trigonal   Formation process: igneous
Chakra: sacral, heart, throat, third eye   Correspondences: water, spirit, Moon, Venus, Neptune, Cancer, Libra

Physical healing: supports healthy skin, eyes, epithelial tissue; reduces inflammation, redness, and fluid retention; regulates metabolism; soothes digestive system; improves sleep

Psychological healing: integrates heart and mind, calms overactive emotional states, soothes racing mind, reduces internal conflict, helps communicate feelings effectively

Spiritual healing: offers insight into possible karmic causes of emotional and mental patterns, calms overactive solar plexus chakra, catalyzes inner alchemy through the union of polar forces, lifts vibration of the environment, strongly stimulates psychic senses, facilitates communion with the Divine

Rose Quartz, Elestial

Formula: SiO_2 with aluminum (Al), phosphorus (P), and trace minerals
Hardness: 7   Crystal system: trigonal   Formation process: igneous
Chakra: heart, higher heart, soul star   Correspondences: earth, air, fire, water, spirit, Venus, Neptune, Virgo, Libra, Pisces

Physical healing: soothes nerves; excellent balance for brain, thymus, thyroid, gonads, and pancreas; supports bones, especially marrow

Psychological healing: master emotional healing stone; draws forth feelings of well-being, joy, and contentment; supports all processes of change and transition with divine love

Spiritual healing: encourages personal development, compassion, and love for all beings; clears and aligns the aura and chakras with the power of unconditional love

Note: Sometimes called pink quartz, rosa quartz, and crystalline rose quartz. Its structure and composition differ from regular rose quartz, although it exhibits similar properties. See also elestial quartz (p. 201).

Rose Quartz, Lavender

Formula: SiO_2 with trace minerals   Hardness: 7
Crystal system: trigonal   Formation process: igneous
Chakra: heart, higher heart, crown
Correspondences: water, spirit, Venus, Taurus, Libra, Aquarius

Physical healing: synchronizes hemispheres of brain, promotes health of nervous system, helpful for endocrine system, regulates blood sugar, assists recovery from addiction

Psychological healing: stimulates emotional insight and perception; improves communication; enables discernment of true motives, behavioral patterns, and unspoken feelings; releases heartache, grief, and trauma; lends strength to overcome abuse

Spiritual healing: instills deeper connection to higher self; cultivates compassion, empathy, humanitarianism, and unconditional love; purifies environment; aligns subtle bodies and chakras; facilitates psychic development

Rose Quartz, Star

Formula: SiO_2 with trace minerals   Hardness: 7
Crystal system: trigonal   Formation process: igneous
Chakra: heart, higher heart, crown   Correspondences: water, spirit, Venus, Jupiter, Taurus, Libra, Sagittarius

Physical healing: treats conditions of heart, blood, circulatory system, lymph, and thymus; alleviates disorders of sensory organs; promotes health of reproductive systems; alleviates gender dysphoria

Psychological healing: promotes overall emotional balance; encourages loving, positive attitude; transcends emotional pain and anguish; invites hope and optimism

Spiritual healing: instills deep compassion and universal love; promotes interdependence, harmony, peace, and planetary healing; expands psychic awareness

Ruby

Formula: corundum (Al_2O_3) with chromium (Cr)
Hardness: 9   Crystal system: trigonal
Formation process: igneous or metamorphic
Chakra: root, heart   Correspondences: fire, Sun, Leo, Cancer

Physical healing: revitalizes, tones, and strengthens body; resonates with muscles, heart, cardiovascular system, adrenals, spleen, and reproductive system; accelerates wound healing; promotes blood production; infuses body with life force; helps fight infection; reduces pain, fatigue, and lethargy

Psychological healing: invigorates mind; generates emotional strength; helps you to breathe through pain and trauma; clears stale emotions; fosters decisive action; stimulates attraction, passion, and sensuality; counteracts depression

Spiritual healing: strengthens and activates root chakra, stimulates flow of vital energy and kundalini, protects heart chakra, invites understanding of divine love, prevents stagnation in aura

Ruby, Star

Formula: corundum (Al_2O_3) with chromium (Cr) and rutile (TiO_2)
Hardness: 9   Crystal system: trigonal (ruby), tetragonal (rutile)
Formation process: igneous   Chakra: root, heart, third eye
Correspondences: fire, spirit, Sun, Cancer, Leo, Sagittarius

Physical healing: powerful ally for heart and circulatory system, mitigates stress-related illness, improves libido and fertility

Psychological healing: dissolves suppressed anger; invites hope, optimism, and overall emotional healing; excellent for assisting recovery from trauma and abuse; lessens tendencies toward self-harm or self-neglect

Spiritual healing: stone of luck, protection, and guidance; transforms pain, darkness, and chaos into light and order; taps into current of infinite abundance; points to divine love and light hidden within material world

Ruby in Fuchsite

Formula: corundum (Al_2O_3) with chromium (Cr) in fuchsite [$K(Al,Cr)_3Si_3O_{10}(OH)_2$] and kyanite ($Al_2SiO_5$) Hardness: 2.5–9 Crystal system: trigonal (ruby), monoclinic (fuchsite), triclinic (kyanite) Formation process: metamorphic Chakra: heart Correspondences: air, fire, Venus, Uranus, Aquarius

Physical healing: supports cardiac, joint, cartilage, skin, and immune health; balances metabolism; helpful for rheumatism and arthritis; improves sleep

Psychological healing: offers emotional strength, lights fire of passion and courage, supports inner strength and determination, improves common sense and problem-solving skills, helps budding relationships flourish

Spiritual healing: protects aura and heart chakra, aids communication with animal guides and spirit teachers, helps you act on intuitive and psychic information

Note: see also fuchsite (p. 125) and green kyanite (p. 161)

Ruby in Kyanite

Formula: corundum (Al_2O_3) with chromium (Cr) in kyanite (Al_2SiO_5) Hardness: 4.5–9 Crystal system: trigonal (ruby), triclinic (kyanite) Formation process: metamorphic Chakra: all, especially root, heart, third eye Correspondences: air, fire, Sun, Mercury, Gemini

Physical healing: reduces tension in neck and shoulders; supports health of gums and mouth, trachea, esophagus, and lungs; strengthens immune system; detoxifies lymph; calms nervous system

Psychological healing: facilitates communication of emotions; balances heart and mind; enables better understanding of emotions; improves emotional endurance, coping skills, and patience

Spiritual healing: aligns willpower with divine love and divine will; balances and aligns subtle bodies and anchors into the heart; integrates intuition and psychic senses with logic; improves meditation, astral travel, lucid dreaming, and manifestation

Note: see also blue kyanite (p. 161)

Ruby in Zoisite (Anyolite)

Formula: corundum (Al_2O_3) with chromium (Cr) in green zoisite [$Ca_2Al_3(SiO_4)(Si_2O_7)O(OH)$] Hardness: 6.5–9
Crystal system: trigonal (ruby), orthorhombic (zoisite)
Formation process: metamorphic Chakra: root, heart
Correspondences: earth, fire, Sun, Moon, Cancer

Physical healing: treats conditions of heart and circulatory system; regenerates, fortifies, and energizes body; excellent for overall healing; promotes fertility

Psychological healing: releases stagnant emotions; instills compassion and empathy; dissolves drama, disagreement, and discord; releases long-term emotional trauma; encourages reconciliation; promotes passion and understanding in romance

Spiritual healing: brings complementary energies into harmony, helps you to actualize your dreams, eliminates roadblocks on path to enlightenment, promotes communication with guides, releases past-life patterns, promotes joy

Note: see also zoisite (p. 265)

Rutile

Formula: TiO_2 Hardness: 6–6.5 Crystal system: tetragonal
Formation process: igneous or metamorphic Chakra: all, especially third eye Correspondences: earth, air, fire, water, spirit, Mercury, Venus, Taurus, Gemini

Physical healing: strengthens respiratory and endocrine systems; alleviates allergies, asthma, and irritation of mucous membranes; improves reproductive and sexual health; carries healing to root of disease or imbalance

Psychological healing: strengthens willpower, creativity, and charisma; improves communication; stimulates mental powers; reduces procrastination and aimlessness

Spiritual healing: strongly protects, repairs and seals aura, removes attachments and intrusions, stimulates psychic development, magnifies personal power, grounds higher energies, amplifies manifestation, catalyzes spiritual growth

Sandstone

Formula: mostly quartz (SiO_2), feldspar (variable), and calcite ($CaCO_3$) **Hardness:** variable **Crystal system:** mostly trigonal or monoclinic **Formation process:** sedimentary **Chakra:** sacral, throat **Correspondences:** earth, air, Mercury, Gemini, Libra

Physical healing: reduces water retention; improves health of bones, eyes, and circulatory system; hastens healing of open wounds; relieves tension in neck and shoulders; alleviates headaches

Psychological healing: dissolves procrastination, stubbornness, and abrasive attitude; helps in learning from the past; instills patience; eases grief; helps in recognizing subconscious patterns; boosts memory

Spiritual healing: represents death and rebirth; attunes to earth energies; facilitates meditation, divination, and spirit communication; connects to ancestral realm; reveals hidden symbols, messages, or information

Sapphire, Black

Formula: corundum (Al_2O_3) with titanium (T) **Hardness:** 9 **Crystal system:** trigonal **Formation process:** igneous **Chakra:** earth star, root, third eye **Correspondences:** earth, air, Moon, Saturn, Capricorn

Physical healing: strengthens nervous and circulatory systems and sensory organs; relieves pain and inflammation; improves function of the large intestine; alleviates ulcers, blood clots, boils, bruises; hastens healing of broken bones

Psychological healing: stabilizes the mind; comforts grief and loss; reduces shame, guilt, or blame resulting from trauma; reduces anxiety about self-image, especially related to age; releases fear of death and dying; helpful for transitions

Spiritual healing: reduces tendency to be psychically drained by work and tragedy; facilitates death and dying process and releasing of earthbound spirits; helps you stay grounded during chaotic times; strongly protects against dark forces, especially helpful for working with spirits

Sapphire, Blue

Formula: corundum (Al_2O_3) with iron (Fe)   Hardness: 9
Crystal system: trigonal   Formation process: igneous or
metamorphic   Chakra: throat   Correspondences: air, water,
Mercury, Saturn, Jupiter, Taurus, Virgo

Physical healing: supports health of nervous system and sense organs, especially
the eyes; strengthens walls of blood vessels; relieves headaches, disorders
affecting balance, parasites, neurological conditions, and chronic degenerative
conditions; supports weight loss

Psychological healing: strongly nourishes and purifies mind and mental body;
improves mental clarity, focus, fortitude, communication, and discipline;
strengthens self-control; reduces gullibility; facilitates learning and study

Spiritual healing: expands and opens mind and spirit; invites peace, hope,
equanimity, harmony, devotion, service, and altruism; cultivates wisdom,
pursuit of truth, and spiritual discipline; releases egoic attachments; improves
psychic abilities; deepens spiritual practice

Sapphire, Green

Formula: corundum (Al_2O_3) with iron (Fe)   Hardness: 9   Crystal
system: trigonal   Formation process: igneous   Chakra: heart
Correspondences: earth, Moon, Saturn, Gemini, Leo

Physical healing: improves health of eyes, endocrine system, and nervous system;
strengthens vision; promotes cellular regeneration; balances overactive
metabolism and high blood pressure

Psychological healing: calms emotional and mental unrest; promotes empathy,
loyalty, trust, and connection; helps in seeing things from another's
perspective; reduces bias, prejudice, and contrarianism; strengthens resolve,
motivation, and willingness to greet life each day

Spiritual healing: increases synchronicities; attracts luck, healing, and good
fortune; enhances inner vision; promotes harmony and understanding among
groups of different backgrounds; attunes to earth energies

Sapphire, Padparadscha

Formula: corundum (Al_2O_3) with iron (Fe) and chromium (Cr)
Hardness: 9   Crystal system: trigonal
Formation process: igneous   Chakra: sacral, heart
Correspondences: fire, Sun, Taurus

Physical healing: beneficial for skin and reproductive system, increases sex drive, boosts fertility, energizes body, prevents burnout

Psychological healing: supports all forms of learning and scholarly endeavors; boosts the mind; attracts inspiration, enthusiasm, and creativity; facilitates expression and communication; removes bias; eliminates shame or guilt surrounding pleasure and sexuality

Spiritual healing: removes obstacles; symbolizes wisdom, abundance, and wealth; teaches surrender, bliss, and deep communion with the universe; improves manifestation

Sapphire, Pink

Formula: corundum (Al_2O_3) with chromium (Cr)   Hardness: 9
Crystal system: trigonal   Formation process: igneous
Chakra: heart   Correspondences: water, Venus, Taurus, Libra

Physical healing: promotes health of nervous and circulatory systems; has a warming effect; reduces pain, tightness, and congestion in chest and lungs; strengthens heart; promotes longevity

Psychological healing: powerful emotional healer; awakens emotional intelligence; brings comfort, resilience, and emotional strength; dissolves grief, pain, worry, loneliness, wanderlust, fear, and disconnection; improves communication and relationships; strengthens emotional boundaries

Spiritual healing: accesses divine, unconditional love; cultivates feelings of connection, harmony, and unity among all beings; helps you attain your life's purpose; magnifies perception of love; instills devotion, altruism, and service

Sapphire, Star

Formula: corundum (Al_2O_3) with rutile (TiO_2)   **Hardness:** 9
Crystal system: trigonal   **Formation process:** igneous
Chakra: throat, third eye, crown   **Correspondences:** air, water, spirit, Moon, Jupiter, Saturn, Sagittarius, Capricorn

Physical healing: strengthens nerves, intestines, brain, and sensory organs; promotes health of bone marrow; purifies blood; assuages nausea

Psychological healing: invites mental and emotional strength; imparts dignity, integrity, responsibility, and honor; stabilizes and organizes mind; enhances communication; reduces feelings of inadequacy, imposter syndrome, and fear of failure

Spiritual healing: helps in navigating life and finding purpose; symbolizes hope, faith, and destiny; helps you attain success through service; protects; confers sovereignty, autonomy, and spiritual strength; connects to heavenly realms

Sapphire, White

Formula: corundum (Al_2O_3)   **Hardness:** 9
Crystal system: trigonal   **Formation process:** igneous
Chakra: third eye, crown, causal   **Correspondences:** air, spirit, Sun, Jupiter, Aries, Sagittarius

Physical healing: stimulates body's natural healing processes; regulates brain, endocrine system, pituitary gland, pineal gland, and nerves; eases dying process

Psychological healing: brings clarity, focus, common sense, and courage to the mind; clears confusion; helps you be a better self-nurturer; minimizes self-criticism, judgment, and blame

Spiritual healing: strengthens inner vision, psychic abilities, and spiritual power; excellent ally for channeling, mediumship, and astral travel; assists past-life regression; imparts discernment, especially regarding spiritual teachings, gurus, and leaders

Sapphire, Yellow

Formula: corundum (Al_2O_3) with iron (Fe)   **Hardness:** 9
Crystal system: trigonal   **Formation process:** igneous
Chakra: solar plexus   **Correspondences:** fire, Sun, Jupiter, Leo, Sagittarius

Physical healing: improves all processes of cleansing and elimination; supports health of skin, lungs, liver, kidneys, bladder, and other organs of elimination; heals digestive system; excellent for cooling sunburn; protects against harmful electromagnetic fields; shields DNA from radiation damage

Psychological healing: improves confidence, optimism, and self-esteem; alleviates depression, anxiety, resentment, grief, and loneliness; boosts intellect, perception, mental acuity, and understanding

Spiritual healing: symbolizes wealth and good fortune; removes obstacles; helps you adapt to shifts in energy from earth, sun, and stars; transforms aura into beacon of light, hope, and positive change for family, community, and planet

Sardonyx

Formula: SiO_2 **Hardness:** 6.5   **Crystal system:** trigonal
Formation process: igneous or sedimentary   **Chakra:** root, sacral
Correspondences: earth, Mars, Saturn, Aries, Virgo, Capricorn

Physical healing: improves conditions of sensory organs, especially ears; strengthens circulatory and nervous systems; alleviates disorders of spine, bladder, kidneys, and prostate; helps body fight viral infections and parasites

Psychological healing: mitigates anger and softens temper, strengthens perception, helps balance cycles of work and rest, reduces feelings of martyrdom and hesitation, helps you stand in your power and enforce boundaries, improves friendships and romantic relationships, sparks decisive action

Spiritual healing: symbolizes justice and victory; cultivates virtue, discipline, and commitment; protects and balances energies; attracts luck in legal matters

Note: Sardonyx may also exhibit properties of black onyx (p. 78) and carnelian (p. 88).

Scapolite

Formula: varies from marialite ($Na_4Al_3Si_9O_{24}Cl$) to meionite ($Ca_4Al_6Si_6O_{24}CO_3$) **Hardness:** 5–6 **Crystal system:** tetragonal
Formation process: igneous or metamorphic
Chakra: third eye **Correspondences:** Mercury, Virgo

Physical healing: beneficial for eyes and vision; supports urinary tract; alleviates tension in shoulders, neck, and upper back; promotes alignment and health of skeletal system; restores flexibility and movement after injury, illness, or surgery

Psychological healing: bolsters intellect, analysis, and willpower; encourages self-reflection, independence, and dedication; releases obsession, denial, fear, and bad habits; helps you to make positive change; supports overcoming self-sabotage; invites inspiration and drive to overcome writer's block

Spiritual healing: helps you pursue freedom, happiness, and spiritual growth; engages your skills to fulfill life's purpose; encourages patience and presence on spiritual path; helps you see bigger picture

Scheelite

Formula: $CaWO_4$ **Hardness:** 4.5–5 **Crystal system:** tetragonal
Formation process: igneous or metamorphic **Chakra:** third eye
Correspondences: earth, air, Uranus, Libra, Aquarius

Physical healing: powerfully heals the brain, nervous system, lymph, lungs, and muscles; improves coordination, fine motor control, and stamina; reduces exhaustion

Psychological healing: encourages recognition of your own needs; dissolves uncertainty and indecision; reveals hidden trauma, abuse, and issues related to conflict and survival; breaks cycles of negative thinking and victimhood

Spiritual healing: helps in accessing inner power and light; encourages higher self-connection; reduces tendency to hold on to others' energy or experiences; erases past-life patterns having a negative impact on present life; improves moral compass

Schist

Formula: variable, typically rich in mica   Hardness: variable
Crystal system: variable   Formation process: metamorphic
Chakra: root, sacral, third eye   Correspondences: earth, air,
Mercury, Gemini, Virgo, Aquarius

Physical healing: improves flexibility; promotes health of nervous system, liver, and adrenals; supports digestive health; balances fluid levels and hastens recovery from dehydration; soothes skin

Psychological healing: imparts mental flexibility; frees trapped, rigid, or stubborn emotions; reduces anger, drama, and tendency to blame others; excellent ally for negotiation, persuasion, and sales; strengthens willpower

Spiritual healing: symbolizes change and new beginnings, strongly shields and protects against negative forces, supports inner and outer processes of transformation, gently increases intuition

Scolecite

Formula: $CaAl_2Si_3O_{10} \cdot 3H_2O$ Hardness: 5–5.5
Crystal system: monoclinic   Formation process: igneous
or sedimentary   Chakra: third eye, crown
Correspondences: air, Saturn, Capricorn

Physical healing: supports skeletal, nervous, and respiratory systems; promotes alignment of spine; helps body expel parasites; excellent sleep aid; improves kidney function; quells overactive libido

Psychological healing: promotes cooperation, harmony, and sense of belonging; improves problem-solving and critical thinking skills; stabilizes mood; encourages relaxation and peace

Spiritual healing: cleanses and opens upper chakras, particularly crown and third eye; stimulates psychic senses; opens mind to higher consciousness; facilitates contact with higher self, angels, spirits, and extraterrestrial intelligences; supports healing the planet

Selenite (Gypsum)

Formula: $CaSO_4 \cdot 2(H_2O)$ Hardness: 2 Crystal system: monoclinic Formation process: sedimentary Chakra: crown, soul star Correspondences: water, air, Moon, Cancer

Physical healing: supports health and alignment of spine, nervous system, and skin; regulates and balances body fluids; hastens recovery after injury or illness of spine and nerves

Psychological healing: initiates emotional release and balance, clarifies confusing emotions, draws light to subconscious, improves judgment, encourages insight

Spiritual healing: opens and activates crown chakra, aligns it with higher chakras; facilitates contact with higher self; taps into inner guidance; clears the aura; enhances meditation; catalyzes psychic development; protects and cleanses home or sacred space

Selenite, Angelwing (Fishtail Selenite)

Formula: $CaSO_4 \cdot 2(H_2O)$ Hardness: 2 Crystal system: monoclinic Formation process: sedimentary Chakra: crown, soul star Correspondences: air, water, Moon, Neptune, Cancer, Pisces

Physical healing: fortifies brain and nervous and skeletal systems; reduces pain, inflammation, and tension; prevents and repairs damage to DNA

Psychological healing: releases insecurity and uncertainty, fills each day with clarity and meaning, instills sense of connection with others to improve all relationships, calms and stabilizes emotions, dissipates tensions and misunderstandings

Spiritual healing: facilitates angelic communication and angelic magic; combs debris from aura; enhances astral travel, contact with spirits, lucid dreaming, and communion with higher self; encourages soul-level healing

Selenite, Desert Rose

Formula: $CaSO_4 \cdot 2(H_2O)$ with sand inclusions   **Hardness:** 2
Crystal system: monoclinic   **Formation process:** sedimentary   **Chakra:** earth star, solar plexus, heart, crown   **Correspondences:** earth, water, Moon, Venus, Taurus, Cancer, Virgo

Physical healing: gently detoxifies body, promotes fertility, relieves fatigue and inflammation, promotes health of connective tissues

Psychological healing: inspires playful, joyful, and loving attitude; deepens appreciation for life; attracts love; helps in seeing the mundane world as inherently magical and whimsical; boosts mental healing; releases old belief patterns and replaces with healthy ones

Spiritual healing: gently grounds; links to the energy of the earth and nature; protects home and land; stimulates plant growth; aids communication with plant spirits, devas, and fairies; supports planetary healing; fosters unconditional love, compassion, and grace

Selenite, Golden

Formula: $CaSO_4 \cdot 2(H_2O)$ with iron (Fe)
Hardness: 2   **Crystal system:** monoclinic
Formation process: sedimentary
Chakra: solar plexus, crown, soul star
Correspondences: air, fire, spirit, Sun, Moon, Cancer, Leo

Physical healing: promotes overall healing and well-being; beneficial for hair, skin, and nails; alleviates conditions of urinary tract; reduces seasonal affective disorder and fatigue

Psychological healing: clarifies the mind; counteracts doubt, confusion, indecision; reduces critical and judgmental attitudes; boosts willpower

Spiritual healing: balances masculine and feminine energies; helps you remain objective and detached when faced with trauma, transition, or pain; supports choosing growth over all other outcomes; aligns personal will with divine will

Selenite, Green

Formula: $CaSO_4 \cdot (2H_2O)$ with copper (Cu), iron (Fe), or chromium (Cr) Hardness: 2 Crystal system: monoclinic
Formation process: sedimentary Chakra: heart, higher heart, crown Correspondences: air, Moon, Venus, Taurus, Gemini, Cancer, Libra

Physical healing: strengthens bones; promotes skin elasticity; improves cardiac health and immune response; helps eliminate toxins, parasites, and free radicals; promotes lactation

Psychological healing: improves self-esteem, insight, and empathy; reduces overly critical nature; dissolves feelings of loneliness, homesickness, and disappointment; promotes forgiveness, reconciliation, and emotional honesty; reduces jealousy; helps you stand up for your beliefs

Spiritual healing: counteracts toxic positivity and spiritual bypassing; instills harmony, connection, and unity among groups of people; draws out feeling of responsibility for the planet; enjoins divine love and divine will

Selenite, Hourglass

Formula: $CaSO_4 \cdot 2(H_2O)$ with sand inclusions
Hardness: 2 Crystal system: monoclinic
Formation process: sedimentary Chakra: sacral, crown, causal Correspondences: air, Moon, Saturn, Cancer, Uranus

Physical healing: helpful for narrowing or stricture of blood vessels and alimentary canal; clears blockages, calcification, and fatty deposits; helps reset and balance rhythm and timing of body's systems

Psychological healing: promotes sense of being safe and nurtured, mitigates tendency to rush and/or procrastinate, fosters greater trust in self and others

Spiritual healing: nourishes spirit, fosters inner peace, encourages better awareness of present moment, awakens memory of innate perfection, helps in shedding karmic baggage to return to state of perfection, assists past-life recall

Selenite, Peach

Formula: $CaSO_4 \cdot 2(H_2O)$ with hematite (Fe_2O_3) and clay inclusions   Hardness: 2   Crystal system: monoclinic
Formation process: sedimentary   Chakra: sacral, crown
Correspondences: water, earth, Moon, Taurus, Virgo

Physical healing: supports skin, hair, and nails; reduces menstrual pain; relieves imbalances of reproductive system; helps body break down and expel stones, calcifications, and other growths; improves appetite

Psychological healing: promotes gentle, playful attitude; furthers enjoyment of simple pleasures; gently transforms emotional makeup; dissolves patterns of abandonment, rejection, and betrayal; fosters forgiveness and acceptance; improves self-image

Spiritual healing: inspires awe, spontaneity, and unconditional love; enables spirit communication; gently stirs past-life memories

Selenite, Phantom

Formula: $CaSO_4 \cdot 2(H_2O)$ with mineral inclusions
Hardness: 2   Crystal system: monoclinic
Formation process: sedimentary   Chakra: crown, soul star
Correspondences: air, Moon, Saturn, Taurus, Cancer, Capricorn

Physical healing: ameliorates childhood disorders and hereditary conditions; improves health of skeleton, joints, and teeth; supports health of ears and strengthens hearing; restores balance and radiant health to body, mind, and soul

Psychological healing: brings light to subconscious; breaks down and clears harmful emotional and mental patterns; supports shadow work, regression therapy, and counseling to achieve psychological balance

Spiritual healing: excellent ally for past-life recall, cord-cutting, and shamanic journeys; transmutes karmic patterns and past-life energies; releases any and all energies that inhibit the soul's most perfect expression

Selenite, Satin Spar

Formula: $CaSO_4 \cdot 2H_2O$ Hardness: 2
Crystal system: monoclinic
Formation process: sedimentary   Chakra: crown, soul star
Correspondences: air, water, Moon, Cancer, Pisces

Physical healing: supports healthy bones, teeth, nails, skin, and hair; balances body's fluids; brings light to physical body to release tension and pain

Psychological healing: improves clarity, focus, and perception; strengthens reasoning skills; reduces fear, obsession, irritation, and anxiety; improves connection and communication

Spiritual healing: cleanses and aligns aura and chakras; helps you to relinquish control and practice surrender; facilitates psychic development, meditation, and channeling; engenders group harmony; clears and protects home

Septarian Nodule

Formula: calcite and aragonite (both $CaCO_3$) in clay or ironstone matrix   Hardness: 3   Crystal system: trigonal (calcite), orthorhombic (aragonite)   Formation process: sedimentary   Chakra: root, sacral, solar plexus, heart   Correspondences: earth, air, fire, water, spirit, Uranus, Taurus, Sagittarius, Aquarius

Physical healing: promotes healthy skin; reduces scar tissue; balances pH; supports digestive and elimination systems; may reduce tumors, growths, and cysts

Psychological healing: improves confidence, self-esteem, and focus; transforms trauma and painful memories; bolsters emotional strength; boosts communication and charisma; helps reprogram the mind for positive change

Spiritual healing: distills wisdom, sensitivity, empathy, and power from experiences; enables perception of higher truth; helps hold space for self and others during transformational experiences; promotes overall healing of body, mind, and spirit; helpful ally for clearing ancestral patterns

Note: also carries general properties of aragonite (p. 65) and calcite (p. 81)

Seraphinite (Clinochlore)

Formula: $(Mg,Fe^{2+})_5Al_2Si_3O_{10}(OH)_8$ **Hardness:** 2–2.5
Crystal system: monoclinic **Formation process:** metamorphic
Chakra: all, especially heart, crown **Correspondences:** earth, air, fire, water, spirit, Mercury

Physical healing: promotes overall healing; corrects systemic imbalances; stimulates cellular regeneration; supports immune health; relieves allergies, sinus pressure, congestion, stiffness, and tension; regulates growth of cancerous cells (as an adjunct to medical treatment) and assists in recovery from radiation therapy and chemotherapy

Psychological healing: brings balance to mind and emotions; dissolves obsession, betrayal, and pain of a broken heart

Spiritual healing: strengthens and purifies aura and chakras; facilitates contact with higher realms, angels, guides, and devas; helps integrate rapid spiritual change; builds order amid chaos; supports planetary healing

Serpentine

Formula: $(Mg,Fe)_3Si_2O_5(OH)_4$ **Hardness:** 2–5
Crystal system: monoclinic **Formation process:** metamorphic
Chakra: root **Correspondences:** earth, fire, Mercury, Saturn, Gemini, Libra, Scorpio, Capricorn

Physical healing: mobilizes and strengthens immune system; promotes healthy digestion and elimination; regulates mineral absorption; treats infection, parasite, candidiasis, and venomous stings; decreases rigidity, inflammation, pain, and cramping; promotes regeneration

Psychological healing: brings clarity and inspiration, encourages compromise and creative problem-solving skills, stabilizes mood swings

Spiritual healing: offers grounding and protection to support transformation; awakens ancient wisdom; attunes to natural world; breaks up stagnant energy; opens chakras, awakens flow of kundalini energy; provides insight into karmic and ancestral patterns; initiates past-life recall; helps access Akashic records

Serpentine with Stichtite

Formula: serpentine [$(Mg,Fe)_3Si_2O_5(OH)_4$] with stichtite [$Mg_6Cr_2CO_3(OH)_{16} \cdot 4H_2O$]   Hardness: 2–5   Crystal system: monoclinic   Formation process: metamorphic
Chakra: all, especially heart and crown
Correspondences: earth, air, Saturn, Virgo, Libra

Physical healing: alleviates pain, cramps, and tension; eases disorders of liver, gallbladder, stomach, and intestines; supports health of kidneys and urinary tract; reduces fatigue; heals at cellular level

Psychological healing: helps in overcoming bad habits, such as nail-biting and teeth-grinding; quiets anxiety, worry, and stress; calms overactive mind and racing thoughts; clarifies and directs willpower toward constructive tasks

Spiritual healing: powerful healer for the land; imbues heart and soul with forgiveness, unconditional love, and illumination; helps ameliorate karma, especially from Atlantis; facilitates past-life recall

Note: see also serpentine (p. 232) and stichtite (p. 243)

Shattuckite

Formula: $Cu_5(SiO_3)_4(OH)_2$ Hardness: 3.5   Crystal system: orthorhombic   Formation process: sedimentary
Chakra: heart, higher heart, throat, third eye
Correspondences: water, air, Venus, Neptune, Uranus, Libra, Aquarius, Pisces

Physical healing: soothes sore throat, inflamed tonsils, and congestion of respiratory system; promotes cardiac health; treats hereditary and genetic illnesses

Psychological healing: enhances perception and communication; breaks through fear, inadequacy, low self-worth; calms emotions; fosters learning, artistic expression, and effective use of speech and language

Spiritual healing: boosts imagination and intuition; enables channeling and spirit communication; makes dreams more vivid and easier to recall; promotes heart-centered spiritual practice; helps you pursue and embody truth

Shiva Lingam

Formula: mostly quartz (SiO_2)   **Hardness:** 6.5–7
Crystal system: mostly trigonal   **Formation process:** sedimentary
Chakra: earth star, root, sacral   **Correspondences:** earth, water, Jupiter, Scorpio, Sagittarius, Aquarius

Physical healing: regulates body fluids; improves sexual health; promotes fertility; reduces pain; strengthens and balances lungs, uterus, and prostate; accelerates healing processes

Psychological healing: ignites creativity and motivation; releases past relationships, childhood trauma, and recurring mistakes; awakens self-respect and compassion; improves self-esteem and body image

Spiritual healing: excellent catalyst for earth-healing, stimulates movement of kundalini energy, balances inner feminine and masculine energies, grounds and anchors the spirit, symbolizes attainment of wisdom, creates atmosphere of sacred space, aligns the self between heaven and earth

Shungite

Formula: mostly elemental carbon (C)   **Hardness:** 3.5
Crystal system: amorphous   **Formation process:** metamorphic
Chakra: earth star, root   **Correspondences:** earth, spirit, Pluto, Scorpio

Physical healing: excellent support for overall healing; particularly helpful for skin, metabolism, digestion, and elimination system; reduces pain and inflammation; protects against harmful environmental energies, including electromagnetic fields; enlivens electrical processes of body

Psychological healing: filters out disharmonious mental and emotional patterns; draws out overactive emotions and thoughts, including fear, worry, and panic; conquers feelings of loss, inadequacy, and failure; encourages better planning

Spiritual healing: offers continuous, dynamic grounding; facilitates manifestation; initiates soul-level healing of the spiritual blueprint; catalyzes purification and spiritual evolution; strongly protects; helps you fulfill your purpose

Siderite

Formula: $FeCO_3$ Hardness: 3.5–4.5
Crystal system: igneous or sedimentary
Formation process: sedimentary Chakra: root
Correspondences: earth, Mars, Aries, Sagittarius, Aquarius

Physical healing: strengthens heart, circulatory system, and lymph nodes; counteracts anemia, low bone density, and poor mineral absorption; improves chronic conditions of digestive system, especially the large intestine; reduces pain, especially in feet and ankles

Psychological healing: stone of assertiveness; lends courage, strength, and stamina; lifts mood and brightens outlook; assuages weakness, shyness, and fear; dispels restlessness, melancholy, and despondency; fosters patience, calm, and levelheadedness

Spiritual healing: grounds and protects; encourages resolve, commitment, and perseverance on spiritual path; supports manifestation; facilitates communication with animals and animal spirits

Silver

Formula: Ag Hardness: 2.5–3 Crystal system: cubic
Formation process: igneous or metamorphic
Chakra: third eye Correspondences: water, Moon, Cancer

Physical healing: regulates fluids; improves health of eyes, stomach, and reproductive system; exerts cooling effect on body; improves assimilation of nutrients; initiates cleansing and purification

Psychological healing: cools temper; strengthens empathy and emotional expression; attunes to subconscious mind; enhances perception, communication; reduces conflict, judgment, and impatience

Spiritual healing: connects to lunar energies, the Divine Feminine, and all currents of magic and mystery; enhances psychic ability, vivid dreaming, and discernment of truth; facilitates astral travel

Slate

Formula: variable   Hardness: 2.5–4
Crystal system: variable   Formation process: metamorphic
Chakra: third eye   Correspondences: earth, Mercury,
Scorpio

Physical healing: facilitates overall healing; promotes healthy skin, nails, and teeth

Psychological healing: facilitates learning; boosts capacity for language, translation, and math; invites pragmatism; prevents emotional overwhelm; helps you change bad or harmful habits

Spiritual healing: taps into ancient wisdom; clears stagnant energy from the aura; facilitates manifestation, psychic development, and magic; offers protection, especially against others' emotions; aids past-life recall and soul-retrieval

Smithsonite, Blue

Formula: $ZnCO_3$ with copper (Cu) and/or cobalt (Co)
Hardness: 5   Crystal system: trigonal   Formation
process: sedimentary   Chakra: sacral, heart, higher heart
Correspondences: water, Moon, Neptune, Cancer, Virgo,
Pisces

Physical healing: regulates endocrine system and hormonal balance; supports healthy metabolism; encourages healthy weight loss; promotes fertility, healthy skin, and wound healing

Psychological healing: soothes stress, grief, heartache, and worry; mitigates shyness and awkwardness; boosts mental clarity and focus; helps in overcoming trauma of abuse; inspires acceptance and expression of gender identity and sexual orientation; invites passion, sexuality, and authentic connection

Spiritual healing: shifts awareness from ego-based love to unconditional love, nourishes inner child, facilitates contact with angelic realm, balances inner masculine forces

Smithsonite, Green

Formula: $ZnCO_3$ with copper (Cu)   Hardness: 5
Crystal system: trigonal   Formation process: sedimentary
Chakra: sacral, heart   Correspondences: water, earth, Venus, Taurus, Sagittarius

Physical healing: improves health of immune system and heart; excellent for sinuses, blood vessels, and digestive system; helps overcome addiction and harmful behaviors

Psychological healing: builds confidence and reduces inhibitions; promotes communication from the heart; helps you act on emotions in healthy ways; excellent balm for grief, anger, bitterness, and heartbreak; encourages kindness

Spiritual healing: facilitates communication with nature spirits and devas, gently stimulates psychic senses, symbolizes new beginnings

Smithsonite, Pink

Formula: $ZnCO_3$ with manganese (Mn) or cobalt (Co)
Hardness: 5   Crystal system: trigonal   Formation process: sedimentary   Chakra: sacral, heart, higher heart
Correspondences: water, Mercury, Venus, Virgo, Libra, Pisces

Physical healing: promotes health of pancreas, heart, and reproductive system; strengthens immune system; soothes conditions of the skin; hastens wound healing; alleviates exhaustion and quells overstimulated nerves; aids recovery from addiction

Psychological healing: promotes forgiveness, trust, and reconciliation; softens unnecessary emotional boundaries; invites emotional mastery; inspires acceptance and expression of gender identity and sexual orientation; heals inner child

Spiritual healing: awakens peace and clarity for personal transformation, helps channel unconditional love, connects to Divine Feminine, balances inner feminine forces

Smithsonite, Purple

Formula: $ZnCO_3$ with manganese (Mn) or cobalt (Co)   Hardness: 5
Crystal system: trigonal   Formation process: sedimentary
Chakra: sacral, heart, third eye   Correspondences: water, spirit,
Jupiter, Neptune, Virgo, Sagittarius, Pisces

Physical healing: improves health of brain and nervous system, alleviates pain

Psychological healing: reduces anxiety and worry; invites diplomacy, tact, and
leadership skills; inspires acceptance and expression of gender identity and
sexual orientation

Spiritual healing: improves psychic senses; encourages past-life recall; balances
inner masculine and feminine forces; gently cleanses aura and chakras of
blocked, stagnant energy

Smithsonite, Yellow

Formula: $ZnCO_3$ with cadmium (Cd)   Hardness: 5
Crystal system: trigonal   Formation
process: sedimentary   Chakra: sacral, solar plexus
Correspondences: water, air, Mercury, Gemini, Virgo

Physical healing: releases illness rooted in psychological imbalance, improves
health of nervous system, alleviates conditions of the inner ear and supports
hearing

Psychological healing: inspires quick wit and sharp mind; releases fear of own
power; clears imprints left by abuse, neglect, anxiety, and trauma; reduces
hesitation and indecision; sparks decisive action and rational thinking; brings
joy and levity

Spiritual healing: taps into ancestral and past-life memories to reclaim lost
wisdom; enhances shamanic journeys, astral travel, and lucid dreaming;
amplifies effects of sound healing, drumming, and ecstatic dance

Smoky Quartz

Formula: SiO_2 with aluminum (Al), lithium (Li), or sodium (Na)
Hardness: 7   Crystal system: trigonal   Formation process: igneous
Chakra: earth star, root   Correspondences: earth, Saturn, Capricorn

Physical healing: promotes overall healing; improves sleep; reduces pain, inflammation, and high blood pressure; helps heal sunburns, asthma, and reproductive health challenges; protects against harmful radiation

Psychological healing: boosts focus, clarity, and intellect; combats stress, spaciness, and lack of follow-through; imparts diplomacy; provides empowerment, grounding, and sense of control

Spiritual healing: excellent for transition, consolidates energy and resources, strengthens and protects aura and chakras, removes unwanted and harmful energies, anchors higher consciousness to material plane, improves manifestation

Sodalite

Formula: $Na_8Al_8Si_6O_{24}Cl_2$ Hardness: 5.5–6   Crystal system: cubic
Formation process: igneous or metamorphic   Chakra: throat, third eye   Correspondences: air, Saturn, Capricorn, Aquarius

Physical healing: promotes health of skeletal, lymphatic, and immune systems; regulates bodily fluids; treats conditions of throat, larynx, bones, ligaments, and cartilage; alleviates insomnia, sluggishness, and depression

Psychological healing: purifies the mind and mental body, encourages expression of bottled-up emotions, sweeps away confusion, helps you access subconscious, initiates pursuit and understanding of personal truth, helps you freely express personality and stand up for beliefs and values, clarifies goals, enhances perception

Spiritual healing: strengthens intuition and psychic development; enhances meditation; promotes idealism, nonattachment, being nonjudgmental; supports inner peace; roots the consciousness in the present moment

Sphalerite

Formula: ZnS **Hardness:** 3.5–4 **Crystal system:** cubic
Formation process: igneous or sedimentary **Chakra:** root, sacral,
solar plexus **Correspondences:** earth, fire, Gemini, Sagittarius

Physical healing: calms nervous system and balances endocrine system; reduces
sensitivity to allergens and environmental toxins; increases physical strength,
stamina, and vital energy; supports recovery from addiction

Psychological healing: sharpens discernment and critical thinking skills; mitigates
effects of disinformation, propaganda, and gaslighting; fortifies recovery from
cults and religious abuse; fosters sense of belonging and support; facilitates
change in career

Spiritual healing: excellent grounding stone; facilitates shifts in consciousness for
trance work, astral travel, and deep meditation; releases earthbound spirits;
prevents psychic burnout and spiritual fatigue; helps assimilate high-vibration
energy

Spinel, Black

Formula: $MgAl_2O_4$ with iron (Fe) **Hardness:** 7.5–8 **Crystal
system:** cubic **Formation process:** metamorphic **Chakra:** earth
star **Correspondences:** earth, Saturn, Taurus, Capricorn

Physical healing: soothes and stimulates digestive and elimination systems;
improves physical strength and endurance; strengthens muscle, bone,
ligaments, cartilage, and tendons; gently detoxifies

Psychological healing: improves discipline and mental focus; purges emotional
baggage; alleviates materialism and tendency to hoard; replaces shame
with healthy sense of modesty; strengthens motivation, follow-through, and
willpower

Spiritual healing: strongly protects, grounds, and stabilizes; dissolves past-life
and karmic patterns; helps to focus during chaotic or fast-paced periods of
transformation; helps in maintaining commitment to spiritual practice

Spinel, Blue

Formula: $MgAl_2O_4$ with cobalt (Co) and/or manganese (Mn)
Hardness: 7.5–8   Crystal system: cubic
Formation process: igneous or metamorphic   Chakra: throat
Correspondences: air, Jupiter, Gemini, Sagittarius

Physical healing: promotes healthy nervous and respiratory systems; strengthens kidneys and bladder; balances acidic states; treats fever, inflammation, burns, bruises, itchiness, and hair loss; cooling for allergies; calms overactive libido

Psychological healing: enhances mental endurance, discernment, perception, and problem-solving skills; offers focus, clarity, and improved memory; eliminates procrastination; imbues relationships with trust, commitment, and enthusiasm; reduces anger; boosts communication

Spiritual healing: boosts inner vision, psychic abilities, and clairvoyance; enlivens imagination and dream states; promotes tolerance and acceptance

Spinel, Red

Formula: $MgAl_2O_4$ with iron (Fe), chromium (Cr)   Hardness: 7.5–8
Crystal system: cubic   Formation process: igneous or metamorphic   Chakra: earth star, root, solar plexus, heart
Correspondences: fire, water, Sun, Mars, Aries, Leo

Physical healing: invigorates, tones, and regenerates entire body; strengthens homeostatic mechanisms; supports functions related to rhythm and timing, including circulatory and digestive systems; strengthens muscle tissue; relieves tingling, numbness, and paralysis in extremities

Psychological healing: facilitates deep emotional release; purges fear, pain, depression, and anger; helps regulate emotions so they are not overwhelming; elicits positive memories for balance and comfort; boosts confidence; helps exercise healthy boundaries

Spiritual healing: invites optimism and compassion; steers toward true happiness and fulfillment; reveals hope in the midst of uncertainty; cultivates balance and stability; promotes tolerance and acceptance; heals conflict and oppression

Staurolite

Formula: $Fe^{2+}_2Al_9O_6(SiO_4)_4(O,OH)_2$ Hardness: 7–7.5

Crystal system: monoclinic   Formation process: metamorphic

Chakra: earth star, root, heart, third eye

Correspondences: earth, Mercury, Gemini, Pisces

Physical healing: excellent for overall health and well-being; fights infection; strengthens bone, muscle, and blood; supports detoxification, regeneration, and creating healthy habits to promote a stronger body

Psychological healing: inspires connection, solidarity, and mutual support; dissolves rigid beliefs; initiates exploration and transformation of self-identity; overcomes feelings of isolation; inspires respect and support for all people; lifts depression

Spiritual healing: traditionally associated with luck, magic, and fairies; protects and grounds; connects to nature and the elements; promotes harmony, cooperation, and intersectional support at the community level

Steatite (Soapstone)

Formula: mostly talc [$Mg_3Si_4O_{10}(OH)_2$]

Hardness: 1–2   Crystal system: mostly monoclinic

Formation process: metamorphic   Chakra: third eye

Correspondences: air, fire, Jupiter, Sagittarius

Physical healing: promotes health of heart, gallbladder, liver, and skin; promotes healthy skeleton, tendons, hair, and nails; soothes upset stomach; alleviates fatigue and insomnia

Psychological healing: soothing and calming; opens the mind to new ideas and behaviors; softens rigid beliefs; alleviates defensive, argumentative, and resentful responses; invites friendly attitude; reduces fear of unknown; boosts confidence after setback

Spiritual healing: boosts psychic ability, especially telepathy; symbolizes rebirth and renewal; facilitates contact with guides and ancestors; connects to spirits of the land; balances yin and yang energies

Stibnite

Formula: Sb_2S_3 Hardness: 2 Crystal system: orthorhombic
Formation process: igneous Chakra: all, especially third eye
Correspondences: earth, Saturn, Pluto, Scorpio, Capricorn

Physical healing: infuses body with vital energy, reduces exhaustion from overwork, helps to alleviate conditions of esophagus and stomach, helps fight infection, detoxifies and purifies body

Psychological healing: liberates mind from fear and doubt, instills courage, helps you reclaim willpower and sovereignty, protects against codependent and vampiric relationships, facilitates emotional release and purification

Spiritual healing: grounds; enhances meditation, astral travel, and spirit communication; provides protection, especially against harmful spirits; removes spirit attachments, cords, and energy implants; integrates higher consciousness into everyday world; facilitates manifestation and transformation; supports spiritual evolution

Note: Stibnite is toxic if mishandled. Wash hands thoroughly after use.

Stichtite

Formula: $Mg_6Cr_2CO_3(OH)_{16}\cdot4H_2O$ Hardness: 1.5–2
Crystal system: trigonal Formation process: metamorphic
Chakra: heart, third eye Correspondences: air, Uranus, Aquarius

Physical healing: alleviates pain, headache, and tension, especially in the jaw; promotes health of brain and nervous system, heart, and pericardium; regulates blood pressure and endocrine system; may curb unhealthy food cravings

Psychological healing: calms stress, worry, and fear; encourages decisiveness and follow-through; assuages loneliness, heartache, and disappointment; inspires harmony, forgiveness, cooperation, and kindness; promotes resilience

Spiritual healing: helps complete karmic cycles, contracts, and soul vows, thereby permanently releasing you from them; expands consciousness; taps into unconditional love; helps with contacting guides

Stilbite

Formula: $NaCa_4(Si_{27}Al_9)O_{72} \cdot 28(H_2O)$ **Hardness:** 3.5–4
Crystal system: monoclinic   **Formation process:** igneous, sedimentary, or metamorphic   **Chakra:** solar plexus, heart, crown   **Correspondences:** water, Moon, Cancer

Physical healing: supports health of intestines, nervous system, and kidneys; balances hemispheres of brain; improves cellular metabolism; detoxifies; treats conditions of sensory organs; soothes sore throat

Psychological healing: exudes calming, gentle energy; promotes self-inquiry; reveals root of fear, anxiety, guilt, and unrest; releases bottled-up emotions; sweeps away confusion; facilitates emotional understanding and expression

Spiritual healing: invites forgiveness and compassion; dispels illusion and delusion; navigates toward authenticity, truth, and integrity; wards off separation and isolation; encourages embracing vulnerability; helps you to follow dreams; facilitates detachment from pain and suffering

Stromatolite

Formula: mostly silica (SiO_2) **Hardness:** 6.5   **Crystal system:** mostly trigonal   **Formation process:** sedimentary **Chakra:** crown, brow   **Correspondences:** earth, water, spirit, Jupiter, Sagittarius

Physical healing: treats conditions of lungs, sinuses, mucous membranes, and large intestine; balances microbiomes of the body; may balance cholesterol; helps eliminate toxins; supports health of brain, thymus, and skeletal system

Psychological healing: releases fear, envy, and superiority; imparts clarity and objectivity about past events, making them learning experiences; removes deeply held beliefs and programming; reduces need to conform to others' expectations

Spiritual healing: powerful earth-healing stone; taps into ancient wisdom, genetic memories, and Akashic records; facilitates past-life recall; promotes grounding and evolution; heals rifts in families, communities, and cultures

Sugilite

Formula: $KNa_2(Fe, Mn, Al)_2Li_3Si_{12}O_{30}$ Hardness: 6–6.5
Crystal system: hexagonal   Formation process: igneous or metamorphic   Chakra: heart, higher heart, third eye, crown
Correspondences: air, Neptune, Uranus, Aquarius

Physical healing: treats neurological conditions, pain, and infection; induces sleep; alleviates toothache and allergies; protects against environmental toxins

Psychological healing: soothing and peaceful; may treat depression, anxiety, and bipolar disorder (as an adjunct to medical treatment); stabilizes and elevates heart chakra; magnifies peace and hope; displaces fear and feelings of being overwhelmed; releases trauma

Spiritual healing: clears out toxic accumulations from aura and chakras; provides additional protection and light; transmutes harmful energies; augments dream state; improves intuition, psychic skills, and visualization

Sulfur

Formula: S_8 Hardness: 1.5–2.5   Crystal system: orthorhombic   Formation process: igneous or sedimentary   Chakra: solar plexus   Correspondences: fire, Sun, Aries, Leo

Physical healing: combats infection, inflammation, cysts, and fever; strongly detoxifies; balances digestive system; warms and invigorates

Psychological healing: purges negative thoughts; assists exploration of subconscious; dispels illusion and confusion; helps you confront shadow self; promotes ability to receive; offers measured option for processing anger and rage; reduces stubbornness, corruption, and greed

Spiritual healing: powerful psychic cleanser; removes foreign attachments, stale energies, and toxic patterns from aura and psyche; heals and prevents leaks or tears in aura; synthesizes heavenly and earthly energies to replenish personal power; traditionally used to break curses and drive away evil

Note: Sulfur can be toxic if mishandled.

Sunstone

Formula: oligoclase ($CaAl_2Si_2O_8$) with hematite (Fe_2O_3) or copper (Cu) **Hardness:** 6–6.5 **Crystal system:** triclinic
Formation process: igneous or metamorphic
Chakra: sacral, solar plexus **Correspondences:** fire, Sun, Leo

Physical healing: promotes health of heart and circulatory system; warms cold extremities; counteracts low blood pressure; treats seasonal affective disorder; assuages lethargy, weakness, and fatigue

Psychological healing: fosters success, joy, optimism, action, and motivation; increases discernment; helps in making healthy decisions; raises sense of self-worth; magnifies leadership skills; resolves depression, melancholy, and gloom; improves memory

Spiritual healing: helps you stay true to yourself, awakens causal body, helps with discovering and attaining life purpose, releases old karmic vows and soul contracts, protects aura and clears obstacles to radiating inner light

Sunstone, Oregon

Formula: plagioclase [$(Ca,Na)[(Al,Si)_2Si_2O_8]$] with copper (Cu) **Hardness:** 6–6.5 **Crystal system:** triclinic
Formation process: igneous **Chakra:** sacral, solar plexus, heart, crown **Correspondences:** fire, Sun, Leo, Scorpio

Physical healing: strengthens heart and blood vessels, strongly energizes without overstimulating, supports cellular regeneration, diminishes growth of unhealthy cells

Psychological healing: strengthens intellect, organization, and alertness; inspires courage, confidence, and exuberant joy; promotes success, especially in career; purges psyche of fear; deepens appreciation of beauty and art

Spiritual healing: eliminates blockages; kindles movement of kundalini; helps assimilate new energies; enhances telepathy; promotes cooperation, unity, and understanding in groups

Note: Oregon sunstone also exhibits the properties of golden labradorite (p. 136).

Sunstone, Rainbow Lattice

Formula: orthoclase ($KAlSi_3O_8$) with hematite (Fe_2O_3) and magnetite (Fe_3O_4)   Hardness: 6–6.5   Crystal system: monoclinic   Formation process: metamorphic   Chakra: all, especially earth star, solar plexus, soul star   Correspondences: earth, air, fire, water, spirit, Sun, Moon, Mercury, Leo, Aquarius

Physical healing: treats conditions affecting DNA and protein synthesis, removes harmful spiritual and etheric programming from cells to invite luminous health

Psychological healing: strengthens reason, intellect, and logic; helps you see the bigger picture; promotes learning, especially languages; alleviates gender dysphoria and other uncomfortable feelings associated with the body

Spiritual healing: stone of initiation, evolution, and mystery; balances yin and yang energies; ally for starseeds; assists channeling, contact with higher self, receiving messages from mineral kingdom, ET communication; kindles Christ-and/or Buddha-consciousness; connects to stellar energies

Tanzanite

Formula: zoisite [$Ca_2Al_3(Si_2O_7)(SiO_4)O(OH)$] with vanadium (V)   Hardness: 6–7   Crystal system: orthorhombic   Formation process: metamorphic   Chakra: all, especially heart, third eye, crown, soul star   Correspondences: air, Jupiter, Sagittarius

Physical healing: treats conditions of nervous system, kidneys, gallbladder, and endocrine system; balances overactive thyroid and adrenals; facilitates healthy weight loss or gain; supports eyes, ears, nose, and throat; improves sleep

Psychological healing: synchronizes heart and mind; alleviates worry, overactive mind, and dull emotions; inspires curiosity, wonder, and focus; brightens imagination

Spiritual healing: cultivates compassion, loving-kindness, and commitment to truth; develops psychic and intuitive abilities; facilitates meditation, purification, and visualization; strengthens chakras and energy field as a whole; helps find greater meaning in life

Tektite (Indochinite)

Formula: mostly SiO_2 Hardness: 5.5–6.5   Crystal
system: amorphous   Formation process: metamorphic
Chakra: all   Correspondences: spirit, Mercury, Gemini

Physical healing: supports health of circulatory system; rids the body of foreign
matter, parasites, and infection; accelerates all healing; strengthens body;
protects against harmful radiation; reduces fever

Psychological healing: inspires fearlessness; helps in facing the unknown; reduces
phobia, anxiety, and panic; releases repressed emotions; promotes friendship

Spiritual healing: balances polarities within; combats materialism and ego; invites
surrender; enhances psychic development, meditation, astral travel, and
visualization; ejects foreign energies and entities from energy field; corrects
chakra deficiencies; improves communication with guides, spirits, angels, and
ETs; taps into wisdom

Thulite

Formula: zoisite $[Ca_2Al_3(Si_2O_7)(SiO_4)O(OH)]$ with manganese (Mn)
Hardness: 6.5–7   Crystal system: orthorhombic
Formation process: metamorphic   Chakra: sacral, heart
Correspondences: air, Venus, Taurus, Gemini, Libra

Physical healing: alleviates childhood illnesses, promotes cardiac health,
strengthens reproductive system, stimulates regeneration after illness or injury

Psychological healing: promotes kindness, joy, pleasure, and love; strengthens
communication; overcomes shyness; enhances confidence and creativity;
harmonizes heart and mind; dissolves anger, arrogance, disagreement, greed,
and fear; deflects burnout in caregivers

Spiritual healing: raises consciousness with unconditional love, allows joy to be a
spiritual practice, inspires compassion and service

Tiffany Stone

Formula: fluorite (CaF_2), bertrandite [$Be_4(Si_2O_7)(OH)_2$], and opal [$SiO_2 \cdot n(H_2O)$]   Hardness: 4   Crystal system: cubic (fluorite), orthorhombic (bertrandite), amorphous (opal)
Formation process: sedimentary   Chakra: third eye, crown
Correspondences: air, Jupiter, Sagittarius

Physical healing: balances lymphatic, immune, and respiratory systems; reduces congestion and inflammation of sinuses and lungs; vitalizing for skin, DNA, brain, bones, and ligaments

Psychological healing: stimulates creativity, innovation, and artistic expression; marries logic and feelings; breaks down persistent mental and emotional patterns; calms overactive emotions; reduces stress; encourages open-mindedness, receptivity, and good communication

Spiritual healing: facilitates effortless transformation, opens third eye, strengthens psychic ability, boosts channeling, helps interpret psychic information

Note: see also fluorite (p. 117) and opal (p. 183)

Tiger Iron

Formula: tiger's eye with black hematite (Fe_2O_3) and red jasper (SiO_2)
Hardness: 5–7   Crystal system: trigonal
Formation process: metamorphic   Chakra: root, sacral, solar plexus
Correspondences: earth, fire, Sun, Mars, Aries, Leo

Physical healing: enhances strength, stamina, and endurance; encourages overall healing, especially of chronic conditions; supports health of circulatory system, muscles, lungs, and bone marrow

Psychological healing: reduces oversensitivity, fear, and difficulty responding to change; bolsters courage and confidence; enhances creativity, focus, and action; reduces arrogance, stubbornness, and conflict

Spiritual healing: strongly grounds and protects, especially empaths; improves manifestation; helps in adapting to planetary and cosmic changes

Note: see also hematite (p. 138), red jasper (p. 156), and tiger's eye (p. 250)

Tiger's Eye

Formula: quartz (SiO_2) with riebeckite [$Na_2(Fe^{2+}{}_3Fe^{3+}{}_2)Si_8O_{22}(OH)_2$] and iron (Fe) **Hardness:** 7 **Crystal system:** trigonal
Formation process: sedimentary **Chakra:** solar plexus, third eye
Correspondences: earth, fire, Sun, Leo

Physical healing: offers relief from pain, lethargy, and overactive adrenal glands; grounds and tones physical body; improves vision and ocular health

Psychological healing: stone of balance and harmony, encourages healthy decision-making skills, bolsters courage, assuages doubt, helps you exercise personal power

Spiritual healing: promotes intuition and spiritual awakening, especially for overly grounded people; represents truth and justice; attracts prosperity and abundance

Tiger's Eye, Blue (Falcon's Eye)

Formula: quartz (SiO_2) with riebeckite [$Na_2(Fe^{2+}{}_3Fe^{3+}{}_2)$ $Si_8O_{22}(OH)_2$] and iron (Fe) **Hardness:** 7 **Crystal system:** trigonal
Formation process: sedimentary **Chakra:** throat, third eye
Correspondences: earth, air, Jupiter, Sagittarius

Physical healing: supports health of eyes, kidneys, spleen, musculoskeletal system, and endocrine system; reduces overactive hormones; alleviates pain; stimulates numb and cold extremities; clears congestion

Psychological healing: balances and calms overactive mind, sharpens decision-making skills, helps in maintaining calm amid crisis or chaos, improves communication with tact and persuasion

Spiritual healing: represents truth, wisdom, and new perspectives; enables seeing the bigger picture; intuitively reveals missing or hidden details

Tiger's Eye, Red

Formula: quartz (SiO_2) with riebeckite [$Na_2(Fe^{2+}{}_3Fe^{3+}{}_2)Si_8O_{22}(OH)_2$] and iron (Fe)   **Hardness:** 7   **Crystal system:** trigonal
Formation process: sedimentary   **Chakra:** root, solar plexus
Correspondences: earth, fire, Mars, Aries, Leo

Physical healing: grounds and invigorates; nourishes circulatory system; treats anemia, inflammation, and poor circulation; improves digestion, metabolism, and vitality

Psychological healing: enhances perception, increases passion and libido, resolves conflict in romantic relationships, helps in overcoming excessive pride and arrogance

Spiritual healing: stimulates energy flow in aura and lower chakras, clears blockages, grounds and nourishes energy field, stimulates quest for self-improvement, brings stamina and vigor to spiritual path

Titanite (Sphene)

Formula: $CaTi(SiO_4)O$ **Hardness:** 5–5.5
Crystal system: monoclinic   **Formation process:** igneous or metamorphic   **Chakra:** solar plexus, third eye
Correspondences: air, spirit, Mercury, Gemini, Scorpio

Physical healing: promotes healthy gums, teeth, bones, and brain; bolsters immune system; helpful for chronic illness; combats infection and inflammation; encourages blood cell production

Psychological healing: sharpens mind, improves learning; cultivates curiosity and wonder; alleviates anger; strengthens willpower and leadership skills

Spiritual healing: helps you discover and follow your own path; facilitates astral travel, psychic vision, past-life recall, and communion with the cosmos; catalyzes shamanic journeys

Topaz, Blue

Formula: $Al_2SiO_4(OH,F)_2$ with iron (Fe)   Hardness: 8
Crystal system: orthorhombic   Formation process: igneous
Chakra: throat, third eye   Correspondences: water, air, Jupiter, Neptune, Sagittarius, Pisces

Physical healing: balances body's fluids; rejuvenates and rehydrates skin; exerts anti-aging influence; supports digestive and nervous systems; alleviates headache, sore throat, and thyroid disorders

Psychological healing: relaxes and opens mind; invites clear, honest communication; encourages confidence, integrity, and reliability; relieves anxiety; helps with embracing change; boosts memory

Spiritual healing: integrates life lessons; draws out the most authentic self; facilitates meditation, communication with spirit guides, and pursuit of wisdom

Topaz, Golden

Formula: $Al_2SiO_4(OH,F)_2$ with iron (Fe) and chromium (Cr)
Hardness: 8   Crystal system: orthorhombic
Formation process: igneous   Chakra: solar plexus
Correspondences: fire, Sun, Leo, Scorpio

Physical healing: improves health of nervous system; improves eyesight, metabolism, and digestion; excellent restorative for conditions of reproductive system and urinary tract (especially kidneys); alleviates exhaustion

Psychological healing: inspires creativity, action, and right use of willpower; embraces individuality and uniqueness; improves communication; enforces healthy boundaries; stabilizes mood swings

Spiritual healing: clarifies intention, magnifies personal power, aligns with divine will, powerfully boosts manifestation, attracts abundance and prosperity, gently protects

Topaz, White

Formula: $Al_2SiO_4(OH,F)_2$ Hardness: 8
Crystal system: orthorhombic Formation process: igneous
Chakra: solar plexus, crown
Correspondences: fire, Sun, Aries, Leo

Physical healing: regulates metabolism; excellent for vitalizing nervous system, digestion, nutrient assimilation, and stress-related conditions related to eating and digestion; soothing for chronic and terminal illness; strengthens and regenerates the body

Psychological healing: prompts self-reflection and understanding of intentions and beliefs underpinning decisions and behaviors; promotes honesty, awareness, emotional balance, confidence, and success

Spiritual healing: associated with wealth, wisdom, and healing; promotes empathy; helps set healthy boundaries; boosts manifestation process

Tourmaline

Formula: $X^+Y^{2+}_3Z^{3+}_6(OH,F)_4(BO_3)2Si_6O_{18}$ Hardness: 7–7.5
Crystal system: trigonal Formation process: igneous or metamorphic Chakra: varies Correspondences: air, Mercury, Gemini

Physical healing: fuels metabolism and immune function; bolsters defenses to environmental sensitivities, such as allergens and pollutants; relieves tension in neck and back; treats conditions of urinary tract

Psychological healing: imparts patience and understanding; combats depression, fear, and stress; facilitates self-discovery; strengthens problem-solving skills

Spiritual healing: protects against and transforms negative energy, clears stagnation, strengthens manifestation process, helps in attaining wisdom

Tourmaline, Black (Schorl)
Formula: $Na(Fe, Mn)_3Al_6B_3Si_6O_{27}(OH)_3(OH,F)$ Hardness: 7–7.5
Crystal system: trigonal   Formation process: igneous or
metamorphic   Chakra: earth star, root
Correspondences: earth, Saturn, Pluto, Scorpio, Capricorn

Physical healing: reduces pain and numbness; protects against harmful toxins, pathogens, and energies; mobilizes immune system; treats autoimmune conditions; calms intestines

Psychological healing: stone of self-discovery, breaks down barriers to the subconscious, helps you find direction in life, offers strength and protection during vulnerable moments, neutralizes stress, moderates OCD (obsessive-compulsive disorder) and anxiety

Spiritual healing: strongly grounds, protects, and purifies; transmutes disharmonious energy in aura and environment; replenishes spirit with earth energy

Tourmaline, Blue (Indicolite)
Formula: $Na(Li_{1.5}Al_{1.5})Al_6(Si_6O_{18})(BO_3)_3(OH)_3(OH)$ with
iron (Fe)   Hardness: 7–7.5   Crystal system: trigonal
Formation process: igneous   Chakra: throat, third eye
Correspondences: water, Neptune, Pisces

Physical healing: promotes balance and movement in circulatory, digestive, elimination, lymphatic, and nervous systems; supports health of bladder and kidneys; alleviates headaches

Psychological healing: releases blocked emotions; facilitates emotional expression, good communication, and self-awareness; soothes grief, crisis, and fear; promotes tolerance, confidence, and freedom; quells overactive mind

Spiritual healing: hastens spiritual growth; improves ethics, trust, faith, and spiritual awareness; aids quest for truth; increases psychic abilities; contacts higher self; offers emptiness and detachment for authentic growth; supports meditation, journaling, and affirmations

Tourmaline, Brown (Dravite)

Formula: $NaMg_3Al_6(BO_3)_3Si_6O_{18}(OH)_3F$ Hardness: 7–7.5
Crystal system: trigonal   Formation process: igneous
or metamorphic   Chakra: earth star, root, heart
Correspondences: earth, Mercury, Gemini, Virgo

Physical healing: offers fortitude and stamina; helps build muscle mass; regenerates tissue; excellent for skin; promotes healthy digestion and elimination; relieves ulcers, constipation, and irritable bowel syndrome

Psychological healing: encourages pragmatism and flexibility, prevents emotional burnout, protects in high-stress environments, instills self-love and acceptance, inspires creativity

Spiritual healing: protects aura and chakras; prevents intrusion of foreign energies, attachments, and entities; grounds and stabilizes; strengthens community bonds; prevents excess and self-denial and offers the middle path

Tourmaline, Green (Elbaite, Verdelite)

Formula: $Na(Li_{1.5}Al_{1.5})Al_6(Si_6O_{18})(BO_3)_3(OH)_3(OH)$ with iron (Fe), vanadium (V), or chromium (Cr)   Hardness: 7–7.5
Crystal system: trigonal   Formation process: igneous
Chakra: heart   Correspondences: earth, Saturn, Capricorn

Physical healing: repairs and restores tissue, especially muscle, tendon, and ligaments; promotes liver health; lowers blood pressure and cholesterol; treats chronic fatigue; regulates digestive, immune, and endocrine systems; excellent for strengthening male reproductive system

Psychological healing: soothes anxiety, invites emotional balance, releases resentment and bitterness, reduces impulsivity, instills patience

Spiritual healing: strengthens inner masculine forces; combats toxic masculinity; instills gratitude, joy, generosity, and respect; helps send loving energy into the world

Tourmaline, Paraíba

Formula: $Na(Li_{1.5}Al_{1.5})Al_6(Si_6O_{18})(BO_3)_3(OH)_3(OH)$ with copper (Cu)
Hardness: 7–7.5   **Crystal system:** trigonal   **Formation process:** igneous
Chakra: heart, higher heart, soul star   **Correspondences:** spirit, Uranus, Aquarius

Physical healing: provides overall balance, animates heart and nervous system, activates body's natural ability to regenerate, accelerates healing process

Psychological healing: relieves stress, tension, worry, and fear; unites heart and mind; invites happiness, peace, simplicity, and personal growth

Spiritual healing: powerful ally for healers; activates and links heart and higher heart chakras; transforms fear into unconditional love; dissolves illusion, chaos, and disconnection; helps see through new eyes; invokes grace, hope, courage, and spiritual strength; facilitates meditation, journeying, visualization, and angelic communication

Note: This stone also exhibits the properties of tourmalines of the same color (green, blue, purple, etc.).

Tourmaline, Pink

Formula: $Na(Li_{1.5}Al_{1.5})Al_6(Si_6O_{18})(BO_3)_3(OH)_3(OH)$ with manganese (Mn)   **Hardness:** 7–7.5   **Crystal system:** trigonal
Formation process: igneous   **Chakra:** heart
Correspondences: water, fire, Mercury, Venus, Libra

Physical healing: promotes health of female reproductive system, improves fertility, soothes symptoms of menopause, protects against environmental radiation, ameliorates varicose veins, reduces hypertension

Psychological healing: encourages feelings of safety and security; helps release emotional walls; promotes harmonious relationships; calms anger, worry, bitterness, stress, and fear; releases old emotional wounds

Spiritual healing: nurtures and balances inner feminine energy, initiates inward flow of love, helps you to embody receptivity and grace, supports caregivers and those who give more than receive

Tourmaline, Purple (Siberite)

Formula: $Na(Li_{1.5}Al_{1.5})Al_6(Si_6O_{18})(BO_3)_3(OH)_3(OH)$ with iron (Fe) and manganese (Mn)   Hardness: 7–7.5

Crystal system: trigonal   Formation process: igneous

Chakra: heart, higher heart, third eye, crown

Correspondences: air, Mercury, Virgo, Pisces

Physical healing: excellent revitalizer for nervous system; alleviates pain and fatigue; supports health of lungs, intestines, and pituitary and thyroid glands

Psychological healing: imparts optimism, self-esteem, and belief in success; refines and strengthens goal-setting, imagination, and problem-solving skills; excellent ally for learning and study; dissolves self-destructive habits

Spiritual healing: symbolizes spiritual freedom, devotion, and hope; enhances visualization and manifestation; strongly transmutes and transforms negativity; helps you attain life purpose

Tourmaline, Watermelon

Formula: $Na(Li_{1.5}Al_{1.5})Al_6(Si_6O_{18})(BO_3)_3(OH)_3(OH)$ with iron (Fe) and manganese (Mn)   Hardness: 7–7.5

Crystal system: trigonal   Formation process: igneous

Chakra: heart, higher heart

Correspondences: water, Mercury, Venus, Virgo, Libra

Physical healing: combats burnout, pain, and hormonal imbalance; heals damaged or infected nerve tissue; excellent for reproductive system; strongly healing and regenerative

Psychological healing: elevates mood, soothes frayed mood; eases anxiety; provides comfort for people experiencing gender dysphoria or exploring gender identity and expression

Spiritual healing: balances incoming and outgoing flow of love, promotes perfect balance between inner masculine and feminine energies, encourages sensitivity to environment without becoming imbalanced by outside forces

Note: see also green tourmaline (p. 255) and pink tourmaline (p. 256)

Tremolite

Formula: $Ca_2(Mg,Fe_2+)Si_8O22(OH)_2$ Hardness: 5–6 Crystal system: monoclinic Formation process: metamorphic
Chakra: heart, third eye Correspondences: air, Mercury, Gemini, Libra, Pisces

Physical healing: supports healthy nervous and respiratory systems, encourages elasticity and youthfulness of skin and collagen
Psychological healing: excellent for communication, connection, and all forms of relationships; increases charisma and personal magnetism; excellent for attracting the right partner; reduces feelings of overwhelm and anxiety
Spiritual healing: taps into ley lines, vortices, and other telluric (earth current) energies; reduces geopathic stress; releases earthbound spirits; stimulates psychic senses; facilitates access to Akashic records and past-life memories
Note: Fibrous specimens should be handled with care.

Turquoise

Formula: $CuAl_6(PO_4)_4(OH)_8 \cdot 4H_2O$ Hardness: 5–6
Crystal system: triclinic Formation process: sedimentary
Chakra: heart, higher heart, throat, crown
Correspondences: earth, air, water, fire, spirit, Venus, Jupiter, Taurus, Sagittarius, Aquarius

Physical healing: master healing stone, alleviates pain, promotes overall healing and regeneration, anti-inflammatory, protects against viral infections, regulates moisture, protects against injury and accidents
Psychological healing: promotes integrity and honesty; facilitates clear and concise communication, helps you speak truth; invokes calm demeanor; balances emotions; dissolves apathy and martyrdom; fosters proactivity and foresight
Spiritual healing: invokes protection, wisdom, insight, and new perspectives; invites compassion toward self and others; helps you adapt to change; makes it easy to see the bigger picture; attracts luck

Ulexite

Formula: NaCaBO   Hardness: 1–2.5   Crystal system: triclinic
Formation process: secondary   Chakra: third eye
Correspondences: air, Mercury, Gemini

Physical healing: supports health of brain, nervous system, and eyes; reduces nausea and lethargy

Psychological healing: detaches from drama; encourages objectivity and willingness to change; strengthens focus, memory, and mental clarity; boosts creativity, reasoning, and problem-solving skills

Spiritual healing: powerfully activates third eye; stimulates psychic senses, especially clairvoyance; helps in seeing alternate realities and timelines; facilitates interpretation of psychic information

Unakite

Formula: feldspar ($KAlSi_3O_8$), epidote [$Ca_2Al_2(Fe^{3+},Al)(SiO_4)$ $(Si_2O_7)O(OH)$], and quartz (SiO_2)   Hardness: 6.5–7
Crystal system: mixture of monoclinic and trigonal
Formation process: metamorphic   Chakra: heart
Correspondences: earth, Venus, Taurus, Libra

Physical healing: treats conditions of liver, gallbladder, and heart; promotes tissue regeneration and overall healing; may shrink tumors (as an adjunct to medical treatment)

Psychological healing: grounds and stabilizes emotional body, harmonizes disparate or conflicting thoughts and emotions, invites compromise, strengthens and heals relationships, gives permission to feel emotions, counteracts self-deprecation and self-criticism, ameliorates anxiety

Spiritual healing: promotes renewal, recovery, and regeneration on all levels; harmonizes opposing forces; cultivates compassion; unifies spirit and matter; helps in exploring true identity

Vanadinite

Formula: Pb(VO$_4$)$_3$Cl   Hardness: 3–4   Crystal system: hexagonal   Formation process: sedimentary
Chakra: root, sacral, solar plexus, third eye
Correspondences: fire, Venus, Mars, Aries, Taurus, Virgo

Physical healing: stimulates and energizes; combats fatigue, exhaustion, and low vitality; withdraws latent illness; reduces inflammation; increases libido; enhances endurance

Psychological healing: calms mind; reduces mental chatter; helps you see underlying beauty of self and world; alleviates despair and isolation; increases self-esteem, creativity, passion, joy, and organization

Spiritual healing: resolves karmic patterns; promotes connection to natural world; anchors soul into the body; facilitates transcendent, ecstatic states of consciousness

Note: Vanadinite is toxic if mishandled.

Variscite

Formula: AlPO$_4$·2H$_2$O   Hardness: 4.5
Crystal system: orthorhombic
Formation process: sedimentary   Chakra: solar plexus
Correspondences: air, water, Mercury, Gemini, Scorpio

Physical healing: improves digestion and detoxification; alleviates nausea, bowel inflammation, and ulcers; calms nervous system; combats impotence, lethargy, and rheumatism

Psychological healing: ensures stable emotional release; counteracts overwhelm and despair; imparts patience, diplomacy, and negotiation skills; boosts confidence, good cheer, and altruism; encourages self-love

Spiritual healing: aligns, purifies, and energizes subtle bodies; draws out conscience and magnifies moral compass; invites sense of belonging; encourages cooperation, harmony, and unconditional love

Vesuvianite (Idocrase)

Formula: $Ca_{10}Al_4(SiO_4)_5(Si_2O_7)_2(OH,F)_4$ Hardness: 6.5
Crystal system: tetragonal   Formation process: igneous or metamorphic   Chakra: heart, third eye
Correspondences: earth, Sagittarius, Capricorn

Physical healing: anti-inflammatory, regenerates, and grounds; treats liver, blood vessels, nerves, and tooth enamel; reduces spaciness and dizziness; improves nutrient assimilation

Psychological healing: ignites curiosity, enthusiasm, courage, and trust; fortifies and bridges heart and will; displaces confusion, fear, and persistent negative thoughts; brings organization and clarity

Spiritual healing: removes facades and false personas to encourage vulnerability and authenticity; dissolves egotism, greed, and materialism; shifts identity toward spiritual self; invites recognition that every moment is a chance to grow and heal

Vivianite

Formula: $Fe^{2+}_3(PO_4)_2 \cdot 8H_2O$ Hardness: 1.5–2   Crystal system: monoclinic   Formation process: sedimentary
Chakra: heart, third eye   Correspondences: water, earth, Pluto, Scorpio, Capricorn

Physical healing: stimulates tissue regeneration; improves immune response; hastens recovery from illness, injury, and general weakness

Psychological healing: engenders peace, tranquility, and forgiveness; softens competitiveness; invites cooperation and tolerance; facilitates critical self-reflection and honesty; emotionally nurturing

Spiritual healing: cultivates strength through surrender; parts the veil between the worlds; intensifies psychic vision, astral travel, and dreams; clears karmic debris; aids past-life recall; facilitates initiation into the mysteries

Wavellite

Formula: $Al_3(PO_4)_2(OH,F)_3 \cdot 5H_2O$ Hardness: 3.5–4
Crystal system: orthorhombic   Formation process: igneous,
sedimentary, or metamorphic   Chakra: solar plexus
Correspondences: air, Uranus, Aquarius

Physical healing: strengthens teeth and bones, supports marrow health and
blood cell production, coordinates hemispheres of brain, regulates body fluids
Psychological healing: provides safe, even emotional release; reduces
attachments to expectation and outside pressures; improves decision-making
skills and sense of follow-through; strengthens family bonds
Spiritual healing: clarifies intuition, extremely centering, enhances clairaudience,
reduces mental chatter during meditation, resolves past-life patterns causing
emotional and spiritual imbalance

Willemite

Formula: Zn_2SiO_4 Hardness: 5.5   Crystal system: trigonal
Formation process: metamorphic   Chakra: sacral, third eye
Correspondences: earth, fire, Mercury, Gemini

Physical healing: protects against environmental pollutants, radiation, and stress;
supports health of eyes; encourages nutrient absorption; promotes sexual and
reproductive health; nurturing during pregnancy
Psychological healing: boosts optimism, enthusiasm, and creativity; promotes
sense of agency and sovereignty in life
Spiritual healing: strongly stimulates third eye; boosts clairvoyance and other
psychic senses; facilitates astral travel, vivid dreams, and meditation; helps
you see the unseen; ignites spiritual development; increases frequency of
synchronicities

Wulfenite

Formula: PbMoO$_4$ Hardness: 3   Crystal system: tetragonal   Formation process: sedimentary
Chakra: sacral, solar plexus   Correspondences: fire, Saturn, Sagittarius

Physical healing: boosts energy, stamina, and metabolism; treats dry skin, injury, muscle atrophy, low sex drive, infertility, impotence; restorative after miscarriage and childbirth

Psychological healing: strengthens creativity, willpower, and inspiration; improves focus, determination, and receptivity; excellent stimulant for writers, artists, and other creatives; overcomes pessimism, self-doubt, and procrastination; excellent support for abuse recovery

Spiritual healing: encourages magical and alchemical practices; inspires authenticity and generosity; transcends old patterns, karmic cycles, and soul contracts; facilitates past-life recall, manifestation, and magical abilities

Xenotime

Formula: YPO$_4$ Hardness: 4.5   Crystal system: tetragonal
Formation process: igneous or metamorphic
Chakra: sacral, third eye   Correspondences: earth, Mercury, Virgo, Aquarius

Physical healing: balances metabolism; improves nutrient absorption; revitalizing for conditions of the intestines, reproductive system, and damage to DNA

Psychological healing: helps you conquers feelings of insignificance, vanity, and paranoia; encourages cautious, careful consideration of details; releases ties to toxic relationships; strengthens willpower; enhances creativity

Spiritual healing: represents adaptation, peace, and realization of inner perfection; grants spiritual assistance for any endeavor; boosts manifestation; magnifies prosperity and abundance; reinforces connection to universe

Note: Xenotime is toxic if mishandled.

Yooperlite

Formula: syenite rock rich in sodalite   Hardness: 5
Crystal system: variable   Formation process: igneous
Chakra: third eye   Correspondences: air, Uranus, Aquarius

Physical healing: accelerates overall healing, repairs damaged tissues and broken bones, improves balance, improves vision and ocular health

Psychological healing: invites self-discovery, creative expression, and childlike wonder; strengthens learning processes; boosts memory and recall; reduces unnecessary restraint; facilitates shadow work; purifies mind to release fear and internal resistance to change

Spiritual healing: uncovers hidden truth and meaning; balances the subtle bodies; removes cords, attachments, and foreign energies and seals aura from harm; prompts egalitarianism, hope, and unity

Zincite

Formula: ZnO   Hardness: 4   Crystal
system: hexagonal   Formation process: igneous
or metamorphic   Chakra: root, sacral, solar plexus
Correspondences: fire, Venus, Taurus, Libra

Physical healing: increases overall vitality, life force, and stamina; stimulates cleansing processes; alleviates overtaxed adrenals, nerve pain, and blood sugar imbalances; heals and balances conditions affecting reproductive systems, sex hormones, and gonads

Psychological healing: evokes creativity, inspiration, and passion; removes blockages to self-expression, artistic pursuits, and sexuality; instills courage; soothing and life-affirming for recovery from sexual abuse

Spiritual healing: stimulates pleasure and enjoyment in the human experience, balances masculine and feminine polarities, provides objective interpretation of intuitive information and subconscious patterns

Zircon

Formula: $ZrSiO_4$ Hardness: 7.5 Crystal system: tetragonal
Formation process: igneous Chakra: root, sacral
Correspondences: earth, fire, Sun, Sagittarius

Physical healing: relieves pain; promotes detoxification, liver function, and recovery from substance abuse; stimulates metabolism

Psychological healing: stone of action, provides comfort during loss and transition, spurs decisive movement toward emotional and mental well-being, releases painful ties to the past

Spiritual healing: both grounding and spiritually expansive; facilitates lucid dreaming, astral travel, and meditation; mitigates egotism, materialism, and unnecessary attachment; helps live each day to the fullest

Zoisite

Formula: $Ca_2Al_3(SiO_4)(Si_2O_7)O(OH)$ Hardness: 6–7 Crystal system: orthorhombic Formation process: metamorphic Chakra: heart Correspondences: earth, Mercury, Gemini, Virgo

Physical healing: promotes regeneration and all-around healing; reduces inflammation, pain; helpful for conditions of the lungs and pancreas; excellent for chronic illness; eases end-of-life transition

Psychological healing: balances willpower; overcomes need for control; helps you unplug from drama; encourages receptivity to constructive criticism; alleviates emotional pain, grief, anger, resentment, and despair

Spiritual healing: transmutes negative energy; encourages spiritual growth and personal development; facilitates surrender to unconditional love and divine will; invokes hope, abundance, service, and inner peace

QUICK-REFERENCE TABLES

The following quick-reference guide offers a concise selection of crystals that correspond to the chakras, elements, planets, and signs of the zodiac. A set of extensive tables is beyond the scope of a pocket guide, so I've narrowed down the stones in this section to represent the most effective and/or most popular choices for each category. If a color or type for a gem is unspecified, you may use any variety. Use these tables as a starting point whenever you are looking for guidance in your practice.

CHAKRA CORRESPONDENCES

EARTH STAR	aegirine ammonite aragonite, sputnik barite	flint hematite magnetite	nuummite petrified wood tourmaline, black
ROOT	black onyx calcite, red garnet jasper	obsidian rhodonite ruby	serpentine smoky quartz tourmaline, black
SACRAL	calcite, orange carnelian copper jasper, mookaite	marble moonstone, peach obsidian, mahogany opal, fire	quartz, tangerine smithsonite sunstone
SOLAR PLEXUS	agate, blue lace amber apatite, golden calcite, gold	citrine malachite prehnite	pyrite tiger's eye topaz
HEART	aventurine, green calcite, mangano emerald jade	kunzite peridot rhodonite	rose quartz ruby in zoisite tourmaline, pink

HIGHER HEART	calcite, cobaltoan hiddenite jasper, porcelain kunzite	lepidolite petalite quartz, lithium	rose quartz, star smithsonite tourmaline, watermelon
THROAT	agate, blue lace amazonite aquamarine calcite, blue	chalcedony, blue chrysocolla lapis lazuli	larimar quartz, rutilated turquoise
THIRD EYE	amethyst apatite, blue apophyllite azurite	charoite celestite fluorite	iolite moonstone sodalite
CROWN	amethyst calcite, optical danburite	fluorite Herkimer diamond moldavite	opal quartz (clear) selenite
CAUSAL	astrophyllite chrysotile gabbro	hematite, rainbow jasper, calligraphy stone kyanite	moonstone, rainbow sapphire, white sunstone, rainbow lattice
SOUL STAR	aragonite, purple charoite Herkimer diamond natrolite	phenakite quartz, amphibole quartz, Lemurian seed	quartz, Tibetan quartz, tourmalinated selenite
ALL CHAKRAS	dolomite fluorite halite kyanite	labradorite moonstone, rainbow opal	quartz seraphinite tanzanite

ELEMENTAL CORRESPONDENCES

EARTH ▽	agate emerald garnet	jade jasper obsidian	rhyolite serpentine
AIR △	amazonite amethyst apophyllite aventurine	celestite fluorite howlite	labradorite lapis lazuli turquoise

FIRE △	agate, fire amber calcite, orange carnelian	citrine malachite opal, fire	pyrite rhodochrosite ruby
WATER ▽	agate, blue lace aquamarine aragonite, blue chalcedony	chrysocolla chrysoprase larimar	lepidolite moonstone smithsonite
SPIRIT ☆	amethyst barite fossil hemimorphite	Herkimer diamond labradorite opal	quartz tektite turquoise
ALL ELEMENTS	chiastolite Herkimer diamond kyanite, blue	labradorite moldavite quartz	septarian nodule turquoise

PLANETARY CORRESPONDENCES

SUN ☉	amber calcite, gold calcite, orange citrine	coral jasper, mookaite peridot pyrite	tiger's eye topaz zircon
MOON ☽	aragonite, white chalcedony magnesite	moonstone opal quartz, girasol	quartz, white selenite stilbite
MERCURY ☿	agate ametrine apatite aventurine	calcite fluorite muscovite	opal tektite tourmaline
VENUS ♀	chrysocolla chrysoprase copper dioptase	emerald malachite opal, pink	quartz, rutilated rhodochrosite unakite
MARS ♂	agate, fire aventurine, red bloodstone bronzite	carnelian garnet hematite	jasper obsidian, mahogany sardonyx

JUPITER ♃	agate, moss amethyst charoite fluorite, purple	iolite labradorite lapis lazuli	sapphire topaz, blue turquoise
SATURN ♄	aragonite black onyx dolomite fossil	galena jet lapis lazuli	obsidian, black petrified wood sodalite
URANUS ♅	amazonite amethyst, pink anhydrite	barite dumortierite fluorite, rainbow	lepidolite meteorite stichtite
NEPTUNE ♆	ammonite aquamarine beryl calcite, blue	coral jasper, ocean larimar	lepidolite opal, blue sugilite
PLUTO ♇	agate, snakeskin aragonite, purple astrophyllite basalt	granite jasper, brecciated kunzite	obsidian shungite tourmaline, black

BIRTHSTONES AND ZODIACAL CORRESPONDENCES

ARIES ♈	agate, fire aventurine, red bloodstone calcite, red	carnelian diamond flint	jasper ruby spinel
TAURUS ♉	agate, tree aragonite, green calcite, green chrysoprase	emerald jasper, picture malachite	rhodonite rhyolite, rainforest unakite
GEMINI ♊	agate ametrine apatite fluorite	jasper, yellow quartz, rutilated sapphire	staurolite tektite tourmaline

CANCER ♋	aragonite, white chalcedony jade, white magnesite	marble moonstone opal	quartz, girasol ruby selenite
LEO ♌	amber calcite, cobaltoan calcite, orange labradorite (golden)	opal, yellow peridot spinel	sunstone tiger's eye topaz, golden
VIRGO ♍	agate, moss jade jasper, ocean	opal, dendritic prehnite sapphire	serpentine tourmaline, brown
LIBRA ♎	aventurine, green calcite, mangano chalcopyrite chrysocolla	morganite opal rhodochrosite	rose quartz tourmaline, pink tourmaline, watermelon
SCORPIO ♏	agate, Botswana bloodstone kunzite obsidian	opal, black pietersite prasiolite	shungite topaz tourmaline, black
SAGITTARIUS ♐	azurite danburite fluorite, purple iolite	kyanite labradorite lapis lazuli	tanzanite topaz, blue turquoise
CAPRICORN ♑	apatite, blue aragonite black onyx dolomite	fossil galena garnet	jet petrified wood smoky quartz
AQUARIUS ♒	amazonite amethyst apophyllite	aventurine, blue barite dumortierite	fluorite, rainbow sodalite stichtite
PISCES ♓	agate, blue lace agate, turritella amethyst aquamarine	fluorite, blue kambaba stone larimar	lepidolite petalite tourmaline, blue

GLOSSARY OF TRADE NAMES, ARTIFICIAL GEMS, AND MISTAKEN IDENTITIES

African turquoise: dyed jasper

agni manitite: pseudotektite (a variety of obsidian) from Indonesia, often claimed to be an authentic tektite

agnitite: heat-treated hematoid quartz from Madagascar

amaranthine: see Chinese charoite

amazez: chevron amethyst from Madagascar

ammolite: trade name for colorful and iridescent ammonite fossils from the Rocky Mountains

anandalite: also called iris quartz and aura quartz; a naturally iridescent quartz whose optical effects derive from structural defects, not inclusions of rhodium

andara: colorful slag (waste glass), often sold for exorbitant prices

ancestralite: banded formation of red jasper and hematite

astaraline: greenish aventurine from Colorado

atlantisite: stichtite in serpentine from Tasmania

aroha stone: a new name for vitalite, a name given to gneiss, a common metamorphic rock

aura quartz: enhanced quartz crystals with iridescent, brightly colored surfaces. Originally, aura quartz was treated with a process called "precious metal anodizing" and was made with metals like gold, silver, platinum, titanium, niobium, and so on. Most aura quartz on the market today is instead either electroplated with titanium or dyed and subsequently coated with polymers. The lattermost variety has no therapeutic value.

auralite-23: amethyst from Ontario, usually with sharp chevrons and beautiful red points from hematite; erroneously said to contain twenty-three minerals

avalonite: trade name applied to two different stones: drusy blue chalcedony and a variety of zoisite

azeztulite: a spurious trade name originally applied to low-quality white quartz; a term currently used to increase the market value of many different rocks, including granite, quartzite, sandstone, aventurine, and citrine

azumar: blue quartzite containing clay minerals

blue scheelite: a mixture of calcite and dolomite from Turkey that does not contain any scheelite

blueberry quartz: artificial glass

cacoxenite: All quartz and amethyst inclusions labeled cacoxenite are goethite.

candy jade: white stone (quartz, marble, etc.) dyed bright colors and sold as jade

cherry quartz: artificial glass, sometimes colored red from the addition of cinnabar

Chinese charoite: low-quality fluorite and quartz, newly rebranded as "amaranthine"

cinnabarite: piemontite in white scapolite; frequently mislabeled as "cinnabar" in quartz

coppernite: igneous rock of indeterminate composition, likely a variety of basalt with iridescent enstatite; often mislabeled as a variety of nuummite from India or China

crocodile jasper: kambaba stone, a variety of metarhyolite

devalite: metamorphic rock consisting of serpentine and quartzite

empowerite: chert or flint

euphoralite: an igneous rock called pegmatite, rich in lithium-bearing minerals such as lepidolite and tourmaline

fire and ice quartz: clear quartz that has been treated by thermal shocking (rapidly heated and cooled) to produce cracks and fissures inside

fordite: layers of paint from automobile manufacturing

gaia stone: artificial green glass. The color comes from small amounts of ash from Mount St. Helens. Also called helenite.

goldstone: artificial glass with particles of copper or other metals

green taralite: andesite, a common extrusive igneous rock with a composition between rhyolite and basalt

green zebra jasper: chrysotile, a variety of serpentine

guardianite: fine-grained igneous rock, similar to granite or aplite

healerite: trade name for high-quality, lime-green serpentine

heartenite: chlorite schist, a common metamorphic rock

hemalyke: simulated hematite derived from powdered ferrite, often magnetic; often used to make fragile, inexpensive rings

illuminite: metamorphic rock, possibly a dense schist

infinite: trade name for serpentine

kiwi jasper: granite from New Zealand

lapis lace onyx: see blue scheelite

lavulite: old trade name for sugilite

Lemurian aquatine calcite: trade name applied to blue-to-aqua calcite from Argentina; also called blue onyx

lepidocrocite: Virtually all material labeled lepidocrocite (usually inclusions inside quartz or amethyst) is actually hematite.

maramalite: serpentinite, a metamorphic rock rich in serpentine, from New Zealand

master shamanite: black limestone

merlinite: refers to one of several stones: black manganese ore, often called psilomelane or romanechite; psilomelane in massive or botryoidal quartz; white agate or white opal with manganese-rich dendritic inclusions. See also mystic merlinite.

Melody stone: see super seven

Mexican onyx: banded calcite, sometimes with dolomite

mystic merlinite: bluish or greyish gabbro from Madagascar, with no relationship to other forms of merlinite

mystic topaz: topaz that has been coated with titanium, similar to aura quartz

new jade: trade name for serpentine, usually referring to a variety called bowenite

obsidian (green, blue, red, yellow, etc.): Man-made glass in bright colors is often marketed as obsidian; note that it does not exhibit the properties of natural volcanic glass. There are minute amounts of natural green obsidian found in several places worldwide; specimens are rare and expensive.

opalite: Artificial glass commonly mistaken for opal or moonstone, which does not exhibit the properties of natural stones. Originally this term replied to low-quality opals but has fallen out of favor due to the prevalence of opalite glass.

orgonite: mixture of resin, metal shavings, and quartz or other crystals believed by some to counteract harmful energies

purple angeline: new trade name for multicolored amethyst and smoky quartz with goethite inclusions; see also super seven

purple Mohave turquoise: turquoise that has been dyed purple and stabilized with bronze and resin

quantum quattro silica: quartz containing various copper-based minerals, including chrysocolla, shattuckite, ajoite, malachite, and dioptase. Most pieces contain only small streaks of shattuckite and little, if any, ajoite.

que será: an igneous rock called llanite

reconstituted quartz: fused silica glass. Since it has been formed into glass, it has no crystal structure and is no longer quartz.

revelation stone: jasper from New Zealand

roswellite: pseudomorph of dolomite after aragonite

rosophia: red or pink granite

sauralite: quartz from New Zealand, often forming beautiful druses, casts, and pseudomorphs

sea sediment jasper: mixture of dyed stone and synthetic resin, sometimes with metallic accents

sentient plasma quartz: exceptionally clear quartz from Colombia

shantilite: agate from Madagascar

Siberian quartz: lab-grown quartz, often available in bright colors

sieber agate: antique slag (glass) byproduct of copper smelting found in Germany

super seven: a trade name applied to multicolored (clear, smoky, amethyst, ferruginous, etc.) quartz with inclusions of goethite, hematite, and rarely rutile. It was erroneously claimed to have seven minerals in its makeup. The name is trademarked and legally applied to only one variety of this quartz from Espiritu Santo, MG, Brazil. Regardless, most pieces labeled as super seven are amethyst or multicolored quartz with goethite and/or hematite inclusions from other locations around the world.

tanzberry quartz: see tanzurine

tanzurine: aventurine from Tanzania available in shades of red and green, sometimes also sold as tanzberry quartz and bliss quartz

terraluminite: granite from Vermont

tijasperite: a recent name applied to tiger iron—a combination of tiger's eye, red jasper, and hematite

transmutite: petrified wood

Transvaal jade: trade name for grossular garnet from South Africa

turquenite: dyed magnesite used as an inexpensive substitute for genuine turquoise

vitalite: trade name for gneiss, a common metamorphic rock

vortexite: spherulitic rhyolite

water sapphire: old term for iolite or cordierite

white moldavite: etched calcite from Arizona that bears a superficial resemblance to moldavite. It is *not* a tektite.

white turquoise: howlite or magnesite

GLOSSARY OF
METAPHYSICAL TERMS

Akashic records: a nonphysical storehouse of the records of all that is, all that was, and all that will be

alchemy: the act of transforming or transmuting one state of being into a higher one

ancestral healing: the act of healing and transforming familial patterns, beliefs, and baggage passed through the ancestral line

angel: spiritual being who acts as a messenger between heaven and earth

astral travel: projecting consciousness beyond the body to explore other places in the physical or spiritual realms

attachment: foreign energies, thoughts, or entities that become attached to the aura; see also cord

aura: the field of subtle energy that surrounds and permeates the body; individual layers, called subtle bodies, comprise the aura, and each contains the blueprint for a different part of our being

causal body: layer of the aura that records our life experiences and karma

chakra: spinning wheel or vortex of energy located along the midline of the body that integrates, processes, and releases life-force in different ways

channeling: process of psychically communicating with or receiving information from a nonphysical entity

clairaudience: psychically hearing sound or other auditory information on the inner planes, derived from the French for "clear hearing"

clairsentience: psychically sensing or perceiving information, derived from the French for "clear feeling"

clairvoyance: psychically perceiving visual information, derived from the French for "clear seeing"

cord: a kind of attachment or energy that links or tethers us to another person, place, or experience; cords may drain us of vital energy or reinforce unhealthy dynamics between people

correspondence: the doctrine of a substance resonating with other principles, symbols, and forces in the universe, such as birthstones corresponding to the signs of the zodiac

deva: spiritual force that oversees all parts of creation; devas act as the oversoul, or overseeing consciousness, of a particular mineral, plant, creature, etc.

Divine Feminine: aspect of the Divine, or Source, related to feminine archetypes; goddess energy

Divine Masculine: aspect of the Divine, or Source, related to masculine archetypes; god energy

elements: the classical energies or forces represented as earth, air, fire, water, and the quintessence (also known as ether or spirit)

emotional body: layer of the aura that processes and stores emotions

empath: someone with heightened ability to feel or perceive the emotions of other people

etheric body: layer of the aura closest to and containing the blueprint for the physical body

geopathic stress: disharmonious or harmful energy created by the disturbance of Earth's natural energy flow, often through construction or otherwise changing the environment

grounding: the process of connecting to the planet's energy to make a complete circuit between the human energy field and that of the Earth; grounding allows you to discharge energies that do not serve and draw nourishment from the Earth

guides: spirits and other nonphysical beings

human energy field: the collection of measurable and subtle energies (e.g., the aura) that surrounds and fills the body

implants: foreign energies, thoughts, or other patterns that are embedded in the aura

karma: the law of cause and effect, which serves as the soul's continuous process of learning from the effects of your actions

kundalini: spiritual energy that dwells at the base of the spine, often visualized as a coiled serpent; activating this energy often accompanies moments of spiritual awakening

lucid dream: a dream in which the dreamer is aware that they are dreaming

manifestation: process of creating change to achieve a particular goal or outcome via the mind and spirit

mediumship: the ability to communicate with the souls of the deceased and other discarnate beings

mental body: layer of the aura responsible for storing, sorting, and integrating thoughts

meridians: pathways for life force that lie close to the skin as described in Chinese medicine

nadis: channels or vessels that pass through the body and aura, through which life force flows, as described in traditional Indian medicine

nature spirits: the spirits and other nonphysical beings that reside in and care for the natural world

past life: past lives represent the previous lives our soul has lived predicated on the idea of reincarnation

planetary healing: sending healing energy to the entire planet

prana: vital energy or life force

psychic attack: conscious or unconscious harm resulting from the negative thoughts or intentions of another person

psychic debris: energy from strong emotions, feelings, spiritual experiences, or even environments that may sometimes get stuck in the aura

shadow self: unconscious part of the self that is out of alignment with the person you are seeking to become; the shadow is often formed through trauma and other lived experience

shadow work: the act of consciously addressing the shadow self for healing and personal growth

shamanic journey: a form of astral travel, usually achieved through a trance or altered state of consciousness wherein you are aided by guides, ancestors, and other spirits

starbeings: extraterrestrial or extradimensional beings from other parts of the universe

starseeds: people experiencing their first incarnation on Earth whose souls come from distant worlds

spiritual blueprint: the template that contains instructions for the health and well-being of the body, as well as the template for life lessons and experiences

spiritual bypassing: avoiding feelings by hiding behind spiritual practices

soul fragments: portions of the soul or spiritual essence broken through the experience of trauma, pain, or suffering

soul retrieval: process of locating and reintegrating soul fragments, often resulting in profound healing

Source: an all-encompassing term for God, Goddess, Creator, or any other Higher Power

subtle body: a layer of the aura with a distinct function, such as the etheric body, astral body, emotional body, mental body, intuitive body, causal body, and soul body; different schools of thought use models of the aura with differing numbers of subtle bodies

subtle energy: energy that cannot yet be measured by science, such as life force, prana, etc.

toxic positivity: dismissing negative or unpleasant emotions with false reassurances

trance: an altered state of consciousness typically achieved through meditation

yin and yang: two complementary forces as described in Chinese philosophy and culture; yin is receptive, dark, and cool while yang is projective, bright, and hot

BIBLIOGRAPHY

Franks, Leslie J. *Stone Medicine: A Chinese Medical Guide to Healing with Gems and Minerals*. Rochester, Vt.: Healing Arts Press, 2016.

Gienger, Michael. *Healing Crystals: The A to Z Guide to 555 Gemstones*. Forres, Scotland: Earthdancer, 2014.

Hall, Judy. *The Crystal Companion: Enhance Your Life with Crystals*. Blue Ash, Ohio: Walking Stick Press, 2018.

———. *The Encyclopedia of Crystals*. Gloucester, Mass.: Fair Winds Press, 2006.

Hugs, Kristi. *Old Rocks, New Names: Synonyms, Trademarks and Marketing Names for Old Favorites and New Minerals*. CreateSpace Independent Publishing Platform, 2018.

Landeck, Horst-Dieter, and Marion Tuchel. *Heilsteine vom Ostseestrand*. Heide, Germany: Boyens Buchverlag, 2010.

Lilly, Simon and Sue. *Essential Guide to Crystals*. London, U.K.: Watkins, 2010.

Melody. *Love Is in the Earth*. Wheat Ridge, Colo.: Earth-Love Publishing, 2007.

Pearson, Nicholas. *Crystal Basics: The Energetic, Healing & Spiritual Power of 200 Gemstones*. Rochester, Vt.: Destiny Books, 2020.

———. *Crystal Healing for the Heart: Gemstone Therapy for Physical, Emotional, and Spiritual Well-being*. Rochester, Vt.: Destiny Books, 2017.

———. *Crystals For Karmic Healing: Transform Your Future by Releasing Your Past*. Rochester, Vt.: Destiny Books, 2017.

———. *Flower Essences from the Witch's Garden: Plant Spirits in Magickal Herbalism*. Rochester, Vt.: Destiny Books, 2022.

———. *The Seven Archetypal Stones: Their Spiritual Powers and Teachings*. Rochester, Vt.: Destiny Books, 2016.

———. *Stones of the Goddess: 104 Crystals for the Divine Feminine*. Rochester, Vt.: Destiny Books, 2019.

Permutt, Philip. *The Modern Guide to Crystal Healing*. New York: CICO Books, 2021.

Raphaell, Katrina. *The Crystal Trilogy* (3 volumes). Santa Fe, N. Mex.: Aurora Press, 1985–1990.

Simmons, Robert, and Naisha Ahsian. *The Book of Stones: Who They Are and What They Teach*. East Montpelier, Vt.: Heaven and Earth Publishing, 2007.